PENGUIN BOOKS
BUILDING MY WORLD

Swraj Paul (Rt Hon. the Lord Paul of Marylebone PC) was born in Jalandhar in 1931. He was educated at Doaba School, Doaba College, Forman Christian College, Punjab University and the Massachusetts Institute of Technology, USA, where he also attended Harvard Business School.

After some years in his family's business, Apeejay, in Calcutta, he went to England in 1966 seeking medical care for his youngest daughter, who tragically died in 1968. He and his family stayed on in England, where he established the Caparo Group, a UK-based international manufacturing business specializing in steel products for industry. Headquartered in London, Caparo operates in the UK, the USA, Canada, India and the UAE.

Swraj Paul is chancellor of the University of Wolverhampton, a position he has held for twenty-six years, making him the longest-serving chancellor of any UK university. He holds sixteen honorary degrees.

He is the author of an earlier autobiography, *Beyond Boundaries*, published in 1998, and a well-received biography of Indira Gandhi, published in 1984.

Awarded the Padma Bhushan by the Government of India in 1983, he was elevated to the peerage and took his seat in the British House of Lords in 1996. He is a Freeman of the City of London and was appointed to the Privy Council by HM Queen Elizabeth II in 2009.

He married Aruna Paul, née Vij, in 1956 (d. 2022) and has three surviving children.

To

*My beloved parents, who I lost too soon but who left
me a legacy of wisdom and kindness.*

*My caring siblings, with whom I shared so much love and
understanding: Stya, Jit, Surrendra, Prakasho, Bimla and Kamla.*

*My dearest Aruna, Ambika and Angad, whose lives helped shape
my destiny and who I miss every day.*

*The tutors and teachers of Doaba School, Forman Christian
College and MIT, who shaped my philosophy.*

*My friend and colleague James Leek, who was with me from the
early days and without whose determination and drive Caparo
would not be what it is today. I miss his insight and wise counsel.*

Contents

1. My Story Begins — 1
2. MIT — 23
3. The Calcutta Years — 39
4. Ambika — 51
5. The Building Blocks of Caparo — 70
6. Inspired by Indira — 108
7. The DCM–Escorts Affair — 162
8. Peerage and Parliament — 189
9. Universities and Education — 221
10. Other Activities Including Government Appointments — 246
11. Angad — 265

12. Aruna	287
13. Where We Are Now and Going Forward	301
Epilogue	317
Acknowledgements	331
Appendix 1	333
Appendix 2	343
Appendix 3	349
Appendix 4	355
Appendix 5	361
Appendix 6	367
Appendix 7	371
Appendix 8	375
Appendix 9	379

1
My Story Begins

My story really begins in 1910 when my father, Amin Chand Payare Lal, moved to Jalandhar, Punjab, and settled there. Known as the 'land of five rivers', Punjab stretched from the north-west frontier of the Indian subcontinent to the borders of Delhi in the interior. The move took him more than 200 miles from his home village of Chang, and it was in Jalandhar that he founded a small business manufacturing metal household and agricultural implements. This was the beginning of our family's fortunes.

It has been ninety-three years since I was born and while many would consider this to be quite a long lifespan, I have experienced it in a rather remarkable form, with a mixture of contentment and despair.

Around the time of my birth, the Indian freedom movement against British colonial rule was forging ahead. In December 1929, the Indian National Congress, at its annual session in Lahore (now in Pakistan), passed a resolution demanding *purna swaraj* or complete independence. In 1930, the icon of the emancipation struggle, Mohandas Gandhi, better known as Mahatma (great soul) Gandhi, spearheaded a mass civil disobedience, which included a defiant and symbolic 240-mile march from his ashram (hermitage) in Sabarmati near Ahmedabad city to Dandi beach on the western coast of India in the Gujarat region. The objective was to gather salt in protest against the British law of 1882, which compelled Indians to buy this staple ingredient relatively expensively, as well as pay tax on it, rather than process it for themselves.

Gandhi and 60,000 of his followers were arrested, and many of the protestors were beaten by the police. It was a demonstration that caught the eye of the world's media. Gandhi's *satyagraha* or passive resistance slowly unified Indians at an emotional level and threw down a gauntlet to the Raj, conveying that its time was running out.

It was in this tumultuous national mood of non-cooperation that I entered the world on 18 February 1931 as the third son and sixth child of my father Payare Lal and mother Mongwati in Jalandhar. I was delivered by a *dai* (midwife) at home, as was the practice in that era, instead of at a nursing home or hospital, of which only a modest one existed in Jalandhar.

Historians have deduced that the whole of Punjab, including what is now Jalandhar district, were part of the celebrated Indus Valley civilization, which is estimated to have existed between 3300 BCE and 1300 BCE. The mention of Jalandhar, however, as per academic chronicles, can be traced back only to 100 CE.

Almost two millennia later, the British annexed it in its effort to overrun the Sikh kingdom in Punjab and established a military cantonment there.

By the time I was born, though, the tide was turning in the opposite direction. The British held on to India—their 'jewel in the crown'—but the Gandhian campaign of the Congress Party had already extracted concessions from the colonialists that had loosened their complete dominance over the country. Moral courage and a spirit of sacrifice had imbued in Indians an increasing desire for liberty.

The British were still largely in control. They had vast resources at their disposal. In 1927, they completed a sixteen-year construction of the impressive imperial city of New Delhi, carved out of both brown and green field lands of Delhi. The older part of Delhi had previously been the seat of the Mughal emperor—the sprawling, fortified complex known as the Red Fort. Self-government for Indians did not appear to be an immediate prospect. Yet, the Indian masses were brimming with a new nationalism which was noteworthy from a historical perspective. It was a heady period in the Indian calendar of the twentieth century.

The antecedents of my family were in the eastern segment of Punjab, which has since 1966 been separated into the state of Haryana. Interestingly, even after fifty-eight years, the two states share the same capital, Chandigarh, which reflects the somewhat unfinished nature of the delineation.

My great-great-grandfather on my paternal side, Jawan Lal, settled in a village called Chang, now in Bhiwani district, where he initially bought and sold vegetables. He then ventured into trading cloth and metalwork. In short, he did well enough to enable his grandson, my grandfather Amin Chand, to diversify into farming.

My mother, the daughter of a merchant, hailed from Charkhi, a village in Charkhi Dadri district not far from the town of Hisar, about 28 miles south of Chang in the direction of the desert area of Rajasthan.

I'd never had the pleasure of meeting my grandparents but in 2005, I was pleased to construct a sports stadium at a women's college in Charkhi to celebrate their lives and my mother's birth.

My grandfather apparently cultivated wheat, rice, cauliflowers and potatoes and ran a dairy farm, which was a common means of livelihood among rural folk in the fertile plains of Punjab, later known as 'the granary' of independent India.

Recalling my ancestors, I am reminded of a story that has become family lore. In summer, when it would be stifling hot inside the brick building of the local school, schoolboys would have their lessons outside under the shade of the trees. At lunchtime, it was the practice of fathers to bring tiffin for their children; in this respect, my grandfather was no different. On one occasion, my grandfather turned up with food for one of my uncles when a maths class was in progress. Amin Chand heard the teacher ask the pupils to add 1,00,000 and 20,000. Sounding quite horrified, he shouted out, 'Stop!' The bewildered master asked, 'Why?' My grandfather replied, 'I don't want my son to know numbers bigger than 100, otherwise he will demand more money. I don't want him to be greedy.'

However, in the early 1900s, agriculture had become comparatively unprofitable. Thus, two of my uncles and then my father, inspired by a spirit of enterprise, travelled to Lahore, which was large and prosperous; it was northern India's biggest city and the capital and nerve centre of the undivided province of Punjab. It was also practical for them to do so, because Amin Chand had three brothers and six sons and the landholding and other assets in Chang were insufficient to support so many men of working age and their growing families.

Their objective was to explore other means of earning. In fact, it was in this metropolis, then known as 'the Paris of the East', with its cultural riches, exotic cuisine and remnants of Mughal architecture, that they learnt the rudiments of commerce.

It was a major departure from the prevailing culture and practice. People who practised any profession other than what their forebears had engaged in were exceptions. A fourth brother, Khemchand, departed Chang for Jalandhar, a developing industrial township. He persuaded his brothers that the market there was less competitive and more promising than the comparatively congested Lahore.

So it was in 1910 that my father settled in Jalandhar, where he commenced a small metal manufacturing business making buckets, tubs and other household implements.

The four brothers were involved in almost identical professions, making agricultural implements, buckets, bathtubs, washbasins and a variety of household items, not to mention brass taps. While they competed with each other in effect, the brothers and their families lived in complete harmony, with no rivalry or rancour between them. Three of my uncles, Khemchand, Bholanath and Nanuram, lived close to our house, while another, Govardhandas, also resided in Jalandhar. A fifth uncle, Lekhraj, stayed back in Lahore, where he died prematurely. My father also had two sisters.

My older siblings were brother Stya (pronounced Satya), sister Prakasho, brother Jit, sister Bimla and sister Kamla, in that order. After me came another brother, Surrendra. Two of our first cousins—children of Lekhraj, who had died early—also came to live in our house in the practice of accommodating the extended family that characterizes the Indian joint family system.

We resided on the first and second floors of a three-storeyed building, number 2, Tanda Road, where the ground floor was my father's company's office and the packaging area for its products. Therefore, despite an upbringing that occurred thousands of miles from Britain, I, like many twentieth-century Britons, literally grew up above the shop! On a vacant plot behind our house, in the backyard of our property, my father established a foundry and steel rolling mill that manufactured the metal and brass ware.

Today, the population of bustling Jalandhar, with its small and medium-sized industries—among them sports equipment manufacturing—is over a million. In the 1930s, it was 50,000–60,000. To compare it to other urban centres in Punjab, it wasn't as big as Amritsar, famous for its Golden Temple, the holiest shrine of the Sikh religion; it was about the size of Rawalpindi, now Islamabad's twin city in Pakistan.

Our life was generally quiet and conventional. But exciting events were stirring the nation and Punjab was integrally part and parcel of this turmoil. Gandhi had galvanized his compatriots with his unique brand of civil disobedience. 'We want swaraj (freedom)!' was the nationalist refrain. To us, though, it had a wider significance—liberation with Gandhian virtues and an evocation of India's cultural past.

My brother Stya, an activist in the resistance to British rule, takes credit for naming me—though it is spelt slightly differently, Swraj, from the standard spelling, Swaraj. My patriotic parents happily agreed.

I believe an individual's emotional intelligence is largely defined by their roots. The insecurities that trouble people later in life begin with the heredity, environment and relationships at play during their formative years. While this may now be textbook psychology, it is also derived from common sense. In this respect, I was particularly fortunate to have been born into a close and caring family.

My father was rightly proud of his growing business and burgeoning family. My siblings and I lived in an affectionate atmosphere and were also blessed with the abiding love of a gracious mother. Consequently, my early childhood was full of happiness and tranquillity.

My father was not fortunate to receive much formal education. But he was a wise and astute man. Ingrained in him was an unambiguous awareness of ethics and principles and he was particular about instilling these in his children. The morals we lived by were charity, discipline, frugality and unity. Our father made sure these values were incorporated into our lifestyle. He was a man of few words and did not overtly preach or sermonize, but made sure we followed a virtuous path.

As a father, he was unfailingly kind-hearted and considerate towards his children. But he also ensured we kept our feet on the ground. He would assign us manual work so that we didn't develop any vanity and would appreciate the dignity of labour. My brother Jit and I were assigned to sweeping the office and factory floor each day. In due course, while I was still a schoolboy, I was drafted into the business as an occasional typist or clerical assistant. We were also allocated some household shopping, like purchasing food and vegetables from the local bazaar.

My father deemed luxury and waste sinful. He did not deny us basic necessities but, like the simple and straightforward Indian men of that generation, he felt frugality was righteous and extravagance a fault. He certainly had the means to provide more. But we children each possessed no more than two or three sets of clothes—one to wear while the others were being washed.

This was clearly a strict regime. We could afford greater comfort but it was not lavished on us. Since then, the world has increasingly gravitated towards instant gratification. I, too, have been indulgent as a parent compared to my father. And while I am still averse to profligacy and ostentation, I have been more amenable to the conveniences of life than my father.

At the same time, I sometimes wonder if my father was right. The consumer society we have built, whether in Britain, in India or anywhere else, has had a damaging effect. Opulence based on credit is unsustainable. The reckless manner of accumulating debt to finance unproductive acquisition is debilitating and its long-term impact is evident. Decades of greed has harmed our environment. I believe the time is at hand when my father's prudence will become compulsory for the preservation of our planet.

Charity was also built into my father's DNA. He strongly believed that surplus money should be directed towards people in need. Just outside the front entrance of our house, he set up a stall. This was for the purpose of providing small items to passers-by, perhaps grains or a snack like roasted peas. The poor, who were hard put to buy these, gratefully picked them up gratis. No count was kept on how many times a person availed themselves of the facility, nor was any reciprocal obligation required. This principle of sharing with others has remained in our family to this day.

It was an unwritten rule that the entire family should assemble at mealtimes to eat together. My mother presided and enjoyed serving us breakfast, lunch and dinner, cherishing this cheerful family gathering. We persevered with this custom long after her death.

But the serenity of my childhood was suddenly shattered. In 1938, my mother passed away in childbirth when I was barely seven years old. It was a terrible blow, unthinkable in my innocence. My siblings and I were moved to the home of one of my uncles to shield us from the funeral ceremonies. I was too young to fully understand what had happened to my mother but I sensed it was disastrous. Contemporary healthcare would have easily prevented the tragedy. But in the 1930s, in a place like Jalandhar, medical amenities were limited and certainly not readily available for home treatment.

It was the first time that life had dealt me a harsh blow. My mother was only in her late thirties and had been omnipresent in my world. Even now, memories of her loving ways linger. She was always simply attired and someone once asked her why she didn't wear any jewellery. She replied, 'My children are my jewels.' The suddenness of her leaving us was a bombshell for the family and left us with an acute emptiness.

The premature departure of near and dear ones since has filled me with grief. My father, my brother Surrendra, my daughter Ambika and my son Angad. All of them taken too soon.

I have tried to comprehend these twists of fate. There are philosophical and religious explanations that offer some comfort. Often, these mitigate the suffering of those who believe in them. I have, however, not found solace in such reasoning. To me, the randomness of death, especially when it visits those whose lives haven't fully unfolded, defies understanding. Its finality, its irrevocability, is hard in a world where one often gets a second chance. Presumably, one day we will learn more about death. But presently, as unfulfilling as it is, we must reconcile ourselves to it being destined, beyond our control. This issue has occupied me more as I have grown older, but the resolution remains as elusive as ever.

In my mother's absence, the bond with my father grew. He was always very fond of me. Now we spent many more hours in each other's company. Apart from school time, I was invariably with him. I even started sleeping in his room at night. The eldest of my sisters, Prakasho, began looking after me and I became very attached to her. When she married in 1941, I was so distraught about her leaving us that my father sent me to live with her at her in-laws' house for a while.

In 1942, Gandhi launched his 'do or die', his 'Quit India' movement against British rule. In fact, the Mahatma visited Jalandhar that year. He even visited our house and joined us for lunch. I was eleven years old and almost overwhelmed by this.

My brother Stya—I called him Bhaiji—who was twelve years older than me, was politically active. In his teens and early twenties, he engaged in anti-colonial activism and was inspired by the Mahatma. Stya was a man of unusual determination and thereby an inspiration to me. Afflicted by polio in infancy, he had to walk with crutches until a final surgery in the 1950s at the Massachusetts Medical Hospital in Boston cured him of his disability. In school, he was a plucky goalkeeper in the hockey team.

One day in 1942, we were sitting around chatting when several policemen in civilian clothes—who we later realized were from the Criminal Investigation Department (CID)—descended on our house. They asked Bhaiji to come with them. Hours passed, but he did not return. We were worried, fearing the worst. My father began inquiries about his whereabouts but drew a blank. The next day, we learnt that Bhaiji had been arrested under an arbitrary British law known as the Defence of India Rule and was now in jail.

Hearing this, my father went to meet the deputy commissioner of Jalandhar, the British administrator of the town, who said he should prevail upon Bhaiji to apologize for joining the freedom movement and then he would be released. My father said he would do no such thing and would rather see his son in prison than ask him to compromise his ideals. In any case, my father knew that even if he suggested such a course, Bhaiji would not relent. Bhaiji's cellmate in jail was Darbara Singh, who later went on to become the chief minister of Punjab.

In those heady times, men and women would endure hardship rather than dishonour their nation. Their families proudly endorsed their bravery, defiance and nationalism. Individuals and groups sunk their differences to join hands in the struggle for independence. In the face of such unity and resolve, the British were in a quandary.

I often wonder what has happened to those qualities of togetherness and patriotism. Why have these values been abandoned in modern-day India? Surely, a race that displayed such an extraordinary effort to gain emancipation can channel this spirit to the task of nation-building. I am afraid that without a return to cooperation and dedication, India may not fulfil its potential. Policies, no matter how enlightened, cannot substitute for commitment.

By the early 1940s, the Second World War was at India's doorstep. Wars are often opportunities for some businesses. Although my father was not making components for the defence industry, he expanded his range of items. He built a new factory to manufacture these new products, which were milk cans and nuts and bolts.

Jit was now fully engaged in the company's operations. He would frequently visit Calcutta (now Kolkata) to negotiate with authorities, as the availability of steel was under government control.

After the war, he made Calcutta his home and lived there for the rest of his life. By that stage, the business had grown much bigger. Indeed, in 1943, during the height of the war, the family decided to buy a car. As children, we either walked or rode a bicycle, while elders used a horse-drawn buggy. Since even a spin in the buggy was exciting, a motorcar was an absolute wonder.

As there were no outlets in Jalandhar selling cars, my father had to journey to Lahore to purchase a second-hand Hudson, an American model, for what was then a princely sum of Rs 3000, which was equivalent to £230 at the time. When my father returned in this handsome vehicle, it was a cause of much celebration in the family and a matter of pride for all of us. It became the talk of the town as only a handful of people owned a car in Jalandhar. My father, normally a stickler for austerity, was nevertheless pleased with his purchase.

But the joy was short-lived. Tragedy struck. My uncle Khemchand, who was particularly close to my father, died of heart failure. This was a crushing blow for my father. On hearing the devastating news, my father rushed to my uncle's house. Clutching the body, he cried in despair, 'Khemchand, I'll bring your meals for you,' he wailed.

We did not grasp what these words meant, or the extent to which the event had affected our father. But it gradually became apparent that he had lost his desire to live. He fell ill, and although he recovered, he was haunted by his promise to Khemchand. Murmuring to himself, he would say he hadn't fulfilled his commitment to his brother. He was inconsolable.

Only three months later, my father and I were alone together on our veranda. Jit was away on business. My sisters were in the kitchen. Suddenly, my father fell off the couch on which he was seated. I raised the alarm and everyone in the house came running. But there was nothing we could do. He too had passed away instantly from heart failure. Without a doubt, the grief that had overwhelmed him had hastened his end. Such can be the impact of the human heart and mind on the body. He was fifty-five and the year was 1944. I was thirteen years old, and my childhood had been cruelly and hastily concluded.

I was well into school by this stage at Labhu Ram Doaba High School, one of the best in Jalandhar. In the early classes, we were instructed in Hindi, but thereafter in English. My father supported the institution as part of his charity work. In 2019, I made a donation to the school for the construction of an administration block. This was inaugurated by my niece, Sushma Berlia, daughter of my brother Stya.

Boyhood to adolescence to adulthood is not always an easy passage. Innocence gives way to consciousness and this in turn concedes to knowledge. The cover is lifted on the sheltered happiness in which most parents bring up their children. In the India of my childhood, and to a certain extent even today, parental love and societal customs insulate young people from the realities of life for a while. Whether this protection is ultimately of value is now a subject for debate; a delay in exposure to the wider world may make one's later entry into it more difficult.

I am convinced that the positives of parental care while growing up outweigh any negatives. It provides reassurance during one's development in an often unforgiving and confusing environment. Since such caring was cut short in my life, I can testify to how traumatic this deprivation can be.

To me, the decade after my father's death was painful. I was thirteen and still somewhat immature for my age. We continued to live in our house as a joint family, but the absence of my parents created a terrible emptiness. My brothers Bhaiji and Jit, both much older than me, did everything they could to alleviate my grief. They were the best surrogate parents, showering me with the emotional and material support so necessary for a boy of my age. Simultaneously, their stewardship of the family businesses was taking us from strength to strength. Jit, especially, was beginning to reveal his financial genius, which would make him one of India's most successful entrepreneurs.

Bhaiji would in due course dedicate his energies to developing quality education in India. He paid particular attention to my schooling. My school was walking distance from our house and my academic record was very satisfactory. When I completed my matriculation in 1945, Bhaiji, who had studied at Government College in Lahore, insisted I enrol at Forman Christian College, an American missionary institution, in the same city for my graduation. This, he felt, would expose me to better instruction than was available in Jalandhar. It would give me insight into a wider world and offer opportunities that didn't exist locally.

The Doaba School, where I studied at both the primary and secondary levels, gave me a solid grounding, which stood me in good stead in the future.

Bhaiji's plan was far-sighted. He and Jit felt I could be more useful to the expanding family business with a higher technical education. The Banaras Hindu University, which possessed a reputed engineering college, was chosen as the target university for my training. In those days, business people generally equipped their children with a basic education and swiftly drafted them into the family business. Experience in the trade was deemed to be more valuable to one's career than higher education. Pursuit of a university degree was atypical and often greeted with mirth among the commercial classes.

Obviously, such thinking has changed dramatically. Self-made parents now generally send their children to business schools to obtain MBAs as a finishing degree. This has become almost essential in a highly competitive and sophisticated business environment. However, I have also known whizz-kids with fancy qualifications make elementary errors that have brought ruin to their employers.

I believe that while superior training is invaluable, this should be a supplement to, not a substitute for, common sense. Experience is an irreplaceable ingredient that academia cannot compensate for. On the other hand, experience can sometimes be a disadvantage. The older we get, the greater the inclination to fall back on irrelevant nostalgia. What we need to derive from experience is less reminiscence, more practicality and a recognition of modernity.

I was admitted to the American Presbyterian Forman Christian College in Lahore to obtain a BSc degree. My father would probably not have sent me to study out of town, but my brothers were from the new generation and more progressive. In the first year, I stayed at the college hostel before moving out to external accommodation.

I had never been away from the family and was often homesick. But I managed to adjust to the circumstances. Regular trips to Jalandhar on Sundays or visits by relatives to Lahore relieved the loneliness. What helped immensely was the kindness of our American principal, Reverend Dr Charles Rice, and his wife Mary. They were Christian missionaries committed to excellence in education. They became quite fond of me and were a source of immense inspiration. Many years later, I was happy to institute a scholarship programme in my late daughter Ambika's name at Forman Christian College.

One of Mrs Rice's brothers, Arthur Compton, had won the Nobel Prize for Physics in 1927 for an invention in electromagnetic radiation. Another brother was president of the world-renowned Massachusetts Institute of Technology in Boston. This was, and still is, one of the United States' finest centres of advanced scientific and engineering studies. Mrs Rice advised and encouraged me to go to America for a shot at MIT. She even brought me the admission form for that purpose. Under her guidance, I began dreaming—indeed, exploring—the possibilities of applying for entry there. With a background in a relatively small town like Jalandhar, thinking of going to the US was equivalent to dreaming about flying to the moon. Fortunately, my academic record was up to the mark; therefore, Mrs Rice could honestly tell MIT so and recommend my case.

At the Kennedy Hall hostel of Forman College, where I was put up, I made new friends and played sports, including tennis. More importantly, I studied physics, chemistry and mathematics.

My brothers were keen that I become an engineer as such expertise would be useful for the development of our business. They were conscious that technology was changing and if our enterprise were to progress, it would need more scientific input.

However, the cost of education overseas was prohibitive so it had been assumed I would enter an Indian university. America was a distant dream and going there, an unlikely prospect.

But before anything concrete happened, India was shaken by the terrible events of Partition in August 1947. The British withdrew and India was divided into two countries, a Hindu-majority India and an Islamic Pakistan. This cut through the heart of the Punjab province. Lahore became a part of Pakistan. Overnight, I became a foreigner in the city, while Jalandhar remained a part of India.

Murderous riots broke out and persisted uncontrolled on both sides of the new border. Assaults on Hindus were taking place all around me in Lahore. In a state of panic, I clambered on to one of the last trains leaving the city to escape eastwards to Jalandhar. As the carriages pulled out of the station, I heard that a Muslim mob had attacked the last compartment, hauling out Hindus and murdering them. Few people had expected Partition to take such an ugly turn.

After that, Hindus and Sikhs seeking to escape Lahore by rail were systematically dragged from their coaches and massacred. There was retaliation against Muslims as they attempted to travel in the opposite direction. It was terrifying and a moment of madness in Indian history. I had been extraordinarily fortunate. Up to 2 million people died in the communal carnage, mostly in Punjab. Hindu refugees streamed into Indian Punjab from Pakistan. Massive camps were set up to receive and accommodate them. The displaced people carried harrowing tales of privation, killings, loss of families and property.

Since it was close to the Pakistan border, Jalandhar was virtually at the forefront of this horror. People were petrified and in a state of immobility. Several of our Muslim friends were butchered—murders that defy description. Protecting them meant instant death at the hands of the maniacal characters that roamed the streets. To do nothing was a horrible admission of powerlessness and inadequacy. I was sixteen and my world had gone up in flames!

The wounds of Partition still sting an entire generation of Indians and Pakistanis. An iron curtain descended between people who had lived in comparative calm for centuries. Whether the division of British India was right or wrong is a complex question. What is obvious is that it created two nations perpetually hostile towards each other, each spending vast sums of money on weaponry rather than on development.

Must everyone with nightmares of Partition perish before a sensible peace is achieved between India and Pakistan? The bitter memories have become a toxic legacy imposed on the consciousness of the two peoples. For those who experienced undivided India, where one could travel freely from Quetta to Dhaka, from the Khyber to Kerala, this is an unmitigated tragedy. It seems that what politics separates, diplomacy cannot enjoin; we are condemned to perpetual antagonism.

The terror I witnessed often comes back to haunt me. Nobody had anticipated the extent of the outburst of violence. It seized us suddenly, as quickly as disease spreads when an evil virus is unleashed. I saw otherwise kind and sensible people metamorphose into monsters. Is the skin of civilization so thin that men can rapidly transform into savages? To those who encountered the India of 1947, places like Bosnia, Ukraine and Gaza are no surprise. And humanity seems no further forward in curbing these extremes.

The upheaval continued in Punjab for the rest of 1947. The influx of refugees and their tragic tales kept the state on tenterhooks. Schools and colleges were closed for almost a year; the students were asked to care for the inmates at the camps and I volunteered. We were busy sometimes for nearly 20 hours a day. It was saddening and strenuous, but strangely also uplifting. It was heart-rending to come into close contact with people who had suffered so much, but it was gratifying as well to make a difference in the lives of such desolate and devastated people. It was my efforts at the refugee camps that awakened me to the importance of community service. It's an ethic that has stayed with me and fortunately I have been able to maintain it.

It was at the camps that I first caught a glimpse of Jawaharlal Nehru, India's legendary first prime minister. It was an interface with greatness. He toured the facilities and spoke to the uprooted people. He appealed for peace. He admonished those who protested and scolded anyone who spoke of revenge.

I sensed the ambivalence of the masses. They loved Nehru but were in a quandary over his message. There was a reaction of both affection and anger in the camps. He was calling for restraint when retribution was the emotion. Nehru did not care about his popularity being affected. He refused to pander to base instincts. It was in the nature of the man to say and execute what he believed was right for a democratic India. His impulse was of a statesman; politics to him was secondary.

It was for such nobility that the youth of my time admired Nehru and why other politicians around him seemed less significant comparatively. Observing him at the camps, little did I contemplate that a day would come when fate would bring me into close contact with his family, especially his daughter and only child, Indira.

It needed one horror to close the chapter of another. The assassination of Mahatma Gandhi in January 1948 shocked the turbulence into silence. He had been an overpowering influence on Indians. We thought of him as immortal. His cold-blooded killing by the Hindu extremist Nathuram Godse—who despised his even-handedness towards all communities, including Muslims—pulverized us. The 'Father of the Nation', India's conscience-keeper, gunned down in public! How ironic that it took such a despicable act to dampen the collective killings. What Gandhi had struggled to achieve in life—not always successfully—he had accomplished in death.

Men of peace sometimes meet a brutal end, for their enemies misunderstand their teachings. This is one of the unedifying lessons of history. It is also true of the South Asian region in general. Why is this part of the world, with its profound preaching of peace from ancient times, so infested with violence? Why have so many of the Indian subcontinent's leaders been assassinated? Unless there is greater contemplation, these awful happenings will destroy the region's spiritual ethos.

In the radically changed circumstances, there was of course no question of returning to Lahore to resume my studies at Forman Christian College. Instead, I picked up the threads at Doaba College in Jalandhar. It was not as famous an institute as Forman, but I gained good experience there. I remember one of the teachers drilling into me the importance of telling the truth. He memorably told me, 'If you tell the truth, you don't have to rehearse it.' In the spring of 1949, I completed my graduation with honours in mathematics, physics and chemistry.

I received exciting news from MIT, which had accepted my application and granted me admission into its engineering course beginning in the autumn of 1949. At first, I was hesitant to inform my brothers. I had kept my correspondence with MIT a secret from them. It would be expensive to go to America and the separation from the family would be for too long. Nobody in our family had ever ventured out of India. I was convinced they would discourage me. To my pleasant surprise, though, Bhaiji and Jit were delighted and were adamant I take up the offer.

I had never travelled farther from Jalandhar than to Lahore in my life, so the thought of going to America, its strangeness, caused me great anxiety. I first had to go to the US embassy in Delhi to obtain my visa. Then about 300 people gathered at the railway station to see me off as I boarded the Jalandhar-Bombay train for the first part of my long journey. In a small town like Jalandhar, it was in those days a very big thing to go from India to America. I was probably one of the first Jalandharis to embark on such a voyage. Never have I received such a roaring send-off! Amid tears and cheers, I bid goodbye to my family and friends.

Bombay was one of India's biggest cities, far more extensive than Lahore. From here, on the first international leg of my journey, I flew to London, where I stopped for a few days to overcome my jetlag. I did not, though, then complete my passage to Boston!

The ancestral home in Jalandhar

Extended family c. 1939. I am in the second row, in the middle

2
MIT

I arrived in London and went to the Great Eastern Hotel near Liverpool Street station, then an independent establishment and now part of the Hyatt chain, where I was booked to stay for about five days. It was an impressive red brick building, characteristic of British architecture. But Britain, yet to recover economically from the Second World War, was still passing through a period of austerity. Nevertheless, it was an amazing, new experience and I was eager to explore.

    British men and women in their own country were noticeably different from their compatriots who ruled the Empire. They were down-to-earth, unaffected, helpful people. They were not imbued with the airs and graces of colonial Britons, who had cultivated an artificial behaviour meant to indicate their superiority over Indians. It may have impressed a few, but it offended many. Perhaps the most lasting impact of this contrived behaviour, with its narrow social aspects, was on the practitioners themselves. Back home in Britain after a lengthy service in the Empire, they found themselves singularly out of place and unable to adjust to the civilities of normal life.

My brothers had good connections in London. Stephen Kay, chief executive of Stewarts and Lloyds, steel tube manufacturers, took charge of me. Our family in India did business with this company. Mr Kay sent me to Glasgow to see their steel tube plant there, which was meant to be an eye-opener for me, aspiring as I was to become a metallurgical engineer. However, what I really witnessed was incessant rain and my recollections of the Scottish city on that visit are rather watery.

I also met William Ricketts. His firm was called Ironside and they, too, traded with our company in India. Assuming that I already knew this—which I didn't—he innocently mentioned that the manager of our Bombay office had gambled heavily and gotten deep into debt. He had to repay these losses and he personally was in no position to honour the obligation, so my brothers Jit and Stya were therefore compelled to do so. This, Mr Ricketts said, had apparently placed our business in a perilous state. The revelation was a bolt from the blue. My brothers hadn't told me anything about this, fearing it would deter me from going abroad. They felt they were being kind because I wasn't involved in the business, so why bother me?

When I heard the story from Mr Ricketts, I was deeply distressed. I felt I couldn't possibly continue with the journey to the United States, given the expense this would involve over an extended period. I informed Jit I was returning immediately. Using the balance of my air ticket, I took the first available flight back to Bombay. All I wanted at that moment was to help my family and not be a financial burden on them.

Jit came to meet me at Bombay airport. After listening to my outbursts for about an hour, he calmly told me I was booked on the next plane out to Boston. He said words to the effect 'Don't worry, we'll manage. You go ahead with your studies.' There was no argument. In retrospect, I am eternally grateful to Jit for his good-humoured but steadfast insistence.

This time, I just took a connecting flight from London. I remember we stopped at Limerick in Ireland en route. This was meant to be for refuelling purposes, but the aircraft also developed some engine problems. We were taken to a hotel while they repaired the plane. From Limerick we flew to Gander, a little island off the American coast. Finally, we reached New York, where I stayed overnight before catching a train to Boston. It was September 1949. I had arrived at the redoubtable Massachusetts Institute of Technology (MIT) to fulfil my dream.

MIT had been founded in 1861 to accelerate the United States' industrial revolution. Regularly listed as the world's number one university, it is a quintessentially American institution, with an innate ingenuity and dynamism. It has invented fundamental technologies for the US and the world and given rise to new industries. It was already a magnet of talent from various parts of the world when I arrived there. Today, it boasts ninety-eight Nobel laureates, among the more recent being Professor Abhijit Banerjee in economics, from my former home city of Kolkata.

My four years at MIT were undoubtedly a turning point in my life. Initially, I was unhappy in the alien surroundings. I was accommodated at the university's student residence and mainly kept to myself. Of course, one of the by-products of my isolation was the ability to immerse myself in my studies.

Asians were few and far between in Boston. There were, if memory serves me right, only seven other Indians at the institute. When we travelled around America and introduced ourselves as Indian, we were inevitably asked which tribe we belonged to.

But gradually the ice began to melt, and I slipped into the mainstream of university life. The teachers were remarkably helpful and friendly. It was an informal style of education, though very demanding. I would be given assignments that I had to submit the very next day. So I beavered away in my room, keeping pace with the requirements, burying myself in textbooks and what we had been taught at the lectures.

Since I had completed a BSc in physics, chemistry and mathematics in India before I entered MIT, I was awarded my bachelor's and master's degrees simultaneously in 1952, i.e., in three years, instead of the standard four years. In 1953, I secured a degree called Mackie in mechanical engineering and metallurgy.

Though I say this myself, I was a reasonably good student. At MIT, they insisted that you master mathematics. One of my professors, Norbert Wiener, would generously give me 100 per cent marks when examining my work. He used to say encouragingly, 'Swraj, I'll be surprised if you ever get less than that.'

Dr Karl Compton was the president of MIT. He was a brother of Mrs Rice, wife of the principal at Forman Christian College in Lahore, who had kindly written to him about me. He was the most senior figure at MIT and generally not accessible to the students. I do not know what precisely she said in her letter about me, but not only did we meet in his private office, but he was also warm and welcoming. Few undergraduate students got an opportunity to meet him one on one.

The smattering of Indian students at MIT at the time naturally gravitated towards each other. I became friends with Krishan Gupta, Arun Prasad and M.S. Pathak, son of G.S. Pathak, later to become vice president of India. M.S.'s brother, R.S. Pathak, became Chief Justice of India, before becoming president of the International Court of Justice at The Hague.

I began to enjoy the environment. The faculty was generous and supportive, my grades were good and I started participating in a variety of campus activities. I played tennis and waited tables at the cafeteria, for which I earned $1 an hour and got the bonus of a free meal. It was pocket money I needed. I was anxious not to overload my family, so I undertook as many part-time jobs as possible.

At various times, I was a waiter, a research assistant and a college instructor. I became an instructor after I obtained my MSc. This was a privilege. I taught those who were training for their bachelor's degree.

In those post-war years, there was a major intake of older students at American universities. MIT was no exception. This was pursuant to a government-funded GI (American servicemen) Education Program to reward soldiers and other veterans of World War II. These were battle-hardened men who had served on various fronts in Europe and Asia. Consequently, they had been compelled to discontinue their studies. Many of them were married, older and more mature compared to the average undergraduate student. Their presence, not to mention their informality, exerted a positive influence on us. Contrary to what I had anticipated, these military men were quite compassionate towards their younger colleagues. Wars are supposed to brutalize people who partook in them. But here was evidence that they could humanize people too.

University life in the US at that time was very different from what it is now. There was much less focus on wider concerns and radical causes. In the aftermath of war, though, new issues gripped America. These were matters like anti-colonialism, gender equality, the environment, multiculturalism and ethnicity, not to mention the green shoots of the civil rights movement in the United States.

Towards the end of my stay, harsher rumblings heralded the onset of a storm. The overtones of McCarthyism reached Boston and the nearby Harvard University was especially scourged by it. Joe McCarthy, a Wisconsin senator, claimed some 200 card-carrying communists worked in the US State department. As chairman of a Senate investigation committee, he conducted hearings on communist subversion in America and probed alleged communist infiltration into its armed forces. It was an infamous witch-hunt based on fabrication. By and large, MIT students remained apolitical and preoccupied with their work. They did not get agitated about public affairs to the extent their counterparts in some of the other universities did. Eventually unsuccessful, McCarthy went into political exile.

My life was calm and untroubled as MIT helped to develop my personality. The constant interaction with people from other cultures broadened my outlook. The intellectual challenges were stimulating and provoked much discussion and debate. The amiability of American youth was infectious.

My friends and I mostly ate at the institute's restaurants. But sometimes, if I felt like having Italian or tasty vegetarian food, there were restaurants nearby. I have never eaten non-vegetarian cuisine and I remember there was an Israeli restaurant which made *chapatis*!

A sense of self-confidence began to grow in me. MIT instils in its students the mantra that you can do anything and nothing is beyond you. I certainly did not possess this self-belief when I left India. The university is famous for its rigorous standards, and this generates the attitude that every challenge can be met, every problem can be solved, all doors will open if you knock hard enough. It was a demanding culture and its effect has stayed with me ever since.

While I was at MIT, my brother Bhaiji or Stya came to Boston for medical treatment. He, as I have mentioned before, was a victim of polio. The cure necessitated him being in hospital for close to six months where he underwent a series of painful and protracted surgeries.

One day, in an effort to cheer him up, we went for a drive to nearby Concord Park. Bhaiji sat on a bench, looking deeply depressed. A stranger walked up and asked why he was so melancholy. Bhaiji explained his condition. To our amazement, the passer-by loosened his clothing and showed us that both his arms and legs were artificial. He told Bhaiji to be grateful that only one of his legs had been afflicted. This was a remarkable morale booster and provided my brother with a much-needed psychological lift.

The care and corrective measures he received provided him considerable relief, without eradicating his disability altogether. He previously needed crutches to walk. Now he was able to walk on both legs for the first time since infancy, albeit with the help of a stick. It was moving to see him stand erect without assistance. We left for India in a joyful mood. Bhaiji lived to the age of ninety-five.

In 1953, I also completed the course requirements for a doctoral thesis. It was, in fact, my intention to return to India for a while, gain some work experience and then come back to MIT to complete my dissertation. But fate dictated otherwise.

Today's affluent parents unwittingly do a disservice to their offspring—many of whom attend US universities—by providing too many comforts to them and by insulating them from reality. They are sent abroad for higher education without much thought to character-building. But have regrets when their children are unable to manage. The fact I wasn't mollycoddled was a blessing. When it came to my children, I was conscious about not allowing them too much luxury in their student days. But they nevertheless enjoyed greater benefits than I had.

Jawaharlal Nehru as prime minister visited Boston while I was a student at MIT. As expressed earlier, I had been greatly impressed by him since my childhood. In my teens, I saw him at first hand when he visited Punjab. Support for Indian freedom was ingrained in our family. A charismatic leader, Nehru really epitomized this movement. He was responsible for winning independence for India along with Mahatma Gandhi. Nehru's sister Vijaya Lakshmi Pandit accompanied him on his trip to Boston, since she was then the Indian ambassador to the United States.

Nehru addressed students from various Boston-based universities. I was in the audience. He talked about India. This was followed by questions and answers. I asked him, 'What guidance do you have to build India?' He replied, 'Build an India we and you can be proud of. You are in a great institution.' Another student asked him, 'Panditji, we learn you stand on your head every day in the morning. What's your reason?' The prime minister jovially replied, 'I can visualize the world better, because the world is topsy-turvy.'

It is because of my attachment to MIT, my gratitude for its contribution to my being, that I have attempted to repay my debt. My first initiative in 1987 was to found the Swraj Paul 1952 Scholarship Fund, providing support for Indian students, or students of Indian origin, to tackle four-year engineering courses.

In May 2022, I was delighted to receive a letter from the vice chancellor for undergraduate and graduate education at MIT on the occasion of the thirty-fifth anniversary of the fund. It said: 'Endowed scholarships are the very foundation of MIT's financial aid program. Your commitment makes it possible for MIT to attract the most talented and deserving students and enable them to fulfil their academic aspirations and make a better world. Thank you for this important investment.'

Accompanying the letter was a kind certificate of recognition. It said: 'Lord Swraj Paul, the MIT community is honoured to mark this auspicious milestone and is grateful for your investment in generations of undergraduates.'

I was also pleased to send funding towards a new building for its Sloan School of Management, which now features the Ambika Paul Mezzanine and the Ambika Paul Study Room.

I additionally extended another endowment of $1 million. My last bequest was $5 million. This was to build a theatre, the 'Swraj Paul PC '52 and Angad Paul '92 Theatre'. In August 2020, Aruna and I were invited to become members of the MIT Charter Society in recognition of our philanthropic commitment to MIT.

Having spent four enlightening years at MIT, I returned to India in 1953. I had saved some money from my wages as a waiter, research assistant and college instructor. So I bought a

Pontiac made by General Motors Company and had it shipped to Calcutta.

I sent two of my sons, Akash and Angad, to MIT. I am now encouraging Angad's widow Michelle to impress upon her children, my grandchildren, to seek admission at my alma mater.

With MIT's eighteenth president Sally Kornbluth in London 2024

Prime Minister Nehru, Vijaya Lakshmi Pandit and
James R. Killian, MIT, 1949

Practical machine shop at MIT in the 1950s

MIT Theatre, *Blitz* article

MIT main building

Picture courtesy MIT archives

MIT Engineering Department, I am bottom left, 1952

Me with fellow MIT mechanical engineering students, 1951

Me as an MIT student, 1952

Me and my Pi Tau Sigma fraternity at MIT

Harvard

Harvard Business School where I went to study management

3

The Calcutta Years

I returned to India from MIT in March 1953. My first assignment in the Apeejay family business was in a construction project away from Jalandhar, which one of my brothers-in-law, Kulwant Rai, was supervising. Punjab was building a new capital, Chandigarh, designed by the French architect Charles-Edouard Jeanneret, better known as Le Corbusier. It was a showpiece venture of independent India because Lahore, the capital of undivided Punjab, had been awarded to Pakistan after Partition.

Apeejay had won a contract to lay a sanitation pipeline grid. The site of Chandigarh in the early stages of its expansion was a vast array of rubble and holes in the ground when I first saw it. For someone fresh from MIT, a labour camp with distant outdoor toilets was something of a culture shock. It was my baptism in Indian business and it took a while to adapt. The work went well. After a few months, there was little more I needed to do, so in late 1953 I relocated to Calcutta, where our

Apeejay Group was now headquartered, to join Jit, who was heading the enterprise. Here I was to spend the next eleven years of my life.

India was in a paradoxical situation. The exhilaration of independence kindled widespread feelings of patriotism and commitment. Public life reflected the enthusiasm and principles of the long struggle for liberty. There was genuine willingness to accept short-term sacrifices in order to create a strong nation which would be prominent in the international community. There was hardly any corruption and expectations for the future were high. Yet, there was a lingering enslavement. We were politically self-governing, but at the same time controlled by British rules and regulations, commercial standards and economic captivity.

The mentality of the bureaucracy, the Indian Civil Service (ICS), a leftover from imperial times, particularly represented this dual thinking. The ICS was integral to building a new India, and indeed was sincere about it, but unable to envision that anything not British could be as good or even sometimes better. All the same, I found involvement in business in India personally stimulating.

Apeejay expanded exponentially. From a moderate-sized firm, we grew into a network of companies with branches and facilities in various parts of the country. We entered several new fields and laid the foundation of what was to become a large, stable chain of concerns. Bhaiji, Jit and I were in due course joined by our youngest brother Surrendra, an energetic and convivial addition, in our endeavours. Surrendra, who had initially joined MIT but then graduated from Brandeis University in the US, was interested in the technical process of manufacturing and in the trading side. The Paul brothers worked smoothly as a team, our complementary skills enabling the effective management of increasingly diverse operations. Our factories continued to turn out high-quality steel products.

Bhaiji spearheaded our expansion into the education sector. He was one of the pioneering industrialists who realized the great role that industry could play in providing quality education. Long before anyone else, Stya was talking of corporate responsibility and emphasizing the integral relationship between ethics and business.

However, in the 1960s, the national economic environment began to deteriorate. Much of the idealism and vigour of the immediate post-independence period was on the wane. Though well-intentioned, a quasi-socialist framework was imposed on the Indian economy. Planning became the watchword of policymaking and government-owned undertakings were positioned as engines of growth. Red tape breeds red tape. An encroaching 'Licence Raj', with its permits, controls and allocated quotas, began to steadily stifle economic dynamism. The bureaucrats seriously thought they were the answer to India's needs. They administered a system that strangled entrepreneurial Indians and denied them the opportunity to give free rein to their talents.

Confiscatory taxation created a parallel economy, and the black market rivalled the open market. Influence-peddling and corruption became endemic, and politicians and their intermediaries were quick to exploit the immorality. Worst of all, an edifice of dependency was erected between the private sector and the government.

A closed circle of political notables, senior public servants and tycoons favoured by the state brought untold and unfair benefits for itself. The country was cheated. Slaying the dragon wasn't easy. The suffocation and suppression of economic buoyancy continued until Indira Gandhi's return to power in 1980, when the need to loosen and modernize dawned on the political leadership, culminating in the landmark reforms of 1991 under the prime ministership of P.V. Narasimha Rao. He really encouraged the Indian industry to forge ahead.

Jit had established a steel tube import business by the time I joined our Calcutta office. India produced only limited amounts of steel and Jit was purchasing substantial quantities of foreign tubing, which were then shipped to Calcutta. His service centre in the city warehoused the products and sold them for use in public works and industry. It was a tough and tedious trade, for the profit margin was dictated by the government and everything was subject to its approval.

The steel controller, a powerful bureaucrat, had to authorize each import licence and only British standard specifications were acceptable. If the steel to be imported did not adhere to these standards, permission to import was denied. This was a senseless leftover from the Raj when everything had to be imported from Britain. Colonized India was a captive market of the United Kingdom. Now, despite India becoming independent, the bureaucracy was unwilling to change.

Ironically, even Britain bought steel with different specifications from continental Europe. But Indian officials insisted that imported steel had to conform to British specifications. Basically, we were told that if we used anything other than British steel, then buildings would collapse. This rigidity extracted a heavy price. India was deprived of the economic benefit of buying equally good steel at a cheaper price elsewhere.

I saw this as absurdly outdated but also as a potential opportunity. With Jit's support and his contacts in the Indian civil service, I undertook to press the authorities to alter their policy. The resistance was incredible. Layer after layer of the bureaucracy adamantly refused to consider any other source of supply but Britain.

Finally, I prevailed on the government to budge. I presented irrefutable technical evidence. My MIT degree was perhaps as convincing to them as my scientific data. The British specification rule was abandoned. Less costly steel became available to India. Apeejay was now free to import European tubing at much lower prices. It was my first success in the commercial world. But many tangles with the bureaucracy were to follow.

Around 1953, there was a global shortage of steel tubing, and it was a struggle to obtain supplies. Jit travelled to and from Europe searching for sources to buy from. While he was away on one of his foreign trips, I was in charge of our operations. One morning, a casually dressed Eastern European gentleman walked into my office. In those days, when the British influence on India was yet to wear off, a jacket and tie was like a calling card; it exuded respectability in the business community. This informal individual announced himself as the deputy trade representative of the Soviet Union in Calcutta. He asked if we wanted to buy steel tubes from Russia.

There was a general impression in international trading circles that Soviet steel was not of the highest quality. But my visitor, Mr Vasiliev, persisted. So I suggested a price which was about 20 per cent below prevailing rates in other advanced countries and said we would buy 2000 tons if he could meet the demand. Mr Vasiliev then left, and I gave the matter no further thought.

Five days later, Mr Vasiliev was back. This time, he had with him a draft purchase contract on a plain sheet of paper.

Partly amused and otherwise sceptical, I signed the scruffy document and retained my copy of the agreement. The whole thing was so unusual that I couldn't be sure if it was for real, and I did not mention the matter to Jit on his return. Three months later, though, a cable arrived stating that 500 tons of steel tubing was ready for shipment from Russia and requesting us to open a letter of credit to guarantee payment. It was no longer a joke!

We were, however, still prisoners of the past. Indian institutions did not at the time transact business in foreign exchange, so Lloyds Bank was our international banker. The general manager at this British bank was a Mr Tebbit. He was shocked at my request for a credit of £30,000 to buy Soviet steel. After consulting his head office in London, he said he could only sanction £5000 and that, too, as a special concession to a very good client. No other foreign bank in Calcutta would do any better.

I contacted Mr Vasiliev and explained the problem. He said he would get back to me and very soon he did, asking me to call on a Mr Chi of the Bank of China, which had a small branch in Calcutta. This was the era of fraternal friendship between the Soviet Union and China, both communist countries. Besides, Mr Chi had studied at Harvard University, also in Boston and knew MIT well. He was willing to undertake the transaction. Thereby, the first shipment of Russian steel arrived in India.

Around Christmas in 1953, I visited the Soviet Union, touring the country for four weeks. I was accorded exceptional hospitality. During my visit, we concluded a purchase agreement at prices much below the international rate. Prior to this, Apeejay had only imported steel tubing. Now it began buying all types of steel. Through our Soviet contacts, we secured access to sources in Eastern Europe. Indeed, we sealed exclusive arrangements with some of them.

However, there ensued an extended tussle with the technical department of the steel controller's office in India. We were told Russian steel billets would crack when processed in India. However, thanks to Jit's persuasive powers and my scientific knowledge, the objection was overcome. In short, Apeejay was now a major force in the distribution of steel in India; our profits reflected this growth. More importantly, India derived many advantages from the competition between the foreign suppliers, something that was missing before our foray into the East European market.

Then, a fortuitous encounter led to Apeejay entering the shipping business. In 1959, I was on a flight from Delhi to Calcutta. Seated beside me was Dr Nagendra Singh, who was director-general of shipping in the Indian government. He told me the authorities were anxious to expand the Indian cargo fleet and that assistance was available to encourage the private sector to do so. I did not, though, take this conversation too seriously.

Shortly afterwards, however, I was in Germany to meet one of our steel suppliers, Willy Schlieker. This gentleman had a controversial past in that he had been a key steel executive during the Nazi era and had been imprisoned by the Allies after the Second World War. He was released in order to play a role in the economic reconstruction of Germany and soon built his own fortune.*

We usually met at his offices in Dusseldorf. But this time, he suggested I go to Hamburg, where he had recently bought a shipyard. When I mentioned the needs of Indian shipping

---

* *Time* magazine article, 26 October 1959.

to him, Schlieker offered to sell a second-hand cargo vessel which was obtainable because its owners had failed to pay its repair bill. I immediately telegrammed Dr Singh. A reply came, promptly offering government support for the purchase. This was a major leap forward for the business and its Apeejay Shipping Line, which is today India's largest privately owned shipping company. In 1960, I was proud to see the Apeejay flag on the mast of the first Indian ship to sail through the St Lawrence Seaway into the Great Lakes of North America.

Nagendra Singh, a lawyer by training, went on to become chief election commissioner of India and then president of the International Court of Justice.

The challenges of business were exciting and enjoyable, though sometimes frustrating. I was entrusted with managing the international operations of Apeejay's steel business, while Jit handled the domestic division. We interacted exceptionally well; his rare acumen in commerce was an enormous asset. For over a decade, I travelled outside India for several months a year, negotiating our steel acquisitions. I got to know a variety of foreign producers and became familiar with the geography of numerous mills, particularly in Europe. In the post-war era, they were the backbone of Europe's economy.

My trips created opportunities for the expansion of Apeejay's ventures. We began to manufacture steel products instead of importing them. We produced different types of tubes, not from iron ore but from rolled steel, at our mill on Hyde Road in Calcutta. We had a separate factory for other products.

Moreover, we diversified into real estate in Calcutta on Park Street, including our head office building and Park Mansions. We also acquired buildings in Churchgate in Bombay, Haddows Road in Chennai and Mathura Road in

New Delhi. We launched Park Hotels, with the first property on Park Street, Calcutta. We went into pharmaceuticals by way of acquiring Martin and Harris as well as into confectionery, cafes and restaurants—perhaps the best known in this category being the purchase of Flury's, an iconic Swiss confectionery and café, also located on Park Street, Calcutta.

The little industry that Payare Lal created in a back garden of Jalandhar had come a long way! Jit played a very important part in this impressive evolution. In 1983, he published his own autobiography, *The Business of Life*, which gives insights into the formation and success of the Apeejay Group.

I again collided with the evolving Indian bureaucratic system in the early 1960s. I had negotiated a collaboration agreement with the renowned multinational cosmetics corporation Revlon. As was the requirement, we had to secure permission from the Government of India to proceed further. Matters were moving well; the authorities wanted only a few adjustments to the deal. Then suddenly, a plethora of obstacles arose. This we discovered was at the behest of a leading local rival belonging to a major conglomerate.

Despite strenuous submissions on my part, I was informed clearance would only be extended if we did not use the Revlon name, logo or trademark. Of course, this significantly defeated the purpose of the tie-up. With the confidentiality of our proposal with the authorities clearly having been violated, the firm putting the spanner in the works contacted Revlon with an assurance that the government objections put to us would be overcome by them and that Revlon would even be allotted 50 per cent of equity in a joint venture without any financial input. Krishna Menon, a firebrand socialist who was defence minister in the Cabinet, heard about the wheeling and dealing and put an end to it. In effect, neither Apeejay nor the group undermining us went ahead with Revlon.

Another cooperation I attempted to promote was with Sheraton Inns for a state-of-the-art Apeejay hotel in Calcutta. We bought acres of then vacant land in Alipore, an upmarket area of Calcutta, for the purpose. This proposed link-up was also scuttled by one of the biggest Indian hoteliers. Anybody who dared to enter territory reserved for the well-established was up against it. The terrain was ring-fenced and well-guarded by the civil service. Much of the land we bought for the hotel was sold. A family house was built on the section we retained and the Paul family residence remains there today.

But while I experienced the cut-throat, educative and intriguing world of Indian business in the 1950s and 1960s, the happiest and most important moment of my thirteen years in Calcutta was my meeting, and marriage to, Aruna Vij in 1956. Aruna, also a Punjabi residing in the city, was charming and exquisite. It was love at first sight! We were married within days. She was a student at Loreto College, a leading Catholic missionary institution, as well as a teacher at Loreto House, which was the school under the same order, the two located in the same compound at Calcutta's Middleton Row. In 2013, Aruna and I were delighted to contribute to the expansion of Loreto College with the building of the Lady Aruna Paul Wing.

Our twin sons Ambar and Akash arrived in 1957. Daughter Anjli was born in 1959. Then came Ambika in 1963. Aruna chose the names of our children, all beginning with the letter 'A'. Our cup was full, until tragedy struck.

Little did we realize how the birth of our beloved Ambika would change the course of our lives entirely.

Youngest brother, Surrendra Paul

My sister Bimla

My elder sister Prakasho

Eldest brother Dr Stya Paul

Elder brother Jit Paul

4

Ambika

Losing a child under any circumstances is an unbearable experience. Ambika, our second daughter and fourth child, gave such delight and great joy to all the family. She shared the same November birthday as our first daughter, Anjli. Ambika's premature passing was therefore an inexpressible tragedy.

Even after so many decades, the memory of the blessing we enjoyed from her being with us remains undiminished. Fifty-six years have passed since losing her but I am yet to come to terms with her absence. I am still searching for an explanation. There are certain experiences in life whose reasons will always be inexplicable, incidents where rationale cannot be penetrated by logic.

All I can say is the agony of Ambika's death indelibly affected me. The sensation is difficult to describe because when sorrow is so personal, it not easy to share with others. At the same time, because of the impact the emotional setback had on my life and career, I shall try to outline this episode.

Ambika was born on the same day as our first daughter and third child Anjli, 12 November, only four years later in 1963. She was an enchanting infant, lively and intelligent beyond her years. She captivated everyone who met her. Hers was an angelic personality, perhaps too ethereal to remain for long in this world. She was engaging and her life progressed quite conventionally until she was two years old.

Around this time, she began suffering from occasional bouts of fever and listlessness. The doctors in Calcutta did not think this was too serious, diagnosing the cause as common childhood ailments. However, because of the disturbing frequency of the illnesses, I wrote to a doctor friend in New York, Clarence Cohen, who replied by return to suggest a variety of tests to eliminate the possibility of leukaemia. I had known Dr Cohen for a long time because he had attended to a business friend's medical needs.

He assured me he would consult one of his colleagues, a specialist in leukaemia, for an opinion. The tests were duly carried out and the doctors in Calcutta did not detect anything untoward. However, when the results were sent to Dr Cohen, his prognosis and that of his colleague was indeed leukaemia, and he recommended treatment in the United States. We decided to follow this immediately.

It was 1966. There were severe controls on travel out of India in order to conserve foreign exchange. Only one family member could accompany a patient on an international trip. Ambika's condition demanded that both Aruna and I go with her. We faced a forbidding set of regulatory obstacles. After tireless efforts, though, I managed to secure some necessary documents to strengthen our application. We also established a precedent of two people being permitted to travel with a patient by Indian authorities.

But having succeeded in making our case, we faced another obstruction. A strike by clerical employees of the Reserve Bank of India (India's central bank) was underway, which meant work at this establishment was at a virtual standstill and the paperwork to obtain authorization for our travel could not be processed. Mercifully, though, an understanding deputy controller of foreign exchange in Calcutta interceded. He wrote out the special permit by his own hand. We left for London the same night.

This was September 1966. It was obviously a long journey to the US. We decided to break the journey in London and consult specialists there first before proceeding to America. By this time, Ambika was very ill and never quite stabilized for any length of time, so we never completed the flight to the US. We immediately admitted her to Middlesex Hospital, which was affiliated to University College London, in central London's Mortimer Street. Here we were told the devastating news that her illness was incurable.

Nevertheless, we prayed for a miracle. We lived in hope, and our faith in Ambika somehow responding to the medicines being administered to her enabled me to function with a semblance of normality. A new drug would induce a remission, this would last for a while and our spirits would rise. Then would come the dispiriting news of a relapse.

I rented an apartment on Upper Wimpole Street, which was a short walk from the hospital. Aruna and I took turns to be at Ambika's bedside. Aruna spent the day with her; I sat by her at night. We saw that leukaemia gradually debilitates its victims, but these weaknesses are interspersed with periodic improvements. Ambika appeared to recover and be near normal at times. She would be cheerful and positive, oblivious of her serious medical state. Now and then, she would draft letters to God in her sweet, baby handwriting, seeking His blessings.

There were times, in fact, when Ambika would be out of hospital. She was even able to occasionally attend school. We did our best to entertain her by taking her to the London Zoo in Regent's Park, which was quite near to our flat. This was a source of amusement and pleasure to her. She was delighted with the antics of the birds and animals and was especially fascinated by the lions and tigers. Most of all, she enjoyed the children's zoo, where she could interact with the more domestic animals like rabbits and goats.

Christmas was approaching. In Calcutta, we used to thoroughly enjoy this festival as a family. Our other children Akash, Ambar and Anjli had been left behind in India. With their school holidays imminent, they were anxious to be with Aruna and me at this time of the year. We, too, very much missed having them with us. According to prevalent Indian government rules, they simply could not join us—such were the restrictions in those days. We were desolate.

As a last resort, I wrote a long, personal letter to Indira Gandhi, then prime minister of India, outlining our misery. I appealed to her, saying as a mother she would understand our plight. Remarkably, the wheels of officialdom began to turn. We had to satisfy some legal requirements and a way was sought to comply with the rules.

An Indian official deputed to find a solution advised me to take up a job in Britain, even if nominally, to change my place of residence from Calcutta to London, which would place me under different applicable regulations, and consequently enable our children in Calcutta to join us.

One of my business contacts, a Midlands steel company, Church and Bramhall, were good enough to add me to their payroll. I promised them I would return the salary they paid me after our children had safely arrived in the United Kingdom. To be honest, I didn't have to do any work. My employment was only paperwork to conform with the Indian government's requirements. Soon, to everyone's relief, our nuclear family was reunited.

Clearly, behind her stern image, Mrs Gandhi was imbued with kindness. An iron exterior is what many people sensed, not her humanity, which was, as our experience showed, quite integral to her being. I wonder if as a woman in a male-dominated world, she felt that to display too much compassion would be misconstrued as weakness and thereby exploited as a vulnerability by her opponents.

The year 1967 was tortuous. Ambika was often in hospital, but every time she was allowed out of it, we believed that things might take a turn for the better. Her serenity gave us hope; we prayed together for her recovery. We took her to the holy Catholic shrine at Lourdes in France. People said if you go to Lourdes, you get cured.

The chief executive of Apeejay's Delhi office was a Christian from the southern Indian state of Kerala. He asked us to go, so we went. Briefly, Ambika was noticeably invigorated, and the pilgrimage became associated with wellness in her mind. When she was admitted to hospital for the last time, she asked to be taken there again.

Ambika's illness and our intense involvement with it brought about an extraordinary psychic empathy between us. But inexorably, she drifted into a critical condition. My helplessness was excruciating. What can torment a father more than to watch life ebb away from a little daughter whom he has brought into this world? How cruel that a child should predecease a parent. But that's the way it was.

Until the final moments, we anticipated something dramatic would happen. Just before the end, the doctors administered an experimental drug which had the potential to prolong life. We held our breath. But it was to no avail.

Ambika's departure in April 1968 left me despondent and devastated beyond words. What was the use of assets, intelligence and money if I couldn't save the life of a loved one at such a tender age? I lost all interest in work and even living. Despair had a numbing effect on me. I retreated into *sanyas* or withdrawal into spiritual contemplation and reflection. My brothers and other relatives were at hand to continuously console me. This was comforting, for without their support I would not have overcome the morbidity that had enveloped me.

For eighteen months, I was practically non-functional. I abandoned my duties as a husband, parent and financial supporter to my family. This is where the value of the Indian joint family system and being part of a family business was a saviour. We went back to Calcutta. I trudged off to the Himalayas to seek solace. I read Bertrand Russell. I found that much of his words mirrored the Hindu way of life, except that Russell was an atheist, whereas I believe in God and destiny.

Philosophies and religions attempt to offer explanations and therefore consolation for premature deaths. To me, its random cruelty on lives which have not fully unfolded is what defies comprehension. In a world where there is often a second chance, its unaccountability is baffling. The mystery haunts me still, yet the answer is as elusive as ever. There are certain experiences in life whose inner truths will always be veiled, occurrences whose sensibility cannot be penetrated by logic or rational inquiry.

Russell's rationality persuaded me that there could be a life for me after Ambika's untimely departure. The message now floating into my mind was: 'Swraj, you were not born to do nothing.'

Another period of introspection followed. I thought about what to do with life. Aruna and I eventually decided we should return to London. The emotional experience with Ambika, her death, which had hit us so hard, was still too painful for us to leave the scene of where it happened. Besides, our other children had liked their schools in London. We thought it would be wise to settle them there.

So, a year and a half after Ambika's passing, a feeling of reconciliation began to develop. The brooding subsided. It now repeatedly occurred to me that I couldn't possibly sit idle and do nothing. After all, I had an engineering degree from MIT. I could not squander this qualification. I had a choice: either to return to India, where our family business was flourishing, or to start afresh. Aruna and I opted for a new beginning and to make England our home. It gradually dawned me that, regardless of the crushing blow of losing Ambika, we should not be defeated. We chose to fight back.

Ambika, though, never left our thoughts. It hurt immensely that her blossoming remained unfulfilled, that an innocence was so cruelly cut short. I have naturally always dearly wished it was otherwise. But then, that's destiny. It changed the course of my life.

I draw some solace from the great Hindu text the *Bhagavad Gita*, which says:

If the slayer thinks he slays
Or the slain thinks he is slain
Both know not the truth of life
Because neither he slays, nor he is slain.

In 1993, I was able to repay my debt to the London Zoo for the happiness and joy it had provided to Ambika. I saw a news item in the papers that said the zoo was threatened with closure because of its critical finances. Noticing this, I wrote to its chief executive, offering to donate £1 million to help it overcome its difficulties and enable it to rebuild. It was a huge amount for me then. The management was sceptical about my offer, about my ability to contribute what was then regarded as a considerable sum. They made checks in respect of my credibility and net worth. Finally, they accepted my proposal and to Aruna's satisfaction and mine, the donation was directed towards the Children's Zoo.

In extending the grant, I recall saying: 'In her last days, Ambika got much happiness from visiting this zoo and sharing its ambience. This is why a part of the zoo is appropriately named the Ambika Paul Children's Zoo and has a special place in our hearts.'

A statue of Ambika in the middle of a pool and water fountain enhances the Zoo's central patio and was unveiled on what would have been her thirty-first birthday in 1994.

In 2006, I assisted the *Into Africa* exhibit at the Zoo to mark our fiftieth wedding anniversary. The following year, I helped the erection of a bridge in the African Aviary and dedicated this to Jennifer Brown, British Labour leader Gordon and Sarah Brown's daughter, who had died soon after birth.

Gordon, later prime minister of the United Kingdom, speaking at a function at the zoo, generously remarked, 'There would be no London Zoo here today were it not for the fact that Swraj kept this zoo going in difficult times.' The Browns are also very sentimentally attached to London Zoo.

Then, in 2009, I provided further support to the development of the Animal Adventure section of the Children's Zoo.

The Zoological Society of London kindly responded to my support by conferring on me an honorary fellowship in June 2019. Thereby, I joined a hall of fame of luminaries no less than Emperor Akihito of Japan, HRH Prince Philip the Duke of Edinburgh and Sir David Attenborough. The citation read out at the award ceremony said:

'For the last thirty years, Lord Paul's support has been key to enabling ZSL and our Zoos to inspire, empower and inform people about wildlife and conservation. Through the Ambika Paul Foundation, the ZSL has received a number of transformational gifts towards projects at ZSL London Zoo.'

The following month, in July 2019, I contributed £1 million towards the redevelopment of the Zoo's aviary, known as the Snowden Aviary, and surrounding area. This is now called the Angad Paul African Reserve after our youngest son, who died unexpectedly and tragically at the age of forty-five.

Finally, I was happy to present another £1 million for what is now named the Lord and Lady Paul Forest Reserve at the Zoo. This opened in August 2022, three months after Aruna's passing.

Each year, for many years, Aruna and I would host an annual tea party at the London Zoo every first Sunday in July in remembrance of our unforgettable visits to it with Ambika. The tradition continues, although, sadly, without the support of my dear wife Aruna. And we also remember our son, Angad.

Wherever Caparo has a factory or building anywhere in the world, we ensure that a tree is planted in Ambika's memory.

Where I live today and where Aruna resided with me for decades, an apartment in Portland Place, was at first a flat we rented, which we later leased and then bought the flat next door, integrating two apartments. My next step was to acquire the freehold of the entire building—which we renamed Ambika House—before gradually purchasing the remaining floors to create accommodation for our children and grandchildren. At the entrance is a marble tablet that says 'AMBIKA PAUL; 12 November 1963 to 19 April 1968; An Angel Who Changed Our Lives; Loved and Remembered Always'.

Stephen Dorrell, secretary of state for health, at the formal opening of the Ambika Paul Children's Zoo, 1994

Me with vice chancellor Caroline Gipps at the Ambika Paul Student Union Centre launch, October 2010

Me with Lady Paul and Sarah Brown for the Ambika P3 unveiling at Westminster University

Jennifer Bridge at London Zoo

London Zoo to open £1m garden for children

By Jenny Rees

A CHILDREN'S enclosure named after a four-year-old girl who died of leukaemia is to be officially opened in London Zoo on Monday.

The Ambika Paul Memorial Gardens will house llamas, camels, ducks, chickens and rare domestic breeds such as Norfolk horned and Leicester long wool sheep, Red Poll cattle and Anglo-Nubian goats.

Children will be able to get close to the animals and pick up rabbits and guinea pigs.

The new £1 million children's zoo has been funded by Mr Swraj Paul, a businessman who moved from northern India to London with his family when Ambika became ill. She often visited London Zoo during the last months of her life before she died in April 1968.

"This is a very emotional time for me," said Mr Paul, 61, of Portland Place, Marylebone.

"Looking at the monkeys and birds brought my daughter such happiness."

He first approached the zoo two years ago when he heard that it might have to close because of financial problems.

"I was very concerned and I wrote to say that if there was any way of saving the zoo I would love to do something in memory of my daughter," he said.

A sculpture of Ambika by Shenda Amery will stand in the Memorial Garden's eight acres of landscaped grounds.

Daily Telegraph, 30 July 1994

DAY IN THE LIFE
NEW LONDON

Animal magnetism

ONE GIRL'S LEGACY BRINGS LONDON ZOO ALIVE FOR OTHER CHILDREN

LONDON Zoo is opening the gates to an enchanted garden for children on Monday. And it is dedicated to the memory of one little girl, Leukaemia victim Ambika Paul spent some of the happiest days of her tragically short life at the zoo seeing her favourites — monkeys and the brilliantly-coloured birds. But she loved all the animals — elephants, penguins, pandas and hippos. And every day she was allowed to leave Middlesex Hospital Ambika insisted her parents take her to see her friends'.

But after more than a year-and-a-half of intensive treatment, her body lost the fight for life. She was a few months short of her 10th birthday.

Now her father, wealthy industrialist Dr Swraj Paul, has funded a new zoo section in ecbmail of his children.

"My wife and I spent a lot of happy times and happy days with Ambika there," he said. "She enjoyed herself so much and I want to do something to give other girls and boys lots of pleasure. Before she started toddling we looked at children's zoos all over the world, and our aim is to make hers the finest one of all."

Ambika's £1 million bequest is part of a programme to transform the 160-year-old Regent's Park zoo. The key theme running throughout: conservation.

Yet only three years ago the historic zoo was itself a threatened species, coming within a few hours of extinction. Dr Jo Gipps was appointed its director, but as he candidly admits, his real job was to be the undertaker to a zoo starved of funds and public interest.

"It was a horrible job but someone had to do it," he says. "It seemed that closure was the only choice. We were not crying wolf, yet I always thought a solution could be found."

Once the zoo's plight became known there was an astonishing turnaround in its fortunes. The Emir of Kuwait weighed in with a £1 million donation allowing the zoo to keep going for another six months.

Then the favourites began clicking up money as thousands of people came to see the animals before the gates closed forever,

following fierce criticisms from welfare groups in the early 1990s.

Senior curator Simon Tonge says: "The animals' welfare must come first, and this is what children are taught."

They don't see chimpanzees tea parties any more, instead they watch animals performing naturally.

The zoo also aims to offer safe haven to endangered species — everything from Britain's field cricket to the Sumatran tiger and the Asian lion. One whole area will be devoted to the wonderfully varied wildlife of Madagascar,

fast vanishing as its forests are ruthlessly eradicated.

Simon Tonge stresses that education plays a vital part in the zoo programme. Young visitors are handed a list of musts to see, including life-size models of the Tyrannosaurus Rex, woolly mammoth and sabre-tooth cat.

BUT it is not just a day trip to a Jurassic Park. Also on the must-see tour is the Arabian oryx and the partula snail. Both are no longer found in their native habitat, but London Zoo's dedi-

cated breeding policy is ensuring their survival for future generations.

Among the latest prized additions to the zoo's success are the dozen youngsters who make up its children's committee. Aged from nine to 14, they meet regularly and post their own ideas to make the Regent's Park grounds even more exciting.

Hilary Mockler, 14, from Tooting, says: "We look at everything, from the palm for the children's zoo to the meals served in the cafe. We feel it is important because the zoo plays such a part in the preser-

vation of animals. We have a big say in what goes on — if we feel something is boring, we say so. We suggest ways of making the zoo more fun. The committee was recruited after market research revealed that one in every three visitors is a child.

Hilary says: "It is very rewarding to play a part and see what goes on behind the scenes.

"You find that the keepers think a lot about how they can make things more interesting for the animals."

(Turn off entry, Page 3

MOIRA MITCHELL

LUNCH WITH THE LIONS

MONKEYS go ape for blackcurrant jam.
BEWARE of light-trunked elephants, in one year alone they snaffled 14 coats, 12 handbags, 10 cameras, eight gloves and five return tickets to Leicester.
REINDEER have fresh lichen specially imported from Iceland.
CRUSTS of bread fed by well-meaning visitors are potential killers because they carry germs which can be fatal to apes and monkeys.
FLAMINGOS and other birds with brilliant plumage have their food supplemented with a dye to keep them in the pink.
KEEPERS once had to feed animals laxatives just before Bank Holidays because they were thrown so many buns and biscuits.
BUSBY the kiwi downs 400lb of worms a year
THE GIANT panda dines on fresh bamboo, with side helpings of steamed bran, maize and egg balls on a bed of boiled rice — all washed down with milk.
FOOD is often pinned up a tree, forcing an animal to climb or reach for it, just as it would in the wild.
LIONS swallow 10lb of meat a day each, with powdered vitamins tucked inside the joints.
BIRDS have the most varied food, including dried flies, locusts, mealworms, dripping, meat and fish, along with feeding pellets and meat.
RHINOS and elephants tuck away 50 bales of hay a week.
OTTERS like an ounce of margarine on their meat to keep them glossy.
FEEDING the 12,000 individual animals (not counting the insect colonies) adds up to around £300,000 a year.
ZOO officials once had to explain to authorities in Athens why a Greek couple had lost their passports and identity cards — an elephant had eaten them.
MONKEYS would starve if they were not fed extra vitamins and minerals.
THE yearly shopping list includes two tons of grapes, 22 tons of fish and 25 tons of bananas.
ANIMALS became beggars and lost the incentive to exercise when visitors were allowed to feed them — forcing the zoo to ban the extras.

KEENA DHILLON

A WALK ON THE WILD SIDE: Clockwise from main picture, Tara Smith, eight, with a pygmy marmoset orphan which has been raised by keeper Sarah Carter; the colourful hyacinth macaws, an endangered species; panda toys are best-sellers in the zoo shop; the popular pony rides; a life-size T. Rex; keeper Andy Hallsworth shows a lema to a group of children.

Daily Express, 30 July 1994

(Left to right) Anjli Paul, Angad Paul, me, Lady Paul and Gauri Paul at the Ambika Paul fountain at London Zoo, 1994

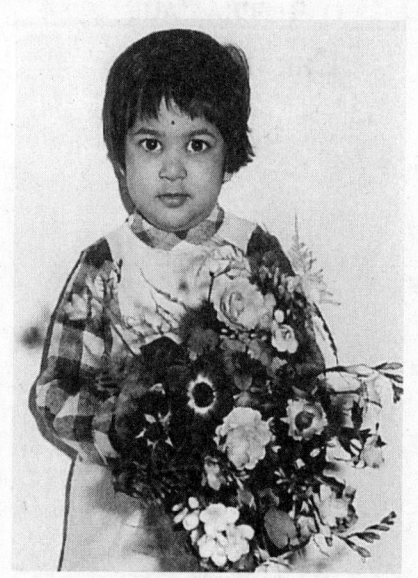

Ambika Paul

Ambika Paul study room at MIT, Boston, USA

Ambika Paul memorial

AMBIKA PAUL CHILDREN'S ZOO

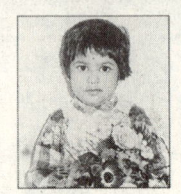

AMBIKA PAUL
MEMORIAL GARDENS

12 NOVEMBER 1994

1500	Guests arrive and visit Ambika Paul Children's Zoo
1600	Unveiling Ambika Paul statue
1630	Tea, Regency Suite
1730	Depart

Ambika Paul Children's Zoo, London Zoo, opened in 1994

Ambika Paul Building, Wolverhampton University

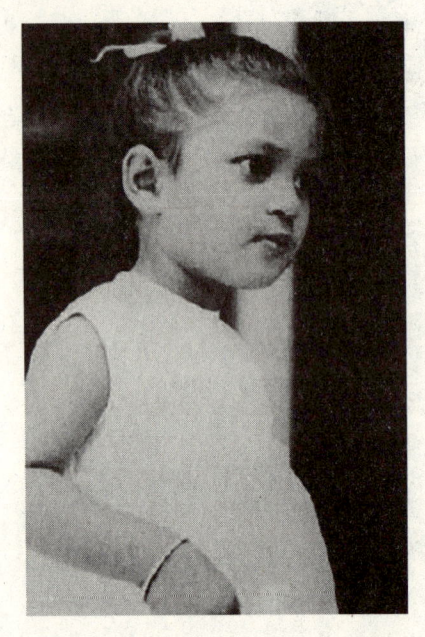

Ambika Paul
1964–1968

Ambika
P3 signage,
Westminster
University

Ambika P3 Award presented to Westminster University for
Best Exhibition Space

5

The Building Blocks of Caparo

Overcoming the loss of Ambika was hard. I was paralysed with grief and coming to terms with it was a long and uneven process.

But the routine of going to an office, absorbing myself in taking decisions and shouldering responsibilities, distracted me from my sorrow. Quite naturally, I looked at the steel sector, for this was my area of expertise. I did not possess capital, but I knew many people in the industry.

Buying and selling steel was a logical first step. I bought steel in Europe and sold it in Britain. I also purchased it in the United States and supplied it to the Continent. It was an entirely one-man operation carried out from a room in an office building on Cannon Street in the City of London. The company's name was simplicity itself: Steel Sales Ltd.

After such trading, I looked at venturing into manufacturing, for which I was equipped with technical know-how from my engineering degree at MIT. A machine that made spiral-welded pipes became available. At the time, this machinery was a new, relatively low-cost method of production. I could not afford to buy this equipment, so I leased it.

The pipes have many applications: water engineering, petrochemical and chemical industries, electric power, agricultural irrigation and urban construction.

Huntingdon in the county of Cambridgeshire, an hour and a half by train from London, seemed a convenient manufacturing location and I was able to rent a building near the railway station there. I borrowed £5000 as capital from Williams & Glyn's Bank and with three workers, started Natural Gas Tubes Limited (NGT) in 1968. One of my staff was Cecil Cargin, who used to work as an executive with a British company in India and had knowledge of the steel industry. He had retired and returned to Britain when I hired him to oversee the new plant.

The steel coils used as raw material were acquired on credit. It was tough going, made harder by the intense scrutiny of a virtual monopolist in Britain's steel tube industry. Stewarts and Lloyds, previously a family business, who had done business with Apeejay in India, had been nationalized to become part of the new British Steel Company and dominated tube production in the country. For reasons I could never understand, they were allegedly unhappy with my little company and deployed an annoying unofficial watch-and-probe on our operations. In due course, they were satisfied that NGT was no threat to them and melted away. But while it lasted, it was an uncomfortable experience.

Each day, I would walk from our flat to King's Cross station and take the train to Huntingdon. I set out with a lot of hope, but not much cash. Our first year sales were a modest £14,000. There were no great visions or extravagant expectations. Basically, the idea was to make some money. I had no income and needed to make a living to support my wife and children. I never thought that one day, this humble factory would be the springboard of what became the Caparo Group. I was, however, convinced that matters would turn out well if I worked hard and persevered.

NGT was created because there was an opportunity in the market. In the late 1960s, there were shortages in the British steel industry. Besides, nobody made spiral welded pipes in the UK and these were having to be imported. The manufacturers at the time did not bother much about customer service. The producer was king. I, on the other hand, was hungry and needed to boost sales. It occurred to me that potential purchasers were likely to respond positively if I provided good service—which was largely missing elsewhere.

My motto was: *the right product with the right quality at the right time.* Our deliveries were prompt, shipments matched orders and quality control was carefully monitored. The reward was commensurate with our approach. I appreciated something that has been a guiding principle ever since: if customers get the attention they need when their times are difficult, they will stay with you when your times are difficult.

A young merchant banker, James Leek, joined Caparo in 1975 as our chief executive and played a key role in our expansion for twenty years. An invaluable associate, his structured thinking blended well with my entrepreneurial outlook. We worked effectively in tandem, planning and implementing corporate strategy.

Born in Birmingham in 1944, James qualified as an accountant with Coopers Lybrand in 1967, specializing in corporate audits and taxation. After a brief spell at a London firm, he moved to the merchant bank Samuel Montagu, where he focused on mergers, acquisitions and corporate reconstruction. By 1972 he had added an MBA from the INSEAD graduate business school in Fontainebleau, near Paris. Returning to London, he teamed up with a couple of former Montagu colleagues and raised enough money to buy the controlling share of a small merchant bank, Close Brothers.

They took over Close Brothers and turned it into a specialized lender to small companies unable to secure loans from bigger banks, so his experience was exactly what Caparo needed.

James joined Caparo in 1975 and by the time he left twenty-two years later, Caparo had grown from a small Huntingdon factory with five employees and annual sales worth £500,000 to a worldwide conglomerate boasting 4000 employees, twenty-five subsidiaries and sales of £350m in steel and engineering products for what the company proudly boasted was 'hundreds of applications and thousands of uses'.

Caparo's tubes and hollow sections are used in pipelines for distribution of oil, gas, petrochemicals, steam, water and air; fire sprinkler systems; heating systems, irrigation schemes; domestic and industrial water and gas distribution/service schemes; coolant and fluid transfer in boilers, power stations, plant and machine tools; hydraulic cylinders; sewage plants; axles, bearings, cable ducts, casings, conveyor rollers, drive shafts, agricultural machinery, storage racks and cargo platforms, machinery and vehicles and children's prams.

By the time James joined me, NGT had expanded satisfactorily and was making decent profits. We were still a small business, but it was evident we needed more capacity to meet future demand. I became aware that relatively significant amounts of longitudinally welded tubes were being imported into Britain and thought about how NGT could begin to manufacture this product. With similar uses to spiral welded tubes, the manufacturing process is more efficient and less expensive. I estimated a new factory was going to cost around £5 million and there was no way NGT, or my personal assets, could underwrite such a capital outlay. So, if we were to grow, we would need to find other means of finance. Fortunately, there were grants and soft loans available for industrial development in depressed regions of Britain. We searched for possibilities and a suitable location. A place called Ebbw Vale in South Wales fitted the bill. Unemployment there was high, and the local economy was in extreme recession. But it was within easy reach of London, where I wished to continue living.

There was, however, a deterrent. I was warned Welsh workers were reputedly troublesome and truculent, which was a reason investors were shying away from the area, and was advised it might be better to find another location.

However, the prominent pro-India politician Michael Foot, who had become a close and helpful friend, was the member of Parliament for Ebbw Vale. He assured me to the contrary. He explained that Welsh labour would react constructively to fair leadership—the extended family policy I believed in. South Wales, he convinced me, would be a good choice.

With assistance from the British government's Department of Trade and Industry and an appropriate financial package, construction was soon underway and a modern 100,000-square-foot plant was built at a town called Tredegar. We imported our new and state-of-the-art machinery from the United States and my younger brother, Surrendra, came across from India to provide invaluable help with the initial commissioning. The inauguration in 1977 by Prince Charles, who was then Prince of Wales, now King Charles III, brought us wide recognition. A further extension to the mill was inaugurated by Mrs Indira Gandhi in 1978.

Stewarts and Lloyds, though, did not take kindly to this new venture. However, as they were our major competitor and as British Steel—of which they were a part—were our principle raw material source, we made a courtesy call on them. We politely asked if they had any advice for us as newcomers. Their response was along the lines that we should 'pack up our machinery and send it back to America as soon as possible'! Despite this negative response, we persevered and, as time passed, our relations with British Steel became excellent.

NGT (later Caparo Tubes) developed into one of Britain's leading manufacturers of welded steel tubes and spiral-welded pipes. It was the largest and most comprehensive of any cold-formed steel producer in the UK. The factory space expanded to over 230,000 square feet, sales grew to tens of millions of pounds, with more than one-third of our output being exported. Never for an instant did I regret my selection of South Wales as our base and our employees totally disproved the notion that they were difficult people to deal with.

With NGT up and running, we began to broaden our horizons and Caparo's business interests became more diversified. In 1979, we formed the Caparo Group as an umbrella for all our investments and in the following year, began an acquisition trail starting with Empire Plantations and Investments and a 26 per cent stake in Singlo Holdings, which then transferred its tea holdings to Empire. The Empire acquisition gave us a major stake in a publicly listed company called LK Industrial Investments. LK was renamed Caparo Industries and provided a greater focus for our operations. Empire Plantations, Singlo Holdings and Assam Frontier were wonderful old companies with Indian tea estate holdings. All ended up controlled by Caparo and were later passed to Apeejay. However, the tea estates would ultimately provide the backdrop to yet another Paul family tragedy—the assassination of my younger brother Surrendra at the hands of Assamese separatist rebels in 1990.

Surrendra was one of India's most dynamic and respected industrialists, and I felt his loss keenly as we shared a very close relationship. Our sisters Prakasho and Bimla remembered fondly that when he was a child, he would often give away his clothes and even his shoes to beggars or to people who he thought needed them more than he. When his family remonstrated with him one day after he had come home in just his underclothes, he said it didn't matter and that he would continue to help other people by giving away his things. He remained a very kind-hearted, generous and gregarious man who was much loved by his family, friends and colleagues.

On his final morning, Surrendra had flown from Kolkata to Mohanbari in Assam to join A.K. Choudhary, director of the Assam Frontier and Singlo companies. He was driven through the estate in the manager's car and got out to inspect the gardens on foot. He approved plans to build a new road across the garden as well as new rotary ovens in the packing plant.

Shortly afterwards, as Surrendra and Choudhary stopped at a petrol station on the way to the next plantation, a blue Jeep pulled up a few yards ahead. A youth with an AK-47 rifle jumped out and fired a stream of bullets into Surrendra's car. Choudhary was badly wounded, but Surrendra died before he reached the nearby hospital.

Sadly, even though Surrendra had resolutely kept out of the politics between the United Liberation Front of Assam (ULFA) and the ruling Asom Gana Parishad government, he had become a victim of the breakdown of law and order that has claimed the lives of many innocent Indians. ULFA terrorists had no quarrel with our family; they simply looked for the publicity that Surrendra's death generated.

In India, the family created endowments at the Indian Institute of Management and established the Surrendra Paul Memorial Lecture. The Surrendra Paul Memorial Fund at Massachusetts Institute of Technology is a gift in memory of Surrendra for student activities in the Department of Mechanical Engineering. In London, we held a memorial service at the House of Commons, attended by John Smith, Labour Party Leader and other parliamentarians.

Going back to our earlier investments in the late 1970s, we bought Osborne Hotel in the coastal resort of Torquay in Devon, southwest England. We later purchased Bignell Park Hotel in Oxford.

We also bought a property at 103 Baker Street, London, the street made famous by Sir Arthur Conan Doyle's 'Sherlock Holmes'. This was an old bank building that was demolished to make way for Caparo House, which became Caparo's corporate headquarters and is still operational today.

In 1979, economic prospects were dismal. Oil prices had reached $40 per barrel—a staggering figure at the time. Interest rates and inflation were soaring in Britain, not to mention considerable industrial unrest. Crude steel production had fallen to 10 million tonnes from 25 million tonnes in 1973. Business confidence was at rock bottom, especially in steel.

However, I felt that if one were to take a long-term view, it was a time for opportunity. A decline in valuations had brought previously high net worth companies within Caparo's reach. Shareholders were willing to consider offers they would have disregarded in better days. If one had faith in the future of British industry, this was the moment to act. The dynamics of manufacturing in steel-based consumer products were changing dramatically. Those who could transform the way companies were managed, who brought efficiency to poorly organized enterprises, had a distinct chance of improving profits and building value. It was a time for calculated risks, when buying companies and upgrading their facilities was less expensive and would deliver a better return on capital, compared to erecting new plants. *Financial Times* described Caparo as 'one of the more predatory companies on the (London) stock market'.

In 1981, Caparo Industries Plc was formed; 75 per cent was held by the Group and we used it to initiate a programme of acquisitions, which brought five significant manufacturers into our fold by the end of the decade. Four of them were purchased through public bids. The total cost was £150 million—paid entirely in cash. The entities were brought under the banner of Caparo Industries Plc, a firm listed on the London Stock Exchange. Caparo held 80 per cent of shares; the rest were in the hands of outsiders.

We first picked up CMT Industrial Group for £14.5 million. This was a medium-sized diversified producer and distributor of pipe fittings, insulation materials and specialized anti-vibration mounts. We had to compete against the might of Hanson Trust to secure the deal. This was encouraging, for it told us that small but flexible entrepreneurs could prevail where size generally triumphed.

We then added the Barton Group to our portfolio for £9.6 million. Barton made steel tubes and allied industrial items. This was followed by Wrexham Wire Company being scooped up for £1.2 million. As its name indicates, it manufactured wire products for industrial applications, from automobiles to beds, and at the Wrexham factory, we managed to increase the output five times quite quickly.

Thereafter, we made our largest domestic investment of £104 million. The Armstrong companies were an engineering chain with worldwide sales. They were the biggest makers of fasteners for the automobile industry in the UK. With Armstrong came two Spanish manufacturers of components for the automotive industry—Caparo's first European establishments.

Buying businesses was only one part of the mission. Each company brought its own ethos with it. To integrate them into Caparo's culture was not always smooth and required adjustment. We invariably made major capital investments and introduced management changes. We reduced overheads and cut costs. Every unit had to pay for itself; there were no cross-subsidies in our group. This disconcerted some executives who were used to a more relaxed system. But the overall results were heartening and validated Caparo's motto that there were few bad businesses, only bad managements.

The shares of Caparo Industries performed well on the London Stock Exchange. I was proud of what we achieved. Business looked rosy. Then came Fidelity. Our advisers, institutional shareholders and brokers recommended we diversify our focus. The argument was that even though we had been successful in the field of industrial engineering and steel processing, and even though we possessed proven management skills, our expertise was still in the realm of what people were calling sunset industries. Metal fabrication was becoming old-fashioned. It was time to enter sunrise industries. The age of hi-tech and consumerism had arrived, and our acknowledged talents would be an asset when applied to the businesses of tomorrow. Why restrict Caparo to the past when a vast consumer boom was on the horizon? It was a plausible pitch.

Fidelity Plc was a well-known consumer electronics manufacturer in north London. It was one of the last surviving British manufacturers of television sets, stereo systems and similar products. The company enjoyed good brand recognition. Although sales were stationary and the management poorly rated, the firm apparently generated a net profit of £1.4 million in 1983. It looked like an attractive proposition. With better administration, revenue could surely increase substantially.

Moreover, improved research and development would potentially enhance Fidelity's franchise. Perhaps its existing technology would be a launchpad for entry into more sophisticated electronics. There was also the prospect of expanding into the consumer electronics market, which was awakening in India and other developing countries. Fidelity's shares were depressed, so we made an offer. Overcoming considerable opposition, we acquired the company for £13.4 million.

After we took over the management, it became clear something was seriously wrong. Our investigations revealed glaring inaccuracies in stocks. Assets were blatantly overstated. Goods in inventory were of unreliable quality.[*] The questions we raised received evasive answers. The true condition of the company was far worse than declared by the sellers, and there

---

[*] Caparo Industries Plc v Dickman [1990] 2 AC 605 House of Lords.

were also elements of fraud. We instituted legal proceedings. We filed three lawsuits: the first, against former directors, alleged fraud. After the passage of seven years, two key directors, Steven and Robert Dickman, were found liable by the London High Court. This, though, gave us little material satisfaction, because after such a long time, the recovery of any money was impossible.

Our case against Touche Ross, Fidelity's auditors, was also protracted. Caparo alleged negligence and sought damages. Touche Ross responded by arguing they owed no responsibility to investors. We lost in the lower court but won on appeal. Touche Ross then challenged this judgment before what was then the highest tribunal in the land, the Law Lords in the House of Lords (before the Supreme Court of the UK came into being in 2009).

The plea was upheld. Indeed, the case generated intense public interest and has become a reference point for the accounting and commercial world. It is looked upon as a landmark judgment,[*] unleashing deep concerns about the responsibilities of auditors and redefining them. Subsequently, Fidelity itself, now owned by Caparo, initiated legal action against Touche Ross. This time, they settled out of court by making a payment.

In the interim, the operations of Fidelity had run into trouble. To revive it, we made major changes in its working practices and injected many efficiencies. In less than three years, overheads were reduced from £7 million to £5.5 million. The struggle for survival may well have succeeded but for market conditions deteriorating sharply.

---

[*] Caparo Industries Plc v Dickman [1990] 2 AC 605 House of Lords.

Fidelity's new problems were caused by competitive imports from South Korea, Hong Kong, Taiwan and China. These were compounded by the fact that exports from such countries were priced in US dollars. The American currency lost value, thereby making Far Eastern products cheaper still. The decline of the dollar was ruinous for us. Fidelity was compelled to cut prices by 20 per cent to merely keep its head above water. The more we sold, the more unviable it was to keep going.

Besides which, there was no sympathy or support from the government. The policy under Prime Minister Margaret Thatcher was to encourage as much open trade as possible with the avowed objective of making British industry more sharp-edged internationally. In many ways, this was a sensible approach, but a painful one for Fidelity.

The policy, though, was flawed in one respect. There was no knowing if other countries were playing by the rules. Many of Fidelity's competitors enjoyed subsidies from their governments, whereas we received no such aid. Clearly, we could not possibly continue in this manner. So, after four traumatic years, we terminated Fidelity's operations. It was a loss for Caparo, but an even bigger loss for Britain. The British consumer electronics industry was sacrificed. Foreign players swept into the British market.

Other parts of our group remained a private company fully owned by me, and all was not doom and gloom for Caparo. In 1985, for instance, we entered into a joint venture with British Steel. At lunch with the latter's chairman, Sir Robert Scholey, I casually asked if we could collaborate. His equally nonchalant reply was to mention a possible project in South Humberside. From this conversation arose United Merchant Bar (UMB), 75 per cent owned by Caparo and 25 per cent by British Steel.

They had already closed three outdated and redundant mills in the area, and wanted to open a new, modern plant in the locality but were unable to do so because of restrictions imposed by the Department of Trade and Industry. They were therefore looking for a partner and Caparo became that partner.

British Steel owned a disused rod mill in Scunthorpe. We reconstructed this into virtually a new facility using the most advanced technology. As planned, UMB produced merchant bar steel flats and angles, which are used primarily in the construction industry. But it was more than another plant— it was a commitment to an industry that seemed to have a fading future.

At the opening of the facility in September 1986, Chancellor of the Exchequer Nigel Lawson described it as 'a modern phoenix rising from the ashes of an outdated sector of Britain's steel industry'. He was prophetic. UMB's performance was outstanding. Production reached 500,000 tonnes in no time, half of which was exported. It was a highly efficient operation, producing superior quality steel at low cost. In ten years, sales increased from £9 million to £72 million. The original capital input had been only £12 million. British Steel, who proved to be cooperative partners, were delighted to receive dividends far in excess of their investment.

In 1991, UMB received the Queen's Award for Export Achievement at a formal presentation held at the site on 10 September that year. The Rt Hon. Neil Kinnock, then leader of the Labour Party Opposition, performed the opening ceremony for further mill expansion. What gave me the most satisfaction was that UMB demonstrated the vitality of British industry, proving that state-owned corporations and the private sector could work harmoniously to create a world-class enterprise in what was until then widely deemed to be a dead-end business.

More horizons beckoned in the late 1980s. I had long been tempted by opportunities in the United States, a country I knew well, but where I had not invested in businesses. Perhaps our greatest endeavour was to break into the American market in 1988.

Our first American acquisition was Bull Moose Tubes in 1988, with its original plants based in Ohio, Illinois, Georgia, Missouri and Ontario. This was followed by Bock Industries in Indiana in 1990. Both were well-known companies, each about thirty years old. Combined, they made Caparo the largest manufacturer of steel tubes in North America. Our capital outlay reached $350 million. As was our custom, we set about improving the facilities and the results were extraordinary. This Caparo-owned Missouri-based steel company has expanded steadily over the ensuing years. It has never recorded an annual loss and today earns at least $50 million a year in profits.

My introduction to futuristic technology occurred at MIT. Now I had returned to the United States, in many people's book *the* land of opportunity, to close the circle of my endeavours in the world of commerce and industry. Our success in a short span made Caparo the largest manufacturer of steel tubes in North America.

Sharon Steel was an old and once well-regarded company formed in 1900, but which had collapsed into liquidation in the 1980s. Its large plant in Farrell in Pennsylvania was shut, its skilled labour force discharged. What remained of the corporate assets was vested in a bankruptcy court. The debacle at Sharon had wreaked havoc in surrounding localities. In late 1994, following a favourable piece on Caparo in the prestigious financial periodical *Forbes*, I received a letter from the Pennsylvania Power and Light Company inquiring whether we would be interested in purchasing Sharon. Pennsylvania had lost a major customer with the demise of Sharon Steel and was anxious to revive this account.

My curiosity was aroused. We examined the steel mill and its other facilities. The State of Pennsylvania indicated its commitment to an economic regeneration of the region. We weighed the pros and cons. If we proceeded, it would be Caparo's largest project, drawing heavily on our resources. I decided to go ahead.

Considerable spadework was undertaken before we acquired Sharon's assets for $26 million. A further investment of $64 million was required to commence production. In June 1995, we formally reopened a plant to start with a capacity of 1.2 million tonnes of hot rolled coil, 600,000 tonnes of cold rolled coil and 100 tonnes of galvanized sheets. Soon, another $180 million was ploughed in for an expansion and improvement programme. It was an inspiring venture for Caparo Steel, not least because our efforts helped to rejuvenate a dispirited local community.

By contrast, India was a bad experience in terms of the resistance I encountered to lawful purchases of publicly listed shares in DCM and Escorts (which I deal with at length later). This somewhat dampened my eagerness to do business in India. I had, of course, undertaken a double purchase of Empire Plantations and Investments and Singlo Holdings, British-owned tea gardens in Assam in north-eastern India. But otherwise, India was a sleeping giant being restrained.

Then, in 1991, new economic liberalization came into being. New technology was now welcome. In July of that year, the communist chief minister of West Bengal, Jyoti Basu, was in London. I had high regard for him, for he was a politician of principle. He was keen to revive Indian Iron and Steel Company (IISCO), a business incorporated in 1918 and located in Burnpur near Calcutta.

IISCO was operating at 25 per cent of its capacity, incurring heavy losses and finding it difficult to continue. Basu's priority was preservation of jobs. If redundancy was necessary, this needed to be done with the cooperation of unions and without animosity. I assured the CM I was prepared to assist.

Basu discussed the matter with the central government, where Santosh Mohan Dev was the minister for steel. We agreed the choice of technology would be mine and no one would be retrenched without their consent. However, the Steel Authority of India Limited (SAIL), which managed IISCO, subsequently shifted the goalpost. It wanted to choose the technology. It became apparent SAIL was not really interested in ceding control. So I withdrew.

Biju Patnaik, chief minister of Orissa (now Odisha), thereafter visited London and proposed a joint venture between his government and Caparo to set up a steel plant in his state. Orissa was a good location with rich natural resources. I was wary of procedural problems, but Patnaik assured me he would deal with this. From my office, he telephoned the Indian Prime Minister P.V. Narasimha Rao, who welcomed the project.

The Foreign Exchange Investment Board approved our application and agreed to a debt ratio of 3:1. Both the prime minister and Finance Minister Manmohan Singh endorsed the venture. Indeed, Patnaik accompanied me to government-owned financial institutions in Bombay to muster the capital. But they presented amazing obstacles. They asked if there would be a demand for steel later in the decade. The most senior civil servant in the Ministry of Steel, Moosa Raza, intervened. But the institutions demanded a 2:1 debt ratio. I told them our technology would be the very best and that we would access this at the lowest possible price. But they were obsessed with the idea that our cost projections were excessive.

I eventually said they could buy the technology and build the plant if they could save us money. There was no response. A hidden hand seemed to be creating hurdles whenever we made any progress. Two years went by and there was still no resolution. I decided to cut our losses and turn our attention to the opportunity in Farrell, Pennsylvania. Patnaik was disappointed. For an international entrepreneur, time is money and there are choices to be made. Game-changing reforms were now law in India and it had, in theory, opened up to foreign investment. But the Indian system was still not fully awake to the facts of economic life in the global marketplace.

Eventually, we established an Indian manufacturing facility in 1994, with my youngest son Angad, who was always fascinated with the history of India and foresaw great potential in India-UK cooperation, casting the foundation of Caparo's business in the country. This was a joint venture with Maruti Suzuki to produce metal components for its motor vehicles factory in Gurgaon near Delhi. This fortunately flourished, and we were thus able to expand steadily in various sectors.

In 1998, led by Angad, we set up a hospitality business under the brand name of AYATTI. Between 2000 and 2018, Caparo Engineering India Limited, a new wing of the group, mushroomed, with manufacturing plants at nine different locations and thereafter at three more. These included joint ventures with Marubeni-Itochu Stell Inc., named Caparo MI Steel Processing Ltd, and Wartsila of Finland for power generation under Caparo Power Ltd. In 2019, we signed a technical assistance agreement with Shin Young Co. Limited of South Korea for our India operations.

The leadership in Caparo India now has my son Akash as chairman and my grandson Arush as vice chairman and chief executive. Our aim is to increase our presence in the territory across automotive, defence, railways, aerospace and domestic appliances sectors. After North America, our prospects look the most promising in India.

Meanwhile, in 1991 in the UK, we made an offer for the publicly held shares in Caparo Industries, which had been listed on the London Stock Exchange. Taking this subsidiary of Caparo Group private was the best answer to an unproductive situation. The stock market operates on short-term results, while the engineering industry requires long-term investments, where payback comes after several years. Our subsequent growth justified the 50 per cent premium we offered over the quoted price of 44 pence per share. Three thousand shareholders expressed satisfaction with their returns at a special general meeting, which approved our move. Managing a public company was an enjoyable experience, but now it was time for an alternative strategy.

By the mid-1990s, the Caparo conglomerate's sales were over £500 million and operating profits more than £50 million. We had 4000 workers in this large family group, whose collective well-being depended on each other and of course, on the management. Within budgetary guidelines, Caparo managers have possessed wide discretion to take 90 per cent of decisions in their respective companies, divisions and departments.

They are imbued with the mantra that progress does not just mean increasing profits. It is in building an organization that is superior to most of its competitors and developing skills in people so that they perform better than their rivals. In the modern business environment, the gifted amateur is more of a myth than a reality. It is practicality, professionalism and training that count.

Caparo encourages its workforce to be flexible. There are no demarcations. Anyone can move to a new area of production if they are capable of this crossover. This is generally easier to implement in a start-up, more complex in an ongoing enterprise. Yet, it is vital for competitiveness and an area in which we have succeeded.

For example, at Armstrong Fastenings, it took almost two years to convince skilled bolt machine setters working on just one machine to move to setting a whole bank of machines. This important change enabled us to compete with Taiwan and Europe. Similarly, at Bock Industries in Indiana, we brought about labour flexibility after twelve months of negotiations with unions. This converted to a 4 per cent decrease in costs and a saving of over a million dollars annually.

Caparo was built on the central premise that we were makers of mass-manufactured steel-based items used by other industries. By constantly enhancing production skills and innovating in sourcing and pricing raw materials, we stayed largely ahead of the game. I avoided operations involving large, one-off capital goods or construction-type products. Make one mistake here and all is lost.

I also generally avoided more fashionable consumer businesses. My style has been to explore companies and products suited to my temperament and perspective.

A judicious use of technology is essential. State-of-the-art equipment may be expensive but in the long run, is also more cost-effective. However, machinery that might be too sophisticated for the people who will be using it needs to be carefully assessed. I have achieved satisfactory results by devoting meticulous attention to machine layout, production and planning to advanced technology. Intelligent use of equipment is as vital as its quality. Machinery must serve the manager, not vice versa.

Advisers, consultants and domain specialists have become all-pervading in today's business world. I am not convinced by them. If I had listened to experts, two of our most profitable ventures would not have taken off. Listen to what they have to say, but don't forget that their input is not a substitute for management's decision-making. Business judgements should be based not merely on evidence, but on faith in a project. An intuitive manager knows their company's potential as well as its limits.

Experience has taught me that while business decisions should be arrived at in a logical manner, logic alone, especially conventional logic, should not be the determining factor. Instinct, an indefinable element, should not be ignored. This is not the same thing as impulse. I prefer to call it holistic analysis: assessments made based on human, cultural and psychological aspects as much as on hard data or factual content. Business schools tend to dismiss this; I believe it is worth considering.

Caparo has operated under strict capital controls, which I term 'weight loss' programmes. Reduction of capital is one way of increasing profits. Income obtained from a lower capital base is higher in value than the same revenue secured from a larger outlay. So Caparo has continually been in pursuit of slimming. This includes trimming overheads. My policy has been to cut overheads below what others think is possible. Let the cracks be repaired as they appear. This is obviously unpopular with executives. But I have rarely seen a bad business with too few overheads or a good one with too many. One of the reasons why Caparo weathered recessions is that we pursued the slogan 'Think lean, act mean, stay keen!'

The key to corporate advancement is leadership. Contrary to textbook theories, there is no standard formula or prescription. A corporate leader doesn't have to be a visionary but must be imbued with vision. This needs to be articulated clearly and adopted diligently. A chief must balance the future with the present, the long-term with the short-term. The real test of a leader is to succeed in the tougher areas of a business rather than the easier ones. Decisiveness is imperative—better a bad decision than no decision. But the basic truth is that few enterprises are successful without effective leadership.

I have always considered work to be a form of religion. Therefore, I have respected my work and have been happiest when engaged in the growth of Caparo. Expansion is the oxygen of business; to stand still is to fall behind. There is no magic potion. The secret is hard work. It is admittedly true that a few people get rich quickly, especially in today's casino-type market and technology-driven scenario. But to sustain this isn't easy. The bubble can burst. In the end, business is about people. Anyone who forgets this could fail. It is an honourable way of life when conducted by honourable people.

The Caparo Ethic or Code of Conduct is attached to this chapter. It was formally drawn up in 2008 but we had already been working on these principles for four decades.

The Caparo Ethic

- Caparo is more than a successful enterprise. It is a story of people, of values and of human effort.
- Working together, we can build Caparo with resolution, fortitude and ability.
- The goodwill and confidence in the efforts of our workers, our suppliers, our customers and our managers are the bedrock of our business.
- Always aspire for excellence; nothing else is good enough.
- Never abandon hope.
- There is no such thing as bad business, only bad management.
- What we like is people who are proud of what they do.
- Our aim and our goal for Caparo is always to be in the top 10 per cent of performers, measured against our industry competitors.
- Success will happen so long as you work hard with integrity.
- Find excitement in industry and in your own job within it.
- Cherish the enduring values of fidelity, truth and integrity.

With Caparo Bull Moose employees at the Missouri Head Office, USA, 2024

UMB Award

United Merchant Bar p.l.c.

CAPARO

Presentation of the Queen's Award
for Export Achievement by
The Lord-Lieutenant of Humberside, Mr. R.A. Bethell

And the Opening of the U.M.B. Mill Expansion by
The Rt. Hon. Neil Kinnock, M.P.

— Tuesday, 10th September 1991 at 11.00 a.m. —

Caparo Group Limited
Caparo House, 103 Baker Street
London W1M 1FD
Telephone: 071-486 1417
Telefax: 071-935 3242
Telex: 8811343 Caparo G

PRESS RELEASE   10 September 1991

CAPARO RECEIVES THE QUEEN'S AWARD

United Merchant Bar, a subsidiary of Caparo, the company owned by Indian-born industrialist Mr Swraj Paul today received the coveted Queen's Award for Export Achievement.

Handing over the Award to Mr Akash Paul, Chairman of UMB, the Lord Lieutenant of Humberside, speaking on behalf of Her Majesty the Queen, said: "The Queen's Award is the most prestigious award that can be bestowed upon a company; you can add this to your long list of achievements that you have already gained since you commenced operations here in 1986. May I congratulate you."

Mr Neil Kinnock, the Leader of the Opposition, who also opened a new £5m expansion at the UMB site said:-
"United Merchant Bar is one of the companies of the Caparo Group built up over the last quarter of a century under the leadership of my friend Swraj Paul - a man who is remarkable for his great talent and initiative, for his deep sense of social justice and for the way in which he applies both to the benefit of the community.
This Queens Award for Exports has been won by a young company - an energetic and enterprising five year old. It has been won by success in tough markets abroad and against the background of serious recession at home. The prize, therefore, has special distinction and is worthy of special praise. But we are here not only to honour the achievements of the past. With the formal opening of the new capacity we are also here to look forward to fresh achievements in the future. Surely, this must be the very best way to salute success.
And I am specially glad to celebrate the achievement of United Merchant Bar because it is a manufacturing company - and manufacturing matters vitally to the U.K."

Registered Office:
Caparo House, 103 Baker Street, London W1M 1FD
Registered in England No. 1387694

UMB Award, 1991

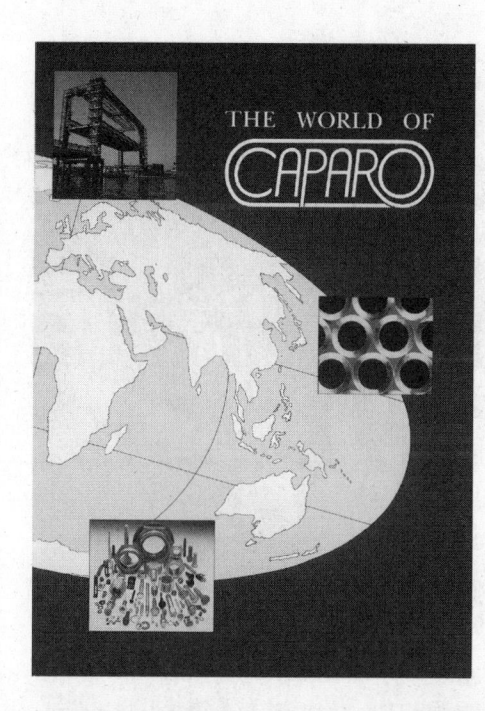

The World of Caparo

The Swraj Paul and Angad Paul Caparo Middle East building, Dubai

NGT plant opening 1977 with HRH Prince Charles

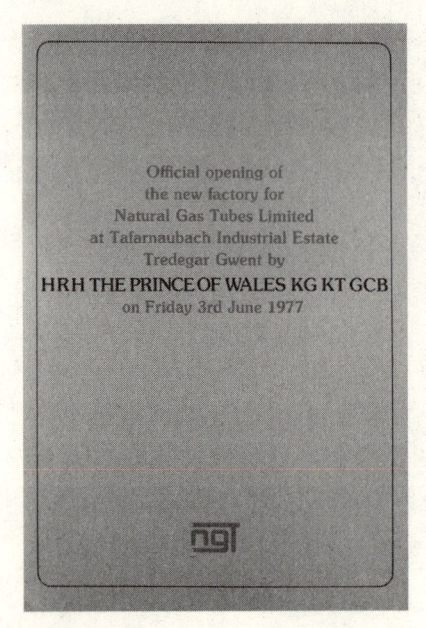

Official opening of
the new factory for
Natural Gas Tubes Limited
at Tafarnaubach Industrial Estate
Tredegar Gwent by
HRH THE PRINCE OF WALES KG KT GCB
on Friday 3rd June 1977

NGT official inauguration, 1977

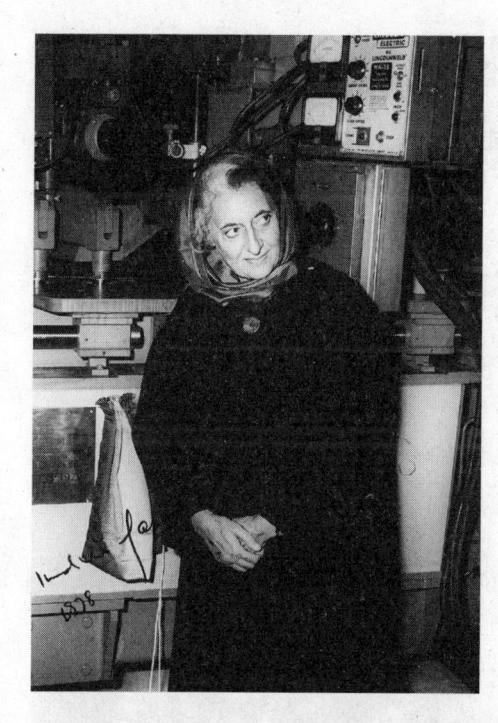

Mrs Gandhi inaugurating the new NGT Mill, Tredegar, Wales, 1978

Gordon Brown, Sarah Brown, Lord Paul, Angad Paul and Lord Digby Jones, UK trade minister, at the inauguration of Caparo India manufacturing facilities, January 2008

Formal inauguration of Caparo India, January 2008

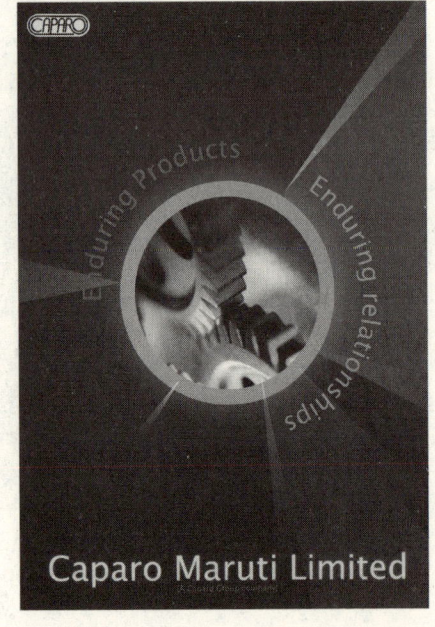

Caparo Maruti

Caparo 25th anniversary—Lady Paul, PM John Major and me

Caparo 25th anniversary

Caparo 25th anniversary—Lady Paul, PM John Major, me, Norma Major, L.M. Singhvi

THE BULL ROAR

FALL 1988

NEWS FOR YOU FROM BULL MOOSE TUBE

BULL MOOSE TUBE ACQUIRED BY CAPARO

On October 18, 1988, the final transaction to sell Bull Moose Tube Company to Caparo Industries, Plc. was completed. Caparo came to the United States to expand its holdings. The direction was to find a product/business that Caparo felt good about and was knowledgeable in. Caparo was looking for a company that was profitable as well as having potential for growth. That is when they discovered Bull Moose Tube Company.

Caparo Industries, Plc. is based in London, England. The company was started in 1968 by Swraj Paul.

When Paul decided to start the company he tried to determine a

Chuck Emmenegger, President and Swraj Paul answer employee questions at Gerald, MO facility.

Swraj Paul meets the employees at the St. Louis Corporate office. Left to right: Fran Bruce (Sales Assistant), Jeff Boyer, (Engineering Consultant), Jane Kelly (Sales Clerk), Swraj Paul and Chuck Emmenegger (President)

James A. Leek, Chief Executive of CAPARO.

(Continued on Page 2)

SWRAJ PAUL HEADS CAPARO INDUSTRIES, Plc.

On October 18, 1988, Caparo Industries, Plc. acquired Bull Moose Tube to add to the list of their other holdings. Caparo Industries, Plc. (Plc. means Public Limited Corporation) is an international group with interests in engineering and steel products. Major companies included as part of this group are as follows:

1. United Merchant Bar located in the United Kingdom is a manufacturer of steel flats, angles and channels.

2. Wrexham Wire manufactures steel wire for fasteners, bedding and seating, ropes, springs and chains.

3. Barton Engineering which has a product range which includes steel tubes, electrical fittings and aluminum castings.

4. Barton Abrasives

This listing as well as other small companies such as Barton Tube in Canada make up Caparo Industries, Plc. which is headed by Swraj Paul. Paul was appointed as Chairman of the Board in 1980. He is a Padma Bhushan which is the Indian equivalent of English peerage and has a honorary doctorate of philosophy.

(Continued on Page 2)

Swraj Paul

ROAR
The Bull Roar is published exclusively for Bull Moose Tube Employees.

Bull Moose Tube acquisition by Caparo, 1988

Caparo Sanand

Caparo Pune

Caparo Pithampur

Caparo MI Steel Bawal

Caparo Maruti Gurgaon

Caparo Maruti Bawal

Caparo Jamshedpur 2

Caparo Greater Noida

Caparo Chennai

Caparo Bawal

Caparo Ayatti Greater Noida

6

Inspired by Indira

Over the years, I came to know Indira Gandhi as a private person. It saddened me that the public image of this remarkable lady, which too often projects her as a tough, power-hungry politician, has permeated much of the press to disguise and even disfigure the warm humanity, the love of family and the sense of fun that were her true characteristics. She seemed to me like an older sister, a wonderful adviser and, in my opinion, the best prime minister I had known up to that time, even surpassing her father, Jawaharlal Nehru, whom I had also known and for whom I had the greatest respect.

Mrs Gandhi, I freely confess, was for me an inspiration. For as long as I can remember, my family and I had been admiring supporters of her and her father. My weekly visits to my brother Stya in jail, when he was detained for nationalist activities, made an indelible impression on me. But, as I recall, I was never bitter towards the British. Rather, I was left with an intense respect, bordering on boyhood hero worship, of leaders of the freedom movement, most of all for Nehru.

I first met Mrs Gandhi in 1957 when Aruna and I visited Nehru in Delhi shortly after marrying, because he wanted to know the thoughts of people like me on how to build India. We had to pluck up the courage to meet him as five years had passed since our brief meeting at MIT, but it was a very harmonious afternoon and Mrs Gandhi served tea. In 1952, Nehru had insisted that I return to India after finishing my education because 'India needs you'.

When Nehru passed away on 27 May 1964, I was still in Calcutta helping my brothers build our family's steel and engineering business. Like most young businessmen of that generation, I welcomed the emergence of Indira Gandhi as minister of information and broadcasting in Nehru's successor Lal Bahadur Shastri's cabinet.

When Shastri prematurely died after only eighteen months in office, I felt the first strong stirrings of political partisanship. Morarji Desai had no doubt he was Shastri's rightful successor. However, people of 'new thinking' in the Congress Party persuaded a still very youthful and visibly reluctant Mrs Gandhi to challenge him for the premiership.

Her strengths were formidable. She was young and brimming with ideas. She had been trained by Nehru to think big and act boldly. Her combination of coolness and poise under pressure contrasted starkly with the feebleness of many of her more senior colleagues. Her self-assurance, her simplicity of style and manner, and above all, her passionate commitment to the modernization of India, made my brothers and I proud to be her contemporaries. For us, she stood for everything that John Fitzgerald Kennedy represented to young Americans of that period: the best hope for all our tomorrows.

We therefore watched the contest between Mrs Gandhi and the ageing Desai with anxious hope and foreboding. I prayed that she would win because I could see little hope for India were it to turn out differently.

Her victory was for me a second milestone on the road to political awareness. It was, I thought then and still believe today, an affirmation of the vision that Nehru provided on India's Independence Day on 15 August 1947: that India, for all its problems of poverty, ignorance and disease, can and will develop as a great power, united in diversity and a force for good in the world.

My first direct contact with Mrs Gandhi took place in 1967. By this time, Aruna and I had moved to London for Ambika's medical treatment. I applied to the Indian government to allow our sons Ambar and Akash and daughter Anjli to join us for a few weeks' holiday. There were strict foreign exchange restrictions in India in those days. Besides, the Indian bureaucracy was somewhat unsympathetic and civil servants found it easy to refuse requests.

In desperation, I took the liberty of writing to the prime minister. I did not harbour much hope of success. Yet, within ten days of writing to her, the bureaucratic machine in Delhi began to respond and the priceless permission was granted. After ten months of separation, Aruna and I were reunited with our children, who had been left behind in Calcutta. Mrs Gandhi's intervention typified what my family and I had always believed Nehru's daughter would be: a leader with a warm heart, able and willing, despite the pressures of her official life, to temper bureaucracy with humanity. She generally acted with the same dispatch that characterized her father to clear bureaucratic roadblocks in matters big and small.

Droughts in 1965 and 1966 had ruined harvests in India. Millions of Indians faced starvation. India badly needed food supplies from the United States but would not desist from condemning the American military involvement in Vietnam. Mrs Gandhi, though, made a strong impression on President Lyndon Johnson, which paved the way for food aid from the US to India. I was struck by Mrs Gandhi's personal impact on Washington on that trip. Johnson sent an urgent request to Congress to authorize more assistance to India. LBJ, as he was called, also presented a state yacht belonging to former US President Harry Truman to Mrs Gandhi. This was absorbed into the Indian Navy for oceanic research.

In 1971, she called an early general election, not due for another year, and won a landslide victory. Listening to the results over the airwaves in London, I was excited at the prospect of Mrs Gandhi establishing a clear personal mandate, without having to compromise with petty individuals who for too long had held her back. The UK's *Sunday Times* described her as 'The most powerful woman in the world'.

But within weeks of her triumph, she faced a challenge on India's eastern front. An uprising in East Pakistan against Pakistan's rulers, who belonged to West Pakistan, catapulted India into the middle of hostilities between the ruling Pakistani military junta and Bengalis, who were the main inhabitants of East Pakistan.

Mrs Gandhi's critics claimed the Bengali revolt drew its inspiration from and was sustained by India. This charge was utterly baseless, but as the Pakistan army sought to quell the rebellion by organized burning of villages, destruction of crops, mass shooting of innocent people and the rape of tens of thousands of Bengali women, it rapidly became impossible for India to stand aloof. Especially when millions of East Pakistanis seeking refuge from the terror began pouring into India, mainly the state of West Bengal, overwhelming its public services and posing a terrifying threat of plague, famine and war.

The Indian prime minister would have liked India to stay out of the war. But as she explained to the US magazine *Foreign Affairs*[*]:

'We would normally have welcomed the attainment of freedom by any victims of colonial oppression, but usually it would have very little direct impact on us. Bangladesh however was a part of our sub-continent. How could we ignore a conflict that took place on our very border and overflowed into our own territory?'

India was increasingly spending millions of dollars every day to feed the refugees and provide them with improvised shelter and basic medical care. There was no choice but to levy special taxes, including a surcharge on postal rates, to raise additional revenue to pay for this. However, the conscience of the world community remained distressingly unmoved by the Bangladesh tragedy. Indeed, Pakistan, instead of being rebuked for the atrocities its forces were inflicting on its own citizens, continued to receive military and economic help from the United States.

It was in this context that Mrs Gandhi signed the Indo-Soviet Treaty of Friendship on 9 August 1971. This promised USSR's support to India in the event of a war with Pakistan, which seemed inevitable. The reaction in Washington was harsh. President Richard Nixon moved a US naval fleet menacingly

---

[*] *Foreign Affairs*, 1 October 1972.

close to Indian shores and used language that reinforced the impression in Delhi that US policy was inherently anti-India and pro-Pakistan.

It upset me, as an admirer of many, although not all, aspects of American life, that India should be so condemned by the United States. I was therefore heartened to learn that Mrs Gandhi had decided to undertake a tour of the West to outline India's position. This was the first occasion when I had the chance to speak to her personally. Through my family, I had seen her at formal events in Delhi, but it was not until this visit to London that I had an opportunity to have a direct conversation with her. The introduction came through L.N. Mishra, India's then minister of foreign trade, who happened to be in the British capital. Mishra arranged a meeting for me with the prime minister through her private secretary, R.K. Dhawan.

The appointment was at Claridge's Hotel in London's Mayfair district, which has welcomed many heads of state over the years. Before I entered her room, I spent fifteen minutes talking to Dhawan and another aide, Nathu Ram. Dhawan then took me into her suite. I was immediately struck by her calmness, grace and authority. I sensed an inner strength that set her apart as a natural leader. We chatted primarily about events in England and what I was doing in London. I suppose I spent a total of ten minutes with her, but I left her presence satisfied that I had said everything I wanted to say. Irrespective of how short a time one spent with her, she had the ability to extract from you effortlessly anything useful you had to impart.

On her return from London, the situation in the subcontinent worsened. It escalated into full-scale war between India and Pakistan, pre-emptively provoked by the latter.

However, the Indian army comprehensively overran East Pakistan. Bangladesh came into being. The surrender of the Pakistani forces was hailed as Mrs Gandhi's greatest triumph. It was by any measure a high point in her career.

To me, her finest moment was her decision that India follow Sir Winston Churchill's famous maxim: 'In victory, magnanimity'. Soon after the armistice was signed, she ordered Indian troops to unconditionally withdraw from territory they had liberated from Pakistan. In due course, the Indian military pulled out of what had now become Bangladesh.

To the defeated Pakistanis, she sent a message which could have been plucked out of the peace-loving Nehru's copybook:

'We have no enmity towards you. We have more things in common that those which divide us. We should like to fashion our relations with the people of Pakistan on the basis of friendship and understanding.'

In the winter of 1974–75, I was visiting Calcutta when, on 3 January 1975, I heard on the radio that someone had thrown a bomb at L.N. Mishra in Patna, the capital of Bihar state. To my sorrow, he died soon afterwards in hospital. He was one of the nicest people I have met in politics and should have had a great career before him. His death had been preceded by criticism of him in the press. He told me in private, 'They are using me as their first line of attack and their next line will be Mrs Gandhi.'

For some reason, Mishra had taken a liking to me, so much so that he asked me to accompany him to the United Nations Conference on Trade and Development (UNCTAD) in Santiago in 1972. The problem was getting me the necessary accreditation to attend. He turned me into a journalist and thereby got me access.

On 12 June 1975, I heard on BBC Radio that Mrs Gandhi had lost a case in the Allahabad High Court over an election petition that had been hanging fire since 1971.

Raj Narain, the candidate who lost to her by 1,10,000 votes, charged her agent Yashpal Kapoor, the district magistrate responsible for her constituency Rae Bareli, its superintendent of police and the home secretary of Uttar Pradesh state, of complicity in arranging rostrums, loudspeakers and barricades for her campaign rallies. This—since the last three mentioned were government officials—the court held, was electoral malpractice. In essence, the judgment disqualified her from Parliament and disbarred her from holding public office for six years.

The sentence seemed quite inexplicable. The charge was also that some of her supporters had built a wooden platform from which she had spoken at a rally in the general election, the cost of which had not been included in the expenses statement filed by her. Mrs Gandhi, it was clear, had no personal knowledge of the matter. Nonetheless, she was found guilty under rules governing Indian elections.

The verdict was overkill. It was as if the President of the United States needed to resign for the failure of his supporters to declare the cost of erecting a billboard during a presidential election. Or a British prime minister could be unseated because their agent had overlooked notifying the returning officer about the cost of a piece of carpentry.

I telephoned Dhawan. He told me the court's decision was subject to appeal, but that Mrs Gandhi was seriously considering resigning. Frustrated and alarmed, I flew to Delhi. Only the most extreme members of the Opposition believed she should step down. The Congress Party's view was that it was for Parliament to decide who should be prime minister, not the judiciary. I was told that both houses of Parliament, the Lok Sabha and the Rajya Sabha, would reject a motion to remove her.

When I called on her, it was obvious she was pondering over whether she should resign or listen to her Cabinet colleagues and party, who were advising her to sit tight and appeal the ruling to the Supreme Court. I ventured to suggest there was no reason to resign on such a trivial matter; indeed, that it was absurd of a solitary judge to decide on the fate of a prime minister elected by a democratic process.

I then had a long discussion with Mrs Gandhi's younger son, Sanjay Gandhi. Mrs Gandhi had earlier asked L.N. Mishra to arrange for me to meet Sanjay and to give impartial advice about whether his fledgling car factory Maruti—the subject of a raging political controversy—was feasible. Sanjay showed me around the factory and I was very impressed. I told Mrs Gandhi that Sanjay was a man in a hurry and his enthusiasm would create employment, although his factory would have to buy components manufactured in other countries. Mrs Gandhi was keen for it to go ahead because India needed its own car plant making small cars for the growing population. Those who scoffed at Sanjay's dream were proved wrong when Maruti, with Japanese carmaker Suzuki's participation, became India's largest car manufacturer and still is.

Now, in the wake of the Allahabad judgment, he was clearly worried. He felt certain opportunistic politicians were attempting to exploit the crisis created by the verdict for their personal benefit. He gave me the impression that some leaders in the Congress were pretending to be loyal to his mother, though in truth they were ready to stab her in the back.

Mrs Gandhi decided to appeal the ruling. But there were fears her life could be in danger. Leading the political campaign against her, Jai Prakash Narayan called on the Indian armed forces and police to disobey the government. It was this threat, more than anything else, that prompted Mrs Gandhi to advise the President of India, Fakhruddin Ali Ahmed, to declare a State of Emergency. This meant press censorship and suspension of all political activities outside Parliament.

My reaction to the Emergency was—and still is—that it was a disagreeable necessity. If Mrs Gandhi had not imposed it, governance would have been impeded by motivated civil disorders inspired by her opponents. India would quickly have become ungovernable. If this had happened, those who would have suffered most would have been the poor people. It would not be an exaggeration to say that India's chances of remaining united, democratic and stable would have been slim indeed, had Mrs Gandhi not taken firm action to stop the rot.

At first, most Indians' response to the Emergency was one of relief. Visiting Delhi, I observed it had raised the morale of the civil service, given a clearer direction to nationalized industries and galvanized business and commerce. Corruption, for a while, went out of fashion. Bureaucrats began arriving at their offices on time!

When I met Mrs Gandhi, I was relieved to hear that the Emergency was only a temporary measure, that it would be ended as soon as possible. She questioned me about the reaction in Britain. Aware of various pieces in the internationally influential British press, she was concerned about the portrayal of her as a ruthless dictator, which could potentially damage Indo-British relations. On my return to London, I resolved to do all I could to encourage balanced media coverage.

A few months earlier, Eldon Griffiths, a Conservative Party MP, and I had launched the Indo-British Association (IBA), a forum through which friends of India in Britain and friends of Britain in India could maintain contact with one another. I was determined to do this since my twins Ambar and Akash, while at Harrow, had discovered the school library possessed twenty books on India but none of them had been opened for years.

IBA was conceived as an extension of Nehru's interpretation that the hitherto colonial relationship between Britain and India had transformed into one of friendship and mutual respect. IBA's annual dinners, which became a star attraction in London's Indo-British calendar, were generally held on or around Nehru's birthday, 14 November, a birth date he shared with King Charles III.

The first such event took place on 14 November 1975. It had one overriding purpose: to give leaders in British politics, industry and the arts first-hand exposure to senior Indian ministers' views on the situation in India, instead of the slanted opinion in a section of the British press. Notwithstanding the general hostility of Fleet Street, there was an excellent turnout. Michael Foot, a senior minister in the Labour Party government and a staunch friend of India, declared he had no doubt whatsoever about Mrs Gandhi's devotion to democracy. Reginald Maudling, the Conservative Shadow Foreign Secretary, similarly made no bones about his conviction that sooner rather than later, India would return to normality.

India was represented by its then Commerce Minister Debi Chattopadhyay and Dev Kanta Barooah, president of the ruling Congress Party. The latter unfortunately did not make good use of his opportunity to speak. Instead of detailing India's problems and how Mrs Gandhi was trying to deal with them, he simply indulged in singing her praise in a sycophantic manner, which did her more harm than good.

Not long afterwards, British papers started carrying pieces[*] about Mrs Gandhi using the Emergency to enforce a family planning policy involving forcible sterilization of large numbers of poor people. Most of these stories originated from Opposition politicians in India. The sheer size of India's population has been one of its drawbacks. No responsible person can quarrel about legitimate efforts to curb its explosive growth. That said, the methods adopted by some officials during the Emergency may have gone well beyond the bounds of justice and civil liberty. Many of the horror stories about forced vasectomies were palpably untrue. But that there were improper pressures, and that some young men and women were subjected to bullying by local party officials, anxious to curry favour with their superiors, cannot, I think, be in doubt.

The tragedy is that this sort of behaviour is all too typical of India's bureaucracy. The further one moves out of Delhi, the more likely it becomes that even the most benign and well-intentioned policies will be carried out with little respect for the personal dignity of those at the receiving end.

The question that was constructively posed was, to what extent was Mrs Gandhi aware of the excesses? And if she was unaware of them, was it not her duty, as prime minister, to find out?

During a visit to Delhi in the middle of the Emergency, Eldon spent nearly an hour talking to the prime minister in her private office on virtually every aspect of her policies. He came

---

[*] Levin, Bernard. 'Series on the Indian Emergency', *The Times*. 1–8 November 1978.

back just as convinced as Foot had been at the IBA dinner that Mrs Gandhi was totally committed to returning India to full democracy. Eldon later wrote to me:

> It is possible that the censorship of the Indian press and radio, combined with the traditional reluctance of Indian officials to tell their superiors anything that might cast a reflection on their own performance, may have cut off the Prime Minister from what was happening at the grassroots. This was doubly unfortunate when, because of the Emergency, Mrs Gandhi was unable to leave Delhi and take the pulse of the nation for herself. Nevertheless, could she not have done more to find out what was going on? In retrospect, perhaps she should have done so. She told me that she wished she had done more to find out exactly what was happening, and I have not the slightest doubt about her veracity and sincerity. It is therefore quite monstrous to allege that Mrs Gandhi at the time knew and approved of the pressures that were applied (and no doubt still are being applied) in the name of birth control in some of India's remote villages. I am quite sure that she didn't and that if she had known she would not have hesitated to put a stop to such conduct at once.

There can be little doubt that the Emergency alienated a majority of the Indian people from the government. As Mrs Gandhi herself put it, 'We managed to annoy all sections of society at the same time.' To her credit, as soon as she was convinced that public order had been restored, she kept her word and advised the President to call a general election.

I saw Mrs Gandhi only once during the electioneering. She clearly felt the tide of opinion was against her, especially in northern India. On 20 March 1977, I rang Dhawan to determine the trends. I asked him to let me speak to Mrs Gandhi. 'We are losing,' she said. Her reaction, though, was not one of sorrow. Instead, she felt relieved. Two days later, she resigned. She told me she was looking forward to seeing more of her family, especially her grandchildren, to 'doing all the things I have not been able to do for a very long time, such as reading and going to Kashmir', above all, to having a rest. After eleven years as prime minister, she was exhausted.

About seven weeks into the Emergency, Bangladesh's leader Sheikh Mujibur Rahman, with whom Mrs Gandhi had established an excellent rapport, and most members of his family, were brutally assassinated in Dhaka in a military coup. Two of Mujib's daughters, Sheikh Hasina and Sheikh Rehana, were fortunately not in the country when the merciless killings took place. There was no way they could return home, for their lives were in great danger. Mrs Gandhi entrusted to me the task of looking after the two sisters. I arranged for them to stay out of harm's way in a flat in London.

Sheikh Hasina became prime minister of Bangladesh, and her younger sister, Rehana, is the mother of Tulip Siddiq, the British MP for Hampstead in London. We remain good friends.

After the Congress' defeat, Morarji Desai, who had parted ways with Mrs Gandhi and her colleagues, cobbled together a new and hurriedly formed Janata Party and, with the aid of Jai Prakash Narayan, fulfilled his ambition of becoming prime minister. Desai immediately set up a judicial commission to investigate charges against Mrs Gandhi, saying that she had abused the Constitution and exceeded her powers as prime minister. Similar charges were laid against Sanjay Gandhi and her chief aide R.K. Dhawan.

I kept in touch with Mrs Gandhi by means of frequent phone calls. A parliamentary by-election arose when an MP vacated his seat. This happened in Chikmagalur constituency in a coffee-growing district of the southern Karnataka state. It was a Congress stronghold; all the same, it was risky for a very recently discredited leader, whose party was still in disarray, to take on a powerful Janata candidate, Virendra Patil, a former Karnataka CM.

Big guns in the national cabinet turned up to campaign against Mrs Gandhi. She was portrayed as a murderess, a dictator and a two-faced witch!* On voting day, there was a record turnout. Out of Parliament for months, the 'Empress of India' spectacularly bounced back. She captured 2,49,376 votes to Patil's 1,72,043.

No sooner had she taken her new seat in the Lok Sabha than the Janata government launched impeachment proceedings against her. She was found guilty of abusing her position as an MP by obstructing, intimidating and harassing officials investigating the previous conduct of her former government.

The Janata government's pursuit of anyone and everyone connected with her extended for a period to my brothers and me as well. Jit was accused of improperly lending jeeps to Mrs Gandhi's party for her use at election time, though he was one of forty others who did the same in kind.

Our family firm Apeejay had followed the general practice in India of offering vehicles to senior politicians of all parties who had difficulty in obtaining transport in rural areas. We were asked to say we had been coerced by the former prime minister's office into providing the jeeps to her party only. Jit refused to record such a statement, for it was patently untrue.

---

* Vivek Haldipur, *Harvard Crimson*, 12 April 1977.

Some companies surrendered to the pressure. Jit maintained the vehicles had been made available voluntarily. This got him into trouble. The Janata men never forgave him for not cooperating in their bid to indict Mrs Gandhi.

Before the Chikmagalur election—its outcome then unknown—a group of Indians had invited Mrs Gandhi to visit London. She accepted, but the Janata government declined to issue her with a passport on the grounds that she was a subject of investigation. Eventually, the authorities relented. But the UK's *Times* newspaper was malicious in its objection to the trip. Bernard Levin, a prominent columnist, accused Mrs Gandhi of 'ruling India under dictatorial powers, achieved by fraud and sustained by . . . force, censorship, lies, corruption, arbitrary arrest . . . harassment and intimidation'. He proceeded to castigate Conservative peer Lord Peter Carrington, later to become British Foreign Secretary; Peter Shore, the incumbent labour secretary of state for environment; Eldon; and me for serving as her 'claque' in Britain and participating in a 'national disgrace' by inviting Mrs Gandhi to speak at an IBA dinner.

Such biased nonsense was widely believed in London. Some of it was picked up in broadcasts to India on BBC's external service. Eldon, as vice chairman, and I, as chairman, of the IBA wrote a letter to the editor of *The Times*. This said in part:

> The case against Mrs Gandhi is still before the Indian courts, and ultimately the Indian Parliament. As yet they have reached no decisions. It is strange that The Times, through the voice of Mr Levin, not only has indulged in trial by journalism but has reached, and published, a verdict while the case is still sub judice.
>
> Mr Levin relies very largely on the arguments against Mrs Gandhi by the Shah Commission . . . We do not for

one moment underestimate the volume, nor do we challenge the veracity of the allegations made to the Commission by Mrs Gandhi's accusers; we are in no position to do so. But we note that Mrs Gandhi has refused to give evidence to the Commission on grounds that it is constitutionally incompetent and politically biased against her. The material before the Commission may therefore be very one sided. So are Mr Levin's articles.

Anyone who cares about freedom and justice in India—and we are just as concerned about these things as you are—is bound to examine his conscience before reaching any conclusions about what happened in India under the Emergency... There were cruelties. There was corruption—just as under the present Janata Government.

But your readers may think as we do, that it is for the Indian people to reach their own decision about the extremely difficult balance between freedom and order in their vast subcontinent; between the strong authority that is required to govern so diverse a country and the liberality that is inseparable from any democracy worthy of the name; between the need to control a population explosion before it condemns millions more to starvation and the right of the individual citizen to procreate as he pleases.

We do not pretend to have answers to these questions. But when the people of Karnataka had their opportunity to comment in last week's by-election in the Chikmagalur constituency, their judgement was unequivocal. Whatever they thought of the Emergency, they chose Indira Gandhi to be their Member of Parliament by the largest majority ever given to any candidate in that seat. For all practical purposes, if she wishes it, Mrs Gandhi is now leader of the

Opposition. Who will say with any confidence that she may not one day become Prime Minister again?'

Mrs Gandhi arrived in London on 12 November 1978. Accompanying her were her daughter-in-law Sonia (wife of her elder son Rajiv and until recently, for a lengthy period, president of the Congress Party), C.M. Stephen, leader of the Congress Parliamentary Party, and Pranab Mukherjee, Opposition leader in India's upper house of Parliament known as the Rajya Sabha. British and Indian journalists crowded the VIP lounge at Heathrow airport to speak to her. One of them asked, 'Are you trying to make a comeback?' She retorted with a subdued smile, 'But where had I gone?'

Outside, members of the Indian Overseas Congress shouted 'Indira Gandhi *Zindabad*' or 'victory to Indira Gandhi'. As we drove out of the terminal complex, we passed a smaller counter-demonstration by Sikhs with black flags showing loyalty to religiously inclined Akali groups in Punjab. The London police kept an eagle eye on both sides and everything passed off peacefully.

During her ten days in the UK, the British government accorded Mrs Gandhi all courtesies deserved by a former prime minister—indeed, even breaking protocol when Prime Minister James Callaghan of the Labour Party received her at his official premises at 10 Downing Street. The Foreign and Commonwealth Office (FCO) was plainly uneasy. The tour received wide coverage in Indian newspapers, which irritated official circles in Delhi. Several ministers in the Janata Party

---

* Letters to the Editor, *The Times*, 10 November 1978.

government in India expressed their displeasure to the British high commissioner about the 'fuss'.

A vengeful Janata Party MP, Ram Jethmalani, a lawyer by profession, in a memorandum to the Indian prime minister, demanded that Mrs Gandhi be jailed forthwith. He also roundly condemned the Indian High Commission in London, because the Deputy High Commissioner Alan Nazareth was present at Heathrow to receive her.* This, in fact, ensured use of the VIP area. Even the High Commissioner, N.G. Goray, a pleasant person, although Desai's political appointee, was criticized for inviting her to tea. Goray, a socialist, also spoke at the IBA dinner in honour of Mrs Gandhi.

The British Home Office was apprehensive that the trip could trigger clashes between pro-Gandhi and anti-Gandhi factions among Indian immigrants in Britain. Such concern was misplaced, albeit there were incidents at her public engagements in the west London suburb of Southall and in the West Midlands city of Birmingham. Sikhs lived in large numbers in both places and were divided in their opinion on Indian politics. But police and intelligence maintained a firm hand and prevented matters from getting out of control.

Callaghan, whom Mrs Gandhi knew from his time as foreign secretary in Prime Minister Harold Wilson's government, informed Eldon he would be pleased to meet Mrs Gandhi in a strictly personal capacity as a former head of a Commonwealth government, but not on any other basis, because of the Desai government's hostility towards her. Deputy Prime Minister Michael Foot, a fan of Mrs Gandhi, urged a solution.

---

* *Indian Express*, 18 November 1978.

So the FCO devised an inventive way forward. Eldon was given a formal appointment to take Stephen to Number 10 in his capacity as leader of Opposition in India and Mrs Gandhi was invited to join them as a sitting MP! 'No publicity please,' the FCO insisted. Eldon had to give an undertaking that there would be no photographs and no press statement about Mrs Gandhi's presence at Number 10. If the Foreign Office thought it would thereby conceal Callaghan meeting Mrs Gandhi from Indian authorities, it was badly mistaken. Every Indian journalist worth their salt learnt of the engagement and wrote about it. Mrs Gandhi, to her credit, did not confirm it when asked by the media about the appointment.

Callaghan welcomed his three visitors with equal warmth. But it was his conversation with Mrs Gandhi that naturally occupied centre stage. Eldon and Stephen happily took a backseat.

There were no protocol issues in respect to Mrs Gandhi's meeting with Margaret Thatcher, then recently elected as Leader of the Opposition Conservative Party. This was the first formal encounter between two people who within a couple of years would be described in the press as the 'two most powerful women in the world'. Eldon, who, as he modestly put it, was present as a silent observer, later noted:

> Superficially, the two ladies could not have been more unlike. Mrs Thatcher was all English rose—fair-headed, blue eyed, pink cheeked. Mrs Gandhi was all Indian enigma, dark hair streaked with grey, complexion brown yet pale, eyes like tiger-stones. Mrs T was severely dressed in black velvet and plaid skirt; Mrs G wore a shimmering sari from which her sandals protruded.

Their conversation styles were utterly different too. Most of the time it was Margaret leading, almost forcing the pace of her discussion, while Indira just sat quietly except for when she interjected a couple of pithy sentences. Her voice was quiet as a whisper; Margaret's was clear as a bell. I was reminded of Kipling's couplet:

'East is East and West is West
But never the twain shall meet.'

Yet meet they did, and very successfully. After their half-hour conversation, a current of fellow-feeling, if that is the right word to describe an unspoken empathy among women, was passing between the two leaders. They had sized one another up. And they both clearly liked what they saw.

On the first evening of Mrs Gandhi's visit, I invited her to have dinner with my family. For a week, Aruna had been worried about the formalities involved in hosting such an important international figure. In the event, her fears were groundless. As soon as Mrs Gandhi entered our flat, everyone felt at ease. She had an extraordinary ability to make herself and everyone else feel at home. My youngest son Angad, then eight years old, was utterly charmed by our distinguished guest.

During her stay in the UK, there were meetings with the Indian community, news media and MPs. The lawmakers asked searching questions about the Emergency. 'What went wrong?' one of them asked. She responded, 'We managed to upset nearly every section of the community simultaneously.' This disarmed the audience and the meeting in the Houses of Parliament went off quite smoothly.

Mrs Gandhi had kindly agreed to perform the inauguration of a new mill at my company Caparo's steel tube plant in South Wales. The original mill had been opened in 1977 by Prince Charles, now King Charles III.

The site, adjoining one of British Steel's strip mills, was in the heart of Michael Foot's House of Commons constituency. Ironically, here was I, a near foreigner and a neo-capitalist, borrowing money from the European Common Market (which was to evolve into the European Union) to build a private factory in the backyard of a senior left-wing Labour politician whose lifetime commitment was state ownership of such facilities. I was pleased and impressed that Foot lent his full support to the venture. He also accepted my invitation to be present at the ceremony, commenting in his speech that his old friend Indira Gandhi should not be written off! He and Eldon, a Conservative, put on a ten-minute display of light-hearted political banter, before Mrs Gandhi stole the show.

As our helicopter approached the Welsh valleys, a blanket of drizzle enveloped us. Our pilot kept circling in vain for a break in the clouds to descend on the landing spot. I must admit, the thought briefly passed through my mind that the future of India could be at stake if anything happened to our honoured guest. What a tragedy it would be if Indira Gandhi was to meet her end in the bleak Welsh hills of Ebbw Vale.

Fortunately, there was no mishap. A Welsh band was laid on for the occasion. Local dignitaries and a gathering of Indians who had travelled 27 miles from the Welsh capital Cardiff greeted her. Clad in a yellow sari, a headscarf and a black coat, Mrs Gandhi pressed a button to set in motion Natural Gas Tubes' second pipe mill. As it happens, the Welsh and Indians had had many things in common in the past, including putting up signs like 'English Go Home!'

In her short speech, Mrs Gandhi recalled an encounter when she was a student at Oxford (in the 1930s):

'Another girl student came into my room and said she would like to discuss our respective nationalist movements. When I asked where she came from, she said, "Wales." Perhaps it was not surprising that she saw in me a fellow spirit. After all, we Indians are sometimes accused of speaking English with a Welsh accent.'

Before returning to London, we took Mrs Gandhi to the huge boulder of Welsh limestone erected on the hill overlooking the town of Tredegar as a memorial to Foot's predecessor as MP of Ebbw Vale, the late Aneurin Bevan. Foot highlighted Bevan's contribution to the post-war Labour government that conceded independence to India. He told me afterwards that when the committee were considering which of his international friends they should invite for the unveiling of the memorial, one name that stood above all others was Indira Gandhi.

The Indian Overseas Congress (IOC) organized a rally in Southall at its Dominion Cinema. The previous evening, we were informed that a gang of professional troublemakers were bent on disrupting the gathering. The IOC inquired if Mrs Gandhi wanted to cancel the engagement. When I asked her, she stressed the meeting must go ahead and that she would attend.

When she arrived at the venue in the afternoon, a noisy 4000-odd people had gathered around it. Many had come from faraway cities and towns to catch a glimpse of her. The police joined hands to form a human chain to prevent those who didn't possess a seat in the theatre from breaking into the building. Mrs Gandhi's supporters broke into applause. Her detractors, like the Akalis, the Marxists and the Maoists, carried banners that said *'Fascist – Murderer – OUT'* and shouted *'Indira Gandhi Nazi'* and *'Fascist GO HOME'*. One of them threw an egg as she entered the cinema. It smashed against the wall, splattering yolk on her black and pink sari.

Inside, there was more pandemonium. Hundreds of demonstrators in the audience rose to their feet as she was introduced, booing and waving black flags. Seated near her on the stage, I estimated that about 10 per cent of those present were creating the din, while the remainder were quietly waiting for her to speak. Undeterred by the cacophony, Mrs Gandhi proceeded with her speech and won huge acclaim. She afterwards remarked, 'What sort of democracy do these people want? They don't want others to speak.'

It was during this visit that I really got to know Mrs Gandhi. I spent most of each day with her. I discovered that everything I had heard or felt about her did her less than justice. I recorded in my diary: 'She is plus everything and minus nothing.'

When we went for a walk along Brook Street and Bond Street to Berkeley Square in Mayfair, every few yards we would be stopped by people—British, Iranians, Iraqis, Eastern and Far Eastern—who would say things like 'Madam, it is an honour to see you'. Others would gush, 'Mrs Gandhi, you are the hope of Asia.'

Before her return to India, she celebrated her sixty-first birthday on 19 November. She was delighted by dozens of children coming to her hotel to sing 'Happy Birthday' to her.

The Sunday Times wrote: 'Paul, who is coordinating the programme at Mrs Gandhi's request from his offices in Portman Square, London, said that more than 50 journalists had requested interviews with the former prime minister. We have also available to us almost every programme on the BBC and ITV,' Mr Paul added. 'But Mrs Gandhi is not giving any interviews. Her political battle is in India, not England.'

On 20 November, as soon as she was back in Delhi, she graciously sent a hand-written letter to me in which she wrote,

> I hardly have the words to thank you for all the trouble you took over my programme. But for your personal interest and constant vigilance the visit would not have been a success. I should like to thank your wife for her hospitality. The first evening at your home was a delightful and relaxing beginning to what turned out to be a most hectic schedule. I was charmed by the children. You should really be proud of them.

On 6 January 1979, she wrote:

> Sonia and I were both charmed by your family. In fact, Sonia repeatedly told me how unlike you were to the normal description of an industrialist.
>
> I very rarely go out, but the other evening I went to a small dinner with one of Rajiv's pilot friends, whose father-in-law is with the World Bank in New York. I was horrified to hear from one of the guests that I had made rude remarks about you in French to Sonia while you were in the room. This ridiculous item has appeared in the 1 January issue of *India Today* magazine. Needless to say, there is not an iota of truth in this.

I replied on 17 January 1979:

> 'I would like to mention that my loyalty to you cannot be and would not be questioned or shattered by this mischievous piece of "so-called" journalism.'

No sooner had she returned than the Lok Sabha's Committee of Privileges pursued her in a partisan manner. She responded:

> The Janata Party knows, the Prime Minister knows, indeed every man, woman and child in Indian knows, that if this drama of impeachment of a former Prime Minister is enacted, its purpose is not to solve any national problem. It is to silence a voice which they find inconvenient. But my voice will not be hushed, for it is not a lone voice. It speaks not for myself, a frail woman, and unimportant persons; it speaks for the deep and significant changes in society which alone can be the basis of true democracy and a fuller freedom. Every insult hurled at me will rebound. Every punishment inflicted on me will be a source of strength to me.

On 19 December 1978, Prime Minister Morarji Desai introduced a motion in the Lok Sabha to find Mrs Gandhi guilty and imprison her.

I was appalled, but quickly became convinced that Morarji Desai and his government had committed a fatal blunder because it made her a martyr in the eyes of scores of millions of Indians who had always felt uneasy over the ditching of the daughter of Jawaharlal Nehru in favour of a squabbling coalition of comparative weaklings.

Members of the Rajya Sabha rushed to the house asking her to speak. She obliged by quoting a British Army song:

> *'Wish me luck as you wave me goodbye*
> *With a cheer, not a tear, in your eye.*
> *Give me a smile, I can keep all the while*
> *In my heart while I'm away . . .'*

That evening, she was taken in a police car to Delhi's Tihar Jail. This struck me like a hammer blow. I frantically wrote letters to heads of government and international organizations pleading with them:

> In the name of human rights, in the name of the stability of India and of the subcontinent, I request you to persuade the Government of India to:
>
> (1) Start governing the country, instead of witch-hunting.
> (2) Stop making Mrs Gandhi a scapegoat for internal bickering of their own party.
> (3) Give her the respect due to a former Prime Minister and national leader.

Looking back, I suppose my efforts seem naïve. I had no experience of politics or diplomacy. Fortunately, more than enough Indians shared these feelings to ensure that she would not stay in jail very long. Within seven days, she was released. She had not given an inch to the government that was hounding her. Indeed, by ill-treating her, the Janata Party government galvanized her resurgence.

In their endeavour to discredit Mrs Gandhi, Indian authorities persevered in gunning for the Paul family. An official attempt was made to even subject me to investigation for allegedly 'bankrolling' her. Ram Jethmalani came to London with two representatives of India's Central Bureau of Investigation. He returned home without a shred of evidence, but with a sizeable flea in his ear. Scotland Yard, who were approached by the agents, told them there was no proof of any wrongdoing on my part either in Britain or in India.

Therefore, they would not attract any support from the London Metropolitan Police. In effect, the muckrakers were told by police in the UK to stay clear of politics and, thereby, asked them to clear off!

On Boxing Day 1978, driving home after lunch with friends, I heard on the car radio Mrs Gandhi had been set free. I rang her residence as soon as I returned to our flat. She answered the phone herself. I was taken aback but congratulated her! Then I asked about her experience in prison. 'You did not let me rest in London, so these people arranged it for me,' she joked.

She corresponded on 9 July 1979, shortly after a holiday in Darjeeling in the eastern Himalayas in the state of West Bengal. She said of a now struggling Prime Minister Desai, 'I doubt he will ever be able to deliver the goods.' The following month, fragmentation in the Janata Party intensified. Desai was compelled to resign. Charan Singh, who was one of his deputy prime ministers, briefly succeeded him, before his government, too, collapsed, paving the way for elections at the turn of 1979–80.

On Christmas Day 1979, I went for lunch with the Gandhi family and found them elated by the impact Mrs Gandhi was making in the election campaign. In the evening, she went to record a party-political broadcast at All India Radio (AIR). I went with her. When she emerged from the studio, people lined the road to greet her with a namaste, the Indian method of greeting with folded hands. I felt certain she was going to win.

Eldon, who, too, was in Delhi, predicted she would return to power with an absolute majority, though a narrow one. The British High Commission disagreed, forecasting her party would be the largest single formation in the Lok Sabha, but would fall short of a clear mandate. I was more optimistic. So were Mrs Gandhi and her son Sanjay, who had been fully into politics since the imposition of Emergency. He had, of course, faced considerable flak for his alleged excesses during that period.

Her elder son Rajiv, who was less interested in public life, preferring his job as an airline pilot, was also inspired to do his bit. He went around Delhi on a motorbike, pasting up Congress Party posters. It could be said this was his baptism in political work.

Campaigning had stopped when I went to see Mrs Gandhi on 5 January 1980 and found her pacing the floor. I ventured to ask what was troubling her. She said, now that canvassing was over, she had nothing to do. Rajiv suggested she should take a short holiday in the paradise of Kashmir until the results started coming out. She quipped that she found holidays too exhausting.

The result was a landslide in her favour. The Janata Party, now split into factions, was decimated. The Congress burgeoned from 72 seats to 350 seats like a phoenix from the ashes. It was a great pleasure to attend the swearing-in ceremony of the new government. That evening, she spoke on AIR in a language reminiscent of her father. Her theme was reconciliation. She urged Indians to abjure hatred and bitterness and return to the task of building India.

Before my departure from Delhi, I went to bid goodbye to Mrs Gandhi at her then 12 Willingdon Crescent home. She was sitting in the dining room, drawing up a list of ministers in her new cabinet. She asked if I would like to become high commissioner in London, or an ambassador somewhere else. You could have bowled me over with a feather! I was an industrialist, not a diplomat. Speeches, receptions and paperwork were not my forte. I therefore expressed my gratitude and said my only desire was to serve her and India in my private capacity. I, thereafter, put it more formally in a letter, which I drafted on my flight back to London:

'I am, frankly, uncomfortable in posts that demand routine and regular patterns; I am, if anything, a man of crisis who prefers to help in solving specific problems. I shall always be at your disposal and available at a moment's notice.'

In fact, according to Dhawan, who rushed to meet me at my hotel thereafter, she was ready to appoint me as a minister in her cabinet but didn't express this, because she felt I would not come back to India.

It was shortly after her return to power in 1980 that I organized an all-expenses-paid visit by the world-famous boxer Muhammad Ali to Delhi as I wanted to surprise Mrs Gandhi with something out of the ordinary.

When Ali arrived at Delhi airport, it was festooned with banners saying: *'The Greatest meets The Greatest.'* The banners continued all the way to Mrs Gandhi's house. We sat in her drawing room with R.K. Dhawan and members of her family. She and Muhammad Ali were on very good terms. Then, when the time came to leave, he lifted her into the air. Laughing, she said, 'Swraj, you never miss an opportunity to surprise me.' I replied, 'Madam, the greatest has come to meet the greatest and lifted you up.'

Later that year, Mrs Gandhi undertook a visit to Tanzania and Zimbabwe, which included a Commonwealth Heads of Government Meeting. I went to meet her there. I remember, she made a point of calling on General Zia-ul-Haq, President of Pakistan, instead of accepting his offer of calling on her, because this was the correct protocol—he was head of state, while she was head of government.

At her suggestion, I travelled back with her to India instead of returning directly to London. The next day, I was invited to lunch with the Gandhi family. Mrs Gandhi enjoyed being with her grandchildren and was utterly devoted to the whole family. Sometimes, when she felt the pressure of work, she would steal time from her office or Parliament to spend an hour with Rajiv's children Rahul and Priyanka. It was fascinating seeing her patiently answering wide-eyed questions about every subject under the sun, listening to their tales about school and the books they were reading, romping with them in the garden where she knew every flower and shrub by name. Few things gave her greater pleasure than reading to her grandchildren.

Mrs Gandhi harboured no resentment against leaders in other countries who had cooled off towards her when she was out of power. But she remembered those who stood by her. She delayed a scheduled trip to Kerala to meet Lord Carrington, who had addressed the IBA dinner in her honour in 1978. At an international meet in Belgrade, she held extended talks with Mrs Thatcher in the latter's hotel room. I was present in the former Yugoslavian capital at the time.

On 23 June 1980, I was awoken by a phone call at 5 a.m. that shocked me out of my senses. I was told that Sanjay, who had helped immeasurably in returning his mother to office, had died in a plane crash. I caught the first available flight to Delhi and found Rajiv and Sonia on the same plane. They had been to Italy to visit Sonia's parents. We landed at about 2.30 a.m. Mrs Gandhi was waiting for us at her residence. Despite her indescribable grief, her concern was to console us.

Sanjay had been intemperate and needlessly forceful during the Emergency. However, three tortuous years of browbeating by the Janata Party government had seasoned him. By 1980, though still strong-willed, he was more balanced and less given to rash judgements and actions. His manner and style were very different from his mother and grandfather; thus, most Indians couldn't quite understand him. He was a young man in a hurry, given to shortcuts, but kept his word and told you exactly what he felt. He was a vegetarian who did not smoke or drink.

His premature death brought Mrs Gandhi closer to his infant son Varun. She now doted on this baby. Sanjay's widow Maneka and the child continued to live with her mother-in-law, which was the norm in Indian society. Unfortunately, differences developed between the two. Tensions also increased between Maneka on the one hand and Rajiv and Sonia on the other.

Since they lived and ate communally under the same roof, the atmosphere became increasingly unpleasant. There were regular disagreements. It became apparent Maneka would leave the house and take Varun with her. She made her move when Mrs Gandhi was in London to inaugurate the Festival of India in 1982.

The news reached the prime minister just as I called to escort her to the IBA dinner, where she and Mrs Thatcher were guests of honour. Mrs Gandhi was suddenly a wounded grandmother who knew her grandchild would now be withheld from her. However, characteristically, she kept calm throughout the evening and made a very effective speech—unrehearsed.

Unsurprisingly, Mrs Gandhi found it difficult to overcome the loss of Sanjay. Rajiv stepped into the breach. He was reluctant to do so. He loved his work as an Indian Airlines pilot and had little desire to leave this for the world of politics. For years, he had shied away from the limelight that shone on his family. He and Sonia, who is of Italian origin, had provided Mrs Gandhi the warmth of a down-to-earth son and daughter-in-law. Politics had been left to Sanjay.

With Mrs Gandhi back in the saddle, Londoners who had cold-shouldered the IBA during the Janata regime began to show more interest in it. Coincidentally, Rajiv's first major exposure to the international spotlight occurred at an IBA function at the Royal Garden Hotel in July 1981, where he was the guest of honour. He made an excellent impression with a refreshing speech.

That was followed by meetings with British MPs and both Indian and British journalists, where he answered questions in a straightforward manner. Prime Minister Thatcher invited him to Downing Street. Sonia, who was also visiting with Rajiv, preferred to go to museums and art galleries with Aruna.

Indo-British bilateral relations were on the rise. But Fleet Street lost no opportunity to exaggerate differences between the two countries. When Mrs Thatcher visited India as prime minister in April 1981, the press corps who went with her sent back stories claiming all she and Mrs Gandhi had done during their meetings was quarrel. Eldon and I knew better. We, therefore, dispatched another letter to *The Times*:

> That Mrs Thatcher and Mrs Gandhi would not see eye to eye over a wide range of East-West issues—Afghanistan, Poland, the United States intervention force—was predictable. Modern India, under almost any Government, is bound to give high priority to good relations with the Soviet Union, just as Britain, under any government we can foresee,

is apt to be broadly pro-American. Mrs Gandhi, too, is just as sensitive about Pakistan and suspicious of Washington's intentions as Mrs Thatcher is sensitive about Ireland and suspicious of Moscow's intentions.

So it was, when the two prime ministers met in New Delhi. Both leaders stated their positions on East-West relations. Both came away with an enhanced appreciation of the other's view and the factors that lie behind them. Why such frank discussions should have been reported as a "row" is beyond us.

Where we hope, and believe, that the prime ministers had their most useful exchanges was in the field of commerce. Both are well aware of the potential for vastly increased trade between an India that needs British technology, investment and buying power, and a Britain which can benefit enormously from 700 million Indians' growing ability to absorb British exports—be they steel plants, jet aircraft, telephone exchanges or support for oil exploration.

That British relations with India need constant care and attention, we have never doubted, but both leaders can take comfort from the abiding things that link our two countries together. The interpretation of so much Indian and British culture. The interdependence of a great deal of British and Indian commerce. Our shared belief in the rule of law and parliamentary elections; above all, the human relationships, personified by a million British graves in India and a million or more people of Indian origin who have made their homes in Britain.

Our letter was published on 4 May. I had meanwhile already received correspondence from Mrs Thatcher and Mrs Gandhi putting the record straight.

The former, writing on 29 April, said, 'I greatly enjoyed my visit to India and my talks with Mrs Gandhi. I much regretted the line taken by the Press.' Then, handwritten, she went on to say, 'I found the visit very interesting and rewarding. Mrs Gandhi was marvellous and went out of her way to give me her time and attention. After Delhi we went to Bombay where the visit was a great success.'

Mrs Gandhi wrote on 30 April, 'Mrs Thatcher's visit was as successful as could be expected, considering the basic differences between our two countries and the briefness of her stay.' She thereafter penned,

> I was extremely cautious in the choice of words and merely expressed the concern of our people ... The purpose of such exchanges between Heads of Governments is not necessarily to come to agreements but to have the opportunity of friendly and candid talks so that respective points of view are clarified. I believe Mrs Thatcher was quite satisfied with the visit. I had left the planning of the programme to the British high commissioner here, presuming that he was in touch with Prime Minister Thatcher. Left to myself I might have arranged things differently.

In 1982, I was asked to assist with the organization of a major exposition of Indian art and culture in the UK. I was a trustee and the chair of the finance committee of the Festival of India, as it was called, a significant joint effort by India and Britain, mainly the endeavour of the Indian government. It opened with a classical concert, an exhilarating performance by Ravi Shankar, the sitar maestro, at the Royal Festival Hall in the

South Bank of London on 22 March and attended by the Prince of Wales, Mrs Thatcher and Mrs Gandhi.

The art show, which was staggering both in its excellence and in the breadth of styles and periods represented, was at the Hayward Gallery, in the South Bank Arts Centre. Nearly 500 paintings and sculptures, two-thirds of which were brought here from India, were arranged to the theme 'the Indian perception of the universe through 2,000 years.' Eight months of exhibitions, festivities and shows followed. The finale was another concert, this time at the London Coliseum on 14 November, attended by Rajiv and Sonia Gandhi.

My own contribution to the festival was to curate an exhibition on Pandit Nehru's life called 'the Nehru Exhibition'; it was formally inaugurated by Mrs Gandhi at Ambika House, Portland Place, London, again in March 1982, as part of her visit.

For my work connected with the Festival of India, I was honoured with a Padma Bhushan, India's third highest civilian award, by Indian President Giani Zail Singh. I travelled to Delhi in January 1983 to receive the prize in the company of Sir Richard Attenborough, who had similarly been recognized for his epic film *Gandhi*. The glittering ceremony took place at Rashtrapati Bhavan, the sprawling President's house at the epicentre of New Delhi atop what is known as Raisina Hill. Afterwards, we were the President's guests at a splendid reception graced by Mrs Gandhi. The days that followed were awash with a frenetic round of private parties and public celebrations.

In September 1983, I went with Mrs Gandhi to the United Nations in New York. There, as chairperson of the

Non-Aligned Movement, she convened a meeting of its member states, numbering more than a hundred. Bilaterally, she met President Ronald Reagan of the US, President Mitterrand of France, President Hosni Mubarak of Egypt and Canadian Prime Minister Pierre Trudeau, father of the current incumbent Justin Trudeau. She also hosted a stylish dinner for twenty-four heads of state or government.

In between, she watched *La Boheme* at the Metropolitan Opera and Ben Kingsley's solo performance on stage in *Edmund Kean*. Kingsley had played the lead role of Mahatma Gandhi in Attenborough's movie. She also found time to shop on New York's Fifth Avenue and bought presents for her grandchildren.

Then she matched wits with a group of writers, painters and philosophers, among them Isaac Asimov, the science fiction author, and Wassily Leontief, winner of the Nobel Prize for Economics. She enthralled them with a description of how she held her broken nose under a sari after she was hit by a piece of brick thrown by a rioter at an election rally in Odisha in 1967.

The next day, an exhibition of photographs of Jawaharlal Nehru opened at India House in New York. I had arranged this with Professor Ralph Buultjens, an old friend of the Nehru-Gandhi family. Unveiling this, Mrs Gandhi poignantly said:

> He was not just a father. He was a teacher; sometimes a remote teacher because he was in prison and I was out, or in another prison. He was my leader too, since I was a member of the (Congress) party of which he was the head, and later, he was my comrade, when I became President of the party. One of the ways I learned most from him was not by what he said or what he did, but by what he made me do. He

always sought to stretch me beyond what I thought was my capacity, and looking back, that was a boon.*

Her energy and vitality were legion. Once, in 1983, she landed in London for a brief unofficial stopover after a long flight from Cancun in Mexico, where she had gone for a North-South Conference. She sighed, 'Swraj, I am really tired, I need some sleep.' As soon as we reached the hotel, I told the security detail she would be resting and therefore not going out. In less than an hour, to our astonishment, she was up and ready to go. She wanted to go for a walk. I told her the security personnel had been given time off from attending to her. She was thrilled. She enjoyed the exercise, chatting and window shopping in central London in a free and informal manner.

It was on this visit that she went to inspect the residence of the Indian high commissioner at Kensington Palace Gardens. The British monarch, Queen Elizabeth II, was about to be hosted there for dinner prior to visiting India to attend the Commonwealth Heads of Government Meeting (CHOGM). Mrs Gandhi was displeased with the state of the furniture in the house, so she immediately went to the internationally renowned departmental store Harrods to order replacements. I went with her. She asked if I could pay for the purchases and the High Commission would reimburse me. Unfortunately, I wasn't carrying enough money to cover the bill. But that didn't matter. The chairman of Harrods, Professor Roland Smith, who was on the board of my company Caparo, was kind enough to say I could settle whenever I liked!

---

* *Indian Express*, 28 September 1983.

In November that year, India hosted the CHOGM. There was tough talking in Delhi between pro-American and anti-American countries following the US's invasion of the Caribbean island of Grenada, a Commonwealth member nation. These, though, were ironed out in a private retreat in exotic Goa, on India's western coast.

Overlooking the surfing waves of the Indian Ocean from the Fort Aguada Beach Hotel, diverse personalities like Kenneth Kaunda of Zambia, Bob Hawke of Australia, Lee Kuan Yew of Singapore and Mrs Thatcher relaxed in the warm glow of India's hospitality. Indeed, they reached agreement on a number of contentious matters.

The informality of this gathering is best illustrated by a snippet of conversation. The leaders were labouring to reach consensus on the wording of the communique and a number of them grew concerned about their wives being kept waiting for dinner, which had been arranged on a ship. 'Don't worry,' said Mrs Thatcher, reminding her colleagues that her husband was on the same boat. 'Denis will take good care of them!' I was later told that he very much did.

In the winter of 1983–84, I attended the plenary session of the Congress Party in Calcutta. I was among a vast throng of well-wishers who went to receive Mrs Gandhi at the airport when she arrived in the city. She, however, spotted me in the crowd and said, 'Oh, you are also here.' I replied, 'Madam, this is my home.'

The Congress was not in power in West Bengal, of which Calcutta was the capital. A government led by the Communist Party of India (Marxist) was. But the reception she received in the metropolis was impressive. Up to 3 million people congregated at her public rally or lined the thoroughfares as she drove in an open jeep to the airport for her return to Delhi.

It was my first exposure to a major party-political conference in India. The experience did not leave me with a desire to repeat it. Arrangements were chaotic, the agenda haphazard and the timetable unreliable. I came away with the overwhelming impression that the Congress Party needed more professional management of its internal affairs. It was encouraging to note, though, that Rajiv Gandhi understood his party had to be brought into the modern world. That the organization and the selection of its candidates for office needed to be improved.

The year 1984 became more difficult for Mrs Gandhi. Sikh separatism raised its ugly head in Punjab, lawlessness abounded. Sikh militants had taken shelter in their holiest shrine, the Golden Temple in Amritsar. A decision was taken to flush them out. Mrs Gandhi agonized deeply over whether to lay siege to the temple complex. She had doubts about its advisability. Had she followed her instincts, the outcome might have been different. But she went along with her advisers, who believed in a swift military strike to end the extremists' resistance.

On several occasions in 1984, I requested Mrs Gandhi to be careful about her security. She said, 'In a democracy, leaders cannot hide from their voters.' She had a lurking premonition of a violent end. She accepted this as a price leaders paid in turbulent times. She took a fatalistic attitude whenever she was warned about threats to her safety.

On 31 October 1984, I was awakened by a phone call from a friend in New York who had seen a news flash about Mrs Gandhi being shot and wounded. My contacts in Delhi confirmed the terrible tidings. I rushed to Heathrow to catch the first plane to Delhi. On the flight, we were informed she had succumbed to a hail of bullets fired by her own bodyguards and that Rajiv had succeeded her as prime minister.

Arriving in Delhi, I went straight to the prime minister's house and sat with her family in the room where her body had been brought from the hospital. Her face, surrounded by flowers, still seemed to be in pain. Her funeral was hugely emotional, and I was left feeling numb by the proceedings. I remember that Mrs Thatcher and Denis were there, and Princess Anne represented the British royal family. The British Opposition leaders Neil Kinnock, David Steel and David Owen were also in attendance. The US Secretary of State was there, the Russian Premier Nikolai Tikhonov, and the Presidents of Pakistan, Bangladesh and Sri Lanka. Up to 1 million people watched Rajiv light the funeral pyre.

Indira Gandhi was far from perfect. She would have been the first to admit that. Yet, whatever shortcomings she may have had, she proved to be an outstanding leader during a very complex and difficult era. Her personal preference was to live in circumstances of almost Zen-like austerity. Both her household and her office were organized strictly for utility. She was a woman of indomitable courage. Her sense of duty was exemplary, and she paid a heavy price for it.

Indira Gandhi became, to me, a personal incarnation of my love for the country of my birth, the personification of my hopes for its future and a strong symbol of the Indian people's continuing relationship with the country of my adoption.

With Lord Mountbatten at the first Indo-British Association dinner in London

The Indo-British Association brochure, 1978

Sonia Gandhi, Mrs Gandhi and me walking in Bond Street, on her visit to London, 1978

Trustees
Sir Michael Walker GCMG *Chairman*
The Rt Hon Lord Aldington KCMG CBE DSO
Mr John Burgh CB
Mr R P Chandaria
The Lord Chitnis
Sir John Cuckney
Mr Maneck Dalal
The Earl of Harewood
Sir Ronald McIntosh, KCB
Mr Swraj Paul
The Rt Hon Kenneth Robinson
H E Dr V A Seyid Muhammad
Dr K S Shelvankar
Mr A J Shepperd

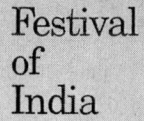

Festival of India

Patrons
The Rt Hon Margaret Thatcher MP
Shrimati Indira Gandhi

Festival of India Office,
Room 64/G Government Offices,
Great George Street,
London SW1A 1AA.
Telephones: 01 233 5986 and 233 3606

31 March 1982

Mr Swraj Paul
Caparo House
103 Baker Street
London W1

Dear Swraj,

Very many thanks for your warm letter of 30 March which has given all of us in the office much pleasure. However, as you know, the credit for the successful start of the Festival is just as much due to you and your Chairmanship of the Finance Committee as to any of us at this end. The great thing is that the Festival has certainly got away to a very good start and I think the fact is we can all take credit for our combined efforts in achieving this result.

Yours ever,

Michael

Michael Walker
Chairman
Festival of India Trust

Sir Michael Walker's letter to me for the Festival of India in London, 1982

Receiving my Padma Bhushan from President Giani Zail Singh, 1983

Presenting a copy of my book on Indira Gandhi to Prime Minister Rajiv Gandhi, 1985

Indira Gandhi, centre, with Muhammad Ali and me on either side, Delhi, 1980

Mrs Gandhi at the opening of the Nehru Exhibition,
Ambika House, London, 1982

Me and Mrs Gandhi at Claridge's, London, 1978

10 DOWNING STREET

THE PRIME MINISTER

24 March 1982

Dear Mr. Paul,

I write to thank you most warmly for the splendid dinner last night. It was a most memorable evening and you and the Indo-British Association are to be congratulated on the admirable arrangements. There have been many gatherings this week to celebrate the Indo-British relationship but the special impact made by last night's dinner will remain long in our memory.

My warm thanks to you, Mrs. Paul and all the Officers of the Association.

Yours sincerely,

Margaret Thatcher

Mr. Swraj Paul.

Margaret Thatcher letter for the Indo-British Association dinner in London, 1982

Indo-British Association dinner, March 1982. (Left to right) Me with Sonia Gandhi, Indira Gandhi, Margaret Thatcher, Eldon Griffiths, MP, and Lady Paul

HER MAJESTY'S GOVERNMENT IN THE
UNITED KINGDOM OF GREAT BRITAIN
AND NORTHERN IRELAND

Visit of Shrimati Indira Gandhi Prime Minister of the Republic of India

21 to 26 MARCH 1982

Indira Gandhi visit to the UK, 1982

PRIME MINISTER

New Delhi
April 14, 1982

Dear Swraj,

    I have returned with pleasant memories of a useful stay in London.

    It was a pleasure to participate in the various functions connected with the Festival of India. I appreciate the personal attention you gave to it and I should like to congratulate you and your colleagues on the excellence and insight with which the Festival was conceived and executed.

    This is the beginning. I am sure that the other events that are planned will generate new avenues of cooperation and goodwill between Britain and India.

    With good wishes,

Yours sincerely,

(Indira Gandhi)

Shri Swraj Paul
103 - Baker Street
London W1M 1FD

Indira Gandhi's letter to me following her London visit, 1982

Indira Gandhi at home in her garden in Delhi, 1957

Speaker's House Westminster London SW1A 0AA

31st March, 1982

My dear Swraj & Mrs. Paul,

My heartfelt congratulations to you on the superb arrangements which you made for Mrs. Indira Gandhi's visit to Britain. I thought that the dinner at the Dorchester was absolutely marvellous, and you presided over the occasion with a dignity and grace that added significantly to the occasion. I cannot say how grateful I am for your invitation to me to join you at the dinner and on the occasion of the unveiling of the plaque in the morning.

Mrs. Gandhi is one of the most remarkable persons I have met. Her serenity is an inspiration, but her energy is a challenge. I am confident that this visit to London will have strengthened the bonds between our two countries, and for this you and your lovely wife have every reason to feel proud.

Ever yours,

George.

Mr. Swraj Paul,
Caparo House,
103, Baker Street,
London, W1M 1FD.

House of Commons Speaker's letter to me regarding Mrs Gandhi's visit to London, 1982

Cartoon of India's Opposition leaders on the visit of Muhammad Ali to Delhi, 1980

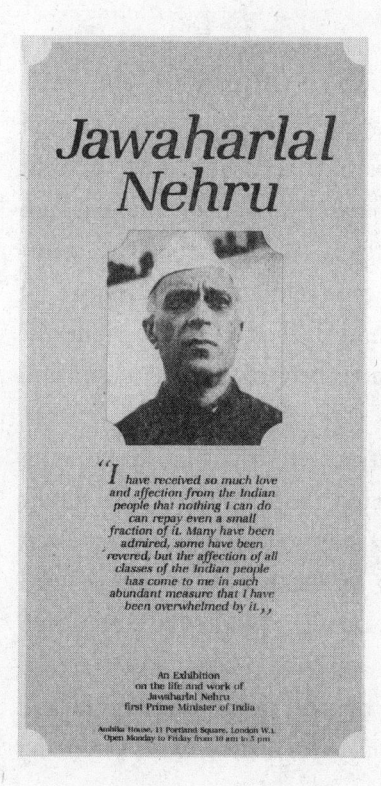

Brochure for the Jawaharlal Nehru Exhibition, 1982

7

The DCM–Escorts Affair

In the 1950s and 1960s, the outlines of modern enterprise were emerging in India. They evolved into the structure that largely defines the Indian industrial landscape today, except that technology has revolutionized the way business is run now. What has changed slightly is that some of the state-owned corporations that were created with the objective of bringing the spirit of nationalism to the larger task of economic development, have in recent decades been slowly privatized and this trend continues.

In the 1950s, state corporations were virtual monopolies in their sectors and were expected to perform in the public interest. The reason for this was that political interference was minimal and management was in the hands of people who possessed outstanding integrity and vision and were committed to industrial modernization.

However, as time went by, matters became distorted and undermined the original mission. The 1960s were a turning point. Major decisions and even many insignificant ones now became subject to ministerial orders. Lethargic administrators were appointed to execute them. Many capable managers quit because they wouldn't tolerate outside interference. Meddling by politicians began to escalate.

Corruption was evident, although not as endemic as it became in the 1970s and beyond. Subservience, not competence, became the preferred criteria for management. The concept of public accountability all but disappeared. Monopoly became a smokescreen to camouflage inefficiency. Consequently, despite the market protection these undertakings enjoyed, their results plummeted to a pathetic level.

In the late 1960s, the state's control was extended to banking and insurance. This was done with worthy motives, the purpose being to bring capital resources to a more diverse set of people than the favoured few. But here, too, a political presence extracted a heavy toll and defeated the good intention. There is nothing inherently wrong with a policy of state ownership of sizeable segments of the economy if this is free of political tinkering and managed by able and dedicated executives who are guided by performance and not corruption and subservience.

Public sector enterprises fail for the same reasons communism and Gandhian approaches have nosedived. At both leadership and citizen levels, it has proved challenging to mould human nature into the selflessness or the self-denial of Gandhi. Such noble attributes of character arise under special circumstances, revolutionary pressures or freedom struggles. In normal situations, the ethic of altruism is not widely prevalent.

The Indian government attempted to uphold national interest without abuse, wrapping the system in a thicket of complex rules and regulations. Ordinances, licences and permits were entangled in red tape and a breed of fixers who manipulated them flourished.

The process of privatization involves danger. Valuable properties can be sold at bargain prices to friendly buyers. Besides, the sale of public sector monopolies to private investors can give rise to an even more oppressive private monopoly. The best way to serve the civic good is to allow competition to break or erode monopolies and broad-base the divested ownership. Thus, alert shareholders will demand accountability from managements and scrutinize affairs for any irregularities. In modern society, where idealism alone seems to be insufficient incentive for lawful corporate behaviour, there is no substitute for greater transparency.

In the environment of government control, another malaise prospered. Profits could be made by pleasing the regulators in certain ways, and certain large private companies did not overlook such opportunities. Efficiencies and skills became irrelevant or secondary where power lay in allocation and protection. Nationalization of financial institutions made them virtual monopolies for large-scale investments. By investing increasingly in major companies and, in a number of cases, converting their loans into equity, the state became a dominant shareholder across the board.

Favoured management with minority stakes continued to enjoy the blessings of these institutions, drawing their incomes and perks without much scrutiny. Just so long as the government investors were kept in good humour, performance was of little consequence. If the executives displeased the financial organizations—which was very rare—there was always recourse to political influence. Union ministries bossed the institutions; politicians bossed the ministries!

This pampered coterie of privileged industrialists was granted preferential access to government handouts. They were a kind of extension of the state but were spared even the limited inspection government corporations are occasionally subjected to. The talents of the owners and managers of these companies were not concerned with superior business administration, but with the art of cultivating and persuading government officials.

In a genuinely dynamic business environment, they would have been tiny; in a protected economy, they were giants. Worst of all, with their stranglehold on the credit and licence system, they impeded the growth of small and medium-sized Indian businesses—enterprises that are competently operated, but which are restricted to utilizing their own capital. The odds against them were overwhelming. The establishment could almost at will, or at its convenience, make or break arrangements, sabotage competitiveness or render the playing field uneven.

My first attempt at investing in India proved to be probably the most controversial in independent India's history up to that point.

After Indira Gandhi returned to office in 1980, she was interested in greater non-resident Indian (NRI) and person of Indian origin (PIO)—generally banded as NRI—participation in the Indian economy, much like the involvement of overseas Chinese in China. The reasons were two-fold. She felt that NRIs needed to be encouraged to be emotionally linked to their motherland. Secondly, that they thereby played a role in improving the Indian economy.

The Indian economy at the time did not generate sufficient wealth to meet the country's development needs. In this situation, it made sense to tap into the resources of NRIs. There were about 20 million such people. Their collective output was equivalent to India's gross domestic product (GDP). Their accumulated savings amounted to between $700 billion and $1 trillion. Besides, an inflow from them was potentially a lightning rod for investment from non-Indian sources, for if NRIs led the way, others were likely to follow.

Mrs Gandhi was dissatisfied with the meagre returns on capital from state-owned businesses. She also concluded that Indian private enterprise was 'more private than enterprising' and was not even domestically dynamic, let alone internationally competitive.

Therefore, her advisers conceived several ideas, one of which was to open Indian firms to portfolio shareholding by NRIs. Up to that juncture, anyone from outside India was excluded from investing in Indian commercial entities. The new policy permitted NRIs, as well as concerns controlled by them, to take stakes in Indian companies on the proviso that the transactions took place through public sector Indian banks.

All my ventures into India were in response to notifications in this respect issued by the Indian government. But the bad publicity it generated, and obstacles created in my path, made me feel there was no genuine commitment to reforms or welcoming of NRI involvement in the Indian economy.

When the government announced the easing of regulations, the Indian private sector seemed to be enthusiastic. In October 1982, a delegation of leading Indian businessmen visited London to promote their stocks to NRIs. The group included Bharat Ram, chairman of DCM (Delhi Cloth Mills, though now diversified) and H.P. Nanda, chairman of Escorts. The team was led by L.K. Jha, a former civil servant and diplomat who was chairman of the Indian Economic Administrative Reforms Commission.

I came to know that an interaction had taken place at the Indian High Commission in London and the delegation vigorously engaged in promoting the purchase of shares in Indian corporations. Furthermore, the promotors specifically underlined that shares of bigger businesses were generally listed on stock exchanges in India and consequently provided investor liquidity. I did not attend this event as I was not interested in entering India at that time. And the reaction in Britain and other western countries to the deputation's presentation was largely indifferent.

Nevertheless, Indian government officials persevered with selling the concept to NRIs. In November 1982, a convention of the Overseas Indian Association in Bombay was addressed by Dr Manmohan Singh, then governor of the Reserve Bank of India, later to become India's finance minister and prime minister. He clearly endorsed the portfolio investment scheme by saying, 'Investors may not like to expose their funds to risks and uncertainties of investing in new ventures, but may like to purchase, through a stock exchange, shares of companies with proven worth.'*

He proceeded to outline the streamlined procedures that would enable investors to remit funds and secure repatriation of them. This was a resounding recommendation from an eminent economist and respected chief central banker of the country.

On 18 December 1982, I was flying to India for a holiday when I met L.K. Jha on the plane. He raised the matter of a window of opportunity having opened for NRIs via the portfolio

---
* *Beyond Boundaries*, Swraj Paul, 1998.

investment route and urged me to take advantage of it. 'Swraj, if people like you, who are so involved with India, are not going to invest, who will?' he asked. I thought about his proposition and decided to allocate a modest outlay.

My brother Jit, head of our family's Apeejay Group in Calcutta, introduced me to Harish Bhasin, a well-known stockbroker who was also chairman of the Stockbrokers Association in Delhi. I asked Bhasin if any company merited investment. He replied that in Delhi there were only two worthwhile enterprises: DCM and Escorts. DCM was a conglomerate with manufacturing capabilities in textiles, sugar, chemicals, rayon, tyre cord, fertilizers, information technology and engineering products. Escorts was the largest producer of agricultural equipment and manufactured engineering products for the railways and construction industry. I asked Bhasin to buy a few shares in each and send me their balance sheets.

My examination of the financial statements was hardly enlightening. They contained minimum tangible information and maximum public relations. The auditors' reports were lengthy and complicated, in sharp contrast to such summaries provided by publicly listed companies in the West. Between January and March 1983, though, I continued to carefully inspect the two companies and obtain information on them. I instructed Bhasin to investigate the extent of the owning families' shareholdings.

The due diligence unearthed that the Rams of DCM, who occupied all senior management posts in the firm, held only a small holding of their own. As for Escorts, he said that the Nandas, who dominated executive positions in it, controlled most of the shares.

That being the case, I felt if I acquired a decent stake in DCM, I might be able to push its top brass to improve performance, for which there was considerable scope. If they did not rise to the task, they could be replaced by competent professionals. Either way, the share value was likely to shoot up. I advised Bhasin to purchase as many shares of DCM as were available. But given his information that the Nanda family owned a majority of shares in Escorts, I told him not to immediately pursue interest in it further.

In April 1983, I visited Delhi once again. This time, I met Rajiv Gandhi, who had become a member of Parliament, replacing his younger brother Sanjay, who had sadly died in a plane crash. I confided in him my recent activity in the Indian stock market. He was enthusiastic and encouraged me to take up as much as possible. 'Buy DCM, buy Escorts, buy Mahindra and TISCO (Tata Iron and Steel Company),' he advocated. 'They are not with us, and we should control them.'

I mentioned to him exactly what I had directed Bhasin to do. I also mentioned it was inadvisable for me to splash out in a hurry. The next day, though, to my surprise, he phoned to say he had checked the Nandas' holdings and that they held only minority shares in Escorts. I delved into the matter and discovered Rajiv was indeed right. So I communicated to Bhasin that he buy as big a stake as possible in Escorts.

As it happened, my investment triggered an escalation in stock prices in both companies. Several directors and members of the Ram and Nanda families sold their shares, delighted by their enhanced value.

Rajiv went a step further. He introduced me to Vivek Bharat Ram, deputy managing director of DCM and son of its chairman Bharat Ram, and revealed to him, 'Swraj owns shares in your company. He will be able to help you and you can do business with him.' I never heard from Vivek again, but he was clearly in contact with Rajiv since they were schoolmates.

By mid-April, news had spread that it was I who was buying shares in DCM and Escorts. There was panic among the Rams and Nandas. The corporate world in India was also shell-shocked and rushed to console the two families. J.R.D. Tata, chairman of the otherwise esteemed Tata Group, exclaimed, 'I could be next!' The Federation of Indian Chambers of Commerce and Industry (FICCI) scrambled to come to the Shri Rams' and Nandas' defence, rallying its member companies for this purpose.

By this time, I had bought 13 per cent of DCM. The Shri Ram family only controlled 10 per cent. Public financial institutions—insurance firms, development banks and unit trusts—held 42.5 per cent. In other words, the Indian government, indirectly with my support or by supporting me, could have dictated terms to the company.

My holdings in Escorts had reached 7.5 per cent. The Nandas commanded less than 5 per cent. The financial institutions owned 54.9 per cent. So again, if the Indian government and I had cooperated, we could have held sway in the group.

A takeover was precisely what the Shri Rams and Nandas feared: that they would be called to account for the way they operated their enterprises and driven out of their plush circumstances. In any case, I possessed more shares than either of them in their respective firms. So, working in tandem with their friends and supporters, they devised a scandalous campaign to stop me.

I was roundly vilified by the news media and sections of the business community in India were in uproar against me. Then, bureaucrats, ministers and even Rajiv were poisoned against me in an attempt to make them oppose me too. Last but not least, my shares were not registered!

The decibel level of the media campaign rose by the day. Newspapers and journalists carried abusive articles with insulting insinuations. I was called a crook, a master of shady deals, a brown Englishman, an upstart, a speculator, a recycler of black money and ill-gotten funds and so on. Allegations were even made that I was using Mrs Gandhi's money stashed away abroad to buy into DCM and Escorts. They dug deep for dirt about me and my family. Unsurprisingly, these sham attempts at investigative journalism found nothing.

Chhotu Karadia, a journalist of Indian origin who wrote a book on the affair in 1984, said,

> Nanda appointed one of his blue-eyed boys, Murad Ali Baig, to head a task force specially set up to spearhead a campaign against non-resident Indians in general and Paul in particular. Their brief was to acquaint the Government, press and (Indian) parliament as well as the shareholders with the 'dangers inherent in the non-resident investment'.

According to Karadia, a strategy was devised at a meeting at the Claridges Hotel in Delhi attended by the Shri Ram and Nanda clans. 'FICCI president Ashok Jain, along with other industrialists, was also present . . . The strategy was to expose Paul and make him a political liability for Mrs Gandhi,' Karadia added.*

---

* *The Swraj Paul Affair*, Chhotu Karadia, Slatecount 1984.

Girilal Jain, editor of *Times of India*, described me as a 'Don Quixote'. *Organizer*, voice of the Rashtriya Sevak Sangh, was offensive in saying: 'Swraj Paul is neither a businessman nor an industrialist. He is simply a speculator.' M.V. Kamath, in the *Telegraph*, asked: 'Why would a brown Englishman want to waste his time trying to expose the shenanigans of his Indian confreres, especially considering that his hands are not clean either?"

Businessmen summoned meetings to disparage NRIs in general and my stock purchases in particular. A coterie from FICCI sought an appointment with Mrs Gandhi 'to discuss Swraj Paul'. This request was turned down. A contingent comprising of, among others, Bharat Ram, H.P. Nanda and Tata, called on Pranab Mukherjee, then union finance minister, on 20 April 1983. They demanded protection. The very people who were previously on a hard sell outside India to invite NRI investment into their companies were now screaming against it. The Shri Rams and Nandas and their cohorts did not spare government officials either.

Then came a bombshell! A key figure who had earlier trumpeted the virtues of the portfolio scheme—Dr Manmohan Singh, the RBI governor—did a volte face. On 26 April, addressing the National Productivity Council in Delhi, he stated, 'It is necessary to protect well-managed companies against takeover bids from abroad.' He added that Indian industry was entitled to 'an assurance from the government that we shall not allow enterprises in India to become a bubble on the whirlpool of international speculation'. The Indian press welcomed this pronouncement in an orchestrated manner. I was frankly rather taken aback by the policy change. Dr Singh

---

* 'Don Quixote', Girilal Jain, *Times of India*, 30 July 1983.

was reputedly a man keen on NRI interest in Indian business. I still wonder what caused the sudden shift of stance.

His speech foreshadowed an RBI diktat. It asserted all past purchases of shares by NRI investors required RBI approval and that it was not sufficient to simply channel these through public sector Indian banks. Punjab National Bank, through which I had made my purchases, pointed out it was ultra vires to enforce the new rule retrospectively. This, though, did not hold good.

Moreover, in the summer of 1983, RBI quite needlessly inquired about my businesses in Britain. Until this was satisfactorily answered, it threatened to withhold payment of monies to my stockbroker Bhasin. This unusual move was obviously designed to discourage further acquisition of shares. I highlighted to the RBI the abnormal and discriminatory nature of its requests, following which it finally desisted from its intrusive behaviour. But the signal was unmistakable: block Swraj Paul. And by so doing, bury a policy which had been proclaimed with so much fanfare. Cleverly, the U-turn was enacted de facto, not de jure.

I complained to Mrs Gandhi about the cavalier manner with which I had been treated. Indeed, I asked if she had authorized a reversal of policy. She appeared puzzled. It seemed various machinations were at play without her knowledge. She indicated she would follow through with an inquiry. If this was instituted, I was not made aware of its outcome. The following year, she met with a tragic end.

DCM and Escorts refused to register the shares I had obtained. On 9 June 1983, Escorts' board rejected the transfer of the stocks. On 15 July 1983, the DCM directors did exactly the same. Such conduct upset a number of people. Stockholders were incensed, small shareholders were troubled, segments of the financial press were critical and there were also concerns within the government. Tata, too, saw the attitude to be a mistake. He assured the annual general meeting of TISCO that his companies completely accepted the principle of free transferability of their shares listed on stock exchanges.

DCM and Escorts not only merely failed to recognize my ownership of their shares but continued to pay dividends to the former holders of these stocks, who had willingly sold them. The financial institutions were aghast. They informed the two companies that they should comply. But DCM and Escorts persisted with their stubbornness.

I was disappointed with Rajiv's role. He had been proactive in prodding me to wade in. But it seems DCM and Escorts got to him. He was possibly discomfited by the fuss generated by them and Indian businesses at large. He might also have realized I would not bend to his whim had I taken charge of the companies. In November 1983, he maintained in the Lok Sabha, the directly elected house of the Indian Parliament, that no NRI should be allowed to corner more than 2 per cent of an Indian company. At the same time, he was telling me this did not apply to me and that he was not combating what I had done.

In contrast, Mrs Gandhi was unambiguous in private and public that government policy remained unchanged and that NRI investments were welcome. She emphasized this so forcefully during a visit to New York in the autumn of 1983 that this was construed as an endorsement of my efforts. When asked if this was the case, she responded, 'You can interpret it as you like, but I stand by government policy which is unchanged.'

One of the components of the 'Stop Swraj' campaign was the creation of a Shri Ram and Nanda-sponsored NRI Investors Committee in London. They issued press releases saying NRIs must develop fresh industries in India and not venture into portfolio investment. Such pronouncements lacked credibility and predictably petered out. Yet, it demonstrated the extent to which DCM and Escorts had gone to foster an atmosphere of hostility towards me.

To counteract the vile propaganda, I began making public statements, which were fortunately quite widely absorbed in India. An amusing aspect of the battle was discord within the Shri Ram and Nanda families. The menfolk had given the impression to their wives and children that they enjoyed controlling shares in the businesses. When the scarcity of their holdings was laid bare, the female partners were furious. They had been deceived. After years of boasting about their secure ownership of their companies, the men were left admitting to their relatives that this was actually not the case.

I toured India for six weeks in July and August of 1983. I delivered dozens of speeches, gave interviews and put out clarifications. It was like electioneering in the financial centres of the country: Bombay, Calcutta and Delhi. The response was heart-warming. Thousands of people came to listen to me or contacted me. Most of them were small shareholders in large, listed companies who had been virtually disenfranchised by managements. Others were concerned citizens who felt that corporate wrongdoers were looting the country. A significant section of younger journalists, disillusioned with their seniors toadying to Indian big business, rallied behind me. Owners of small and medium-sized business egged me on. The youth in general urged me to resist. Even employees at DCM and Escorts lent me their quiet endorsements. A few liberal-minded big industrialists did the same. My brothers Jit and Surrendra were towers of strength to me in the battle I waged.

On 6 August, well over 2000 people gathered to listen to me speak at the All-India Investors Association in Bombay. After my address, the *Sunday Observer* asked me why I was being treated like a film star. I replied to the effect, 'Because for the first time a businessman is calling a spade a spade ... a handful have got together to beat one man. This is the first time they have not been able to down a person.' By the time I departed India, public opinion had turned somewhat in my favour. DCM and Escorts perceived their mudslinging was not working. Yet, they still refused to register my shares.

Karadia wrote about the meeting:

> All hell broke loose. (The Indian) Industrialists hoped that they had contained Paul by pressurising the government to impose a five per cent ceiling on NRI portfolio investments. But when they (the audience) heard Paul thunder with such strong language, their nerves began to quiver again. He would not use such strong language, they reasoned, against India's industrial class without a wink and a nod from Mrs Gandhi.

On 18 September 1983, the RBI put out a circular on policy regarding NRI investment. This stated that any stake acquired after 2 May 1983 could not exceed 5 per cent of the total equity capital of any Indian company. This in consequence legitimized my purchase of shares, since they were made before that date.

Escorts, fearing that the government would force them to register legally procured shares, pre-emptively moved court. They asked the Bombay High Court to declare the RBI notification 'illegal and void' as it, according to them, contravened the Foreign Exchange Regulation Act (FERA), a law that imposed restrictions on overseas monetary transactions. The Finance Ministry, the RBI and PNB responded, refuting Escorts' claim. The case, however, proceeded in the usual protracted manner common in the Indian judiciary.

Meanwhile, Escorts announced it was planning to offer Rs 350 million worth of new shares and debentures. This would mean dilution of the holdings of the public sector financial institutions, who owned more than half of Escorts' shares. The institutions decided not to take the move lying down as it would be a dereliction of their duties as handlers of public funds if they did not contest it.

Any new share issue of the magnitude proposed by Escorts required the assent of existing shareholders as well as the Controller of Capital Issues, a government official who supervised the capital structure of public companies. The institutions informed the Nandas they would oppose their plan. They also served notice that they would seek to replace most Escorts board members—a step they were entitled to, being majority shareholders. Escorts went to court to stop this too.

My tussle with DCM and Escorts was, not unexpectedly, raised in the Indian Parliament. Opposition MPs J.B. Mathur and R.R. Morarka alleged I was investing Mrs Gandhi's money, which had been concealed in Swiss banks. Mrs Gandhi naturally sternly denied the accusation. I was left no choice other than to condemn Mathur and Morarka in the press, citing that if they had made the charges outside Parliament, they would be tantamount to defamation and libel under Indian law. Parliamentary privilege was being abused to voice flagrant lies.

Mathur and Morarka took shelter under the protection the legislature provided. They accused me of restraining their rights as MPs and insulting the Indian Parliament. I wrote to the Speaker of the Lok Sabha contending privileges of parliamentarians did not include irresponsible behaviour. Also, that innocent individuals were defenceless in the face of an MP misusing his or her position. A breach of privilege hearing rambled on for an extended period and eventually came to nothing. All it produced was worthless sensation.

Karadia recorded that at a press conference, Mrs Gandhi was asked if I had the blessings of the government, as alleged by Ram and Nanda. She retorted, 'I deny it most categorically.' When pressed further, she underlined, 'Our concern is not at all with individuals or individual companies but with the country.' Another question posed was as to whether an Indian company could refuse to register shares. She answered: 'That I don't know . . . I will have to find out.'

I returned to India towards the end of 1983. Once again, I took the opportunity to present my case to a wide audience. The feedback was even more energizing. At Delhi University, a sizeable crowd of students rendered a rousing reception, empathizing with my predicament. Wherever I spoke, the reaction was notably favourable.

At the All India Congress Committee session in Calcutta, Mrs Gandhi left no one in doubt that she was disappointed with the conduct of the Indian business community and its contribution to national development. Finance Minister Mukherjee thereafter made it clear to the Calcutta Stock Exchange that the government would not remain a 'silent spectator' to a situation where investors were kept hanging about on the fate of shares purchased by them.

Subsequently, the Committee of Presidents of Stock Exchanges declared that the power of companies to refuse registration of shares should not be used in a 'capricious manner'. They warned of an adverse impact on the investment climate if companies withheld registrations.

DCM and Escorts' intransigence, though, dragged on through 1984. The courts were characteristically and frustratingly taking their time. Although Mrs Gandhi and Mukherjee were positive, there was little emergent government action. Rajiv had by now acquired influence over the workings of the administration. While he was of course telling me everything was fine and would soon work out, I suspected he was assisting my opponents. Nevertheless, I refrained from burdening Mrs Gandhi with any extended discussion on the subject.

In mid-1984, I visited India and, as was my practice, called on Mrs Gandhi. She was distressed. She showed me a memorandum Rajiv had sent her about the DCM–Escorts affair. In it, he accused me of being a conduit for money from one of her aides, and that this money had been used to buy shares in DCM and Escorts. Mrs Gandhi said she knew Rajiv's allegations were untrue. But she was visibly upset. She could not bring herself to confront Rajiv. I requested her to forget about the matter.

A Congress MP close to Rajiv informed me Mrs Gandhi discussed the aide-memoire with her son soon after my meeting with her. She later told the friend, 'Tell Rajiv that once the Nehrus make commitments, they don't go back on their word.'

On that visit, I was staying at the Taj Mahal Hotel, where I received a phone call from H.P. Nanda. He inquired whether we could meet. I invited him to come to the hotel. He, then, suggested we get together on more neutral ground. I told him if his house was neutral enough, I would go there. When we came face-to-face, I asked him to register my shares and manage

Escorts in a manner I deemed fit. Nanda didn't expect such forthrightness and replied he had run his company the way it was normally done in India. He stressed, 'Everybody does this.' I explained to him I didn't own shares with 'everybody' but was a major investor in Escorts. The conversation ended there. I never heard from Nanda again.

When Mrs Gandhi was assassinated at the end of October 1984, matters were still unresolved. The Bombay High Court had delivered a judgment in favour of Escorts. But government officials and financial institutions were anxious to appeal. They were, however, under pressure not to do so. Rajiv, the new prime minister, was in two minds. But the institutions were adamant because they knew they would face criticism and their investments would be at risk if they didn't appeal. A challenge was lodged in the Supreme Court.

In December 1984, India held a general election. Rajiv returned to office with an overwhelming majority. When I met him in January 1985, I said the electoral triumph was his mother's last farewell. He did not like this. He saw it as his own success.

A few days earlier, R.K. Dhawan, a loyal aide of Mrs Gandhi, had been dismissed by Rajiv. I suggested he had been useful to his mother and would be of equal utility to him. The new PM was not impressed by this either.

The DCM-Escorts situation meandered along through 1985. The authorities' litigation with Escorts persisted. So did the public debate over right and wrong. Finally, on 23 December, the Supreme Court spelled out its verdict. The Bombay High Court decision was overturned. The wrangling was over. Escorts had lost.

The Nandas, and by extension the Shri Rams, were directed to register my shares. This duly happened. But H.P. Nanda and his son Rajan were re-appointed for five years as chairman and managing director of Escorts, respectively. These were corporate positions, but because the company was publicly listed, they had to be ratified by the Company Law Board, a Government of India department. The timing of the Nandas' continuance in their executive roles, the speed with which this was approved, implied they had blessings from high places. Both the financial institutions and I were certainly shocked by the turn of events.

When I went to Delhi, Rajiv was out of town. So I met his relative and colleague Arun Nehru. Nothing came of this meeting. Eventually, on 6 January 1986, I called on Rajiv at his residence. He said he knew nothing about the reappointment of the Nandas and that we must find out who was responsible. He then told me I could sell my shares and he would ensure I didn't incur a financial loss. I sensed there was no purpose in fighting the prime minister of India, so I agreed to his proposal.

Rajiv immediately phoned one of his senior aides Gopi Arora, a civil servant, and an intimate of his, Arun Singh, who was also the minister of state for defence. I thereafter met them, and it was agreed I would sell my shares to the Rams and the Nandas without any monetary loss to me. However, the 'no loss' formula soon emerged to be fictional. A full repatriation of my capital consumed a decade. Government permission for foreign exchange transfers was granted only in dribs and drabs. There was no compensation for interest charge suffered or currency devaluation. In effect, I took a hit of Rs 150 million (GBP 15 million). Thus, a dismal affair came to an end.

Nonetheless, the DCM-Escorts matter had a beneficial long-term effect in India. It awoke shareholders to their rights. Firms refusing to register shares came under the scanner. The financial press became more sensitive to malfeasance than before.

Bharat Ram and H.P. Nanda soon retired. The DCM group was carved up by the Ram younger generation. Escorts never quite recovered its reputation.

Khushwant Singh, the reputed writer, sent me a letter in 1996. It said, 'Bharat who was in school with us drops in once or twice a week. He now admits that what you were doing was quite legitimate.'

With brothers Stya and Jit campaigning for Indian shareholders' rights, Delhi, 1983

Times of India cartoon, 6 May 1983

THE HINDUSTAN TIMES
WEEKLY
NEW DELHI, 8/5/83

This is it!
By Sudhir Dar

AND WEAVING MILLS LTD.
ANNUAL GENERAL MEETING

"All clear, Boss... no sign of Swraj Paul!"

Hindustan Times, 8 May 1983

Hindustan Times, 2 February 1984

Indian Express,
28 April 1983

CURRENT ■ July 2, 1983 ■

END OF FIRST ROUND

Breather from take-over

THE DCM and Escorts shares, which had touched the dizzy heights of Rs. 105 and Rs. 84 with the threat of London-based businessman Swraj Paul buying over the two giants, crashed to as low as Rs. 70 and Rs. 62.

The sharp decline was due to the Reserve Bank directive to the Punjab National Bank not to allow the transfer of Rs. 1.1 crore sent in by Paul from London for the purchase of these shares.

Paul has warned the DCM and Escorts bosses that the reprieve is temporary and that is determined to take them over. The ruling party appears to be divided into two powerful camps, one supporting Paul and the other out to rescue the DCM and Escorts. It will be a political battle with the highest involved

Current, 2 July 1983

THE ILLUSTRATED WEEKLY OF INDIA, OCTOBER 25, 1987

PEOPLE

Mrs Gandhi's blue-eyed boy has come a long way. **Swraj Paul**, the corporate buccaneer whose takeover bid of DCM and Escorts is still spoken of with awe, is back in the news. This time, for having been voted the best Asian of the year, by the publishers of Who's Who of the Asian community in Britain. Paul, who ranks among 200 millionaires in Britain, was presented the award at the Hilton, London, on October 22. Other distinguished Asians in the Who's Who are **I G Patel**, director of the London School of Economics, **Lord Chitnis**, **Mohammed Ajeeb**, the former lord mayor of Bradford and **B C Patel**, editor of *New Life*.

Cartoon from *Illustrated Weekly*, 25 October 1987

Chhotu Karadia

THE SWRAJ PAUL AFFAIR

CAPARO DCM

The Swaraj Paul Affair

With Prime Minister Narendra Modi, April 2017

With King Charles III, May 2023

With HM Queen Elizabeth II at the Festival of India inauguration

Times of India cartoon

THE WORLD OF CAPARO

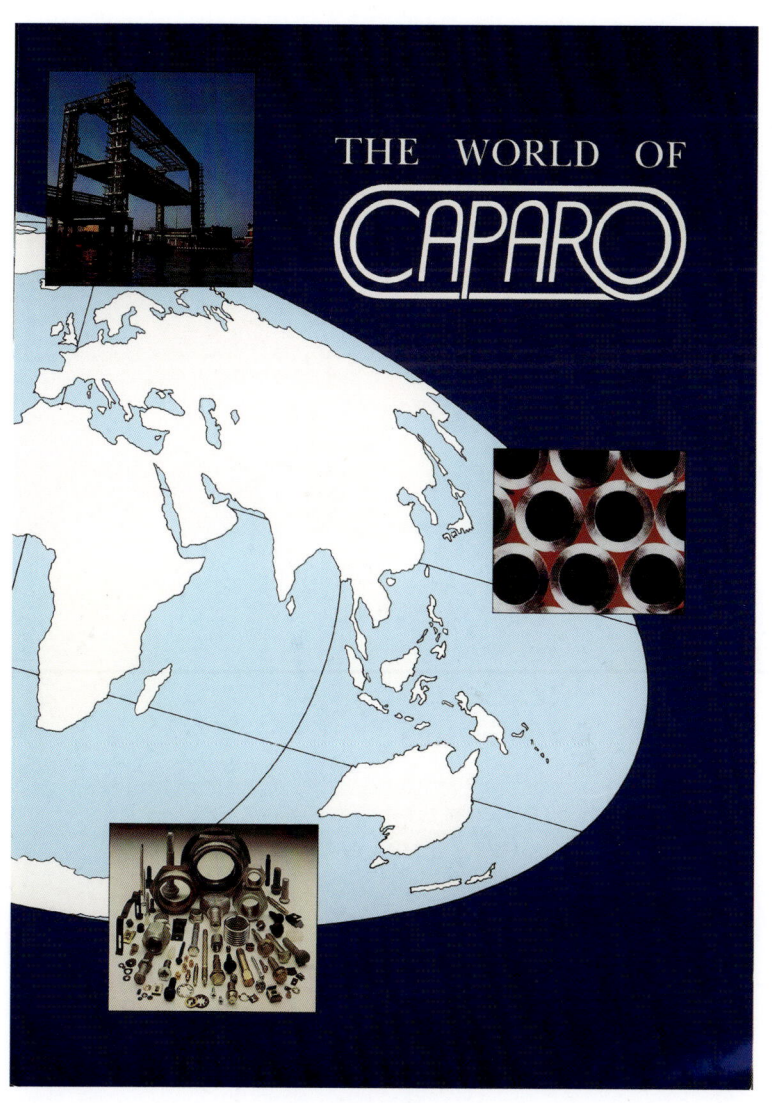

The world of Caparo

Speaking at the Indo-British Association dinner, 1982, with Prime Minister
Indira Gandhi (left) and Prime Minister Margaret Thatcher (right)

Sitting as deputy speaker, House of Lords, 19 December 2008

Presenting an honorary degree to President A.P.J. Abdul Kalam from the University of Wolverhampton, October 2007

Mrs Gandhi speaking at the Indo-British dinner in November 1978 with me, Michael Foot, MP, and Lady Paul

Me with Lady Paul and our daughter Anjli Paul at the Ambika Paul Building, University of Wolverhampton

The Lord Paul and Angad Paul Theatre, Kresge Auditorium,
MIT, Massachusetts, USA

Lady Paul and me unveiling the Lord Swraj Paul Building
at the University of Wolverhampton

Formal House of Lords robes

CAPARO

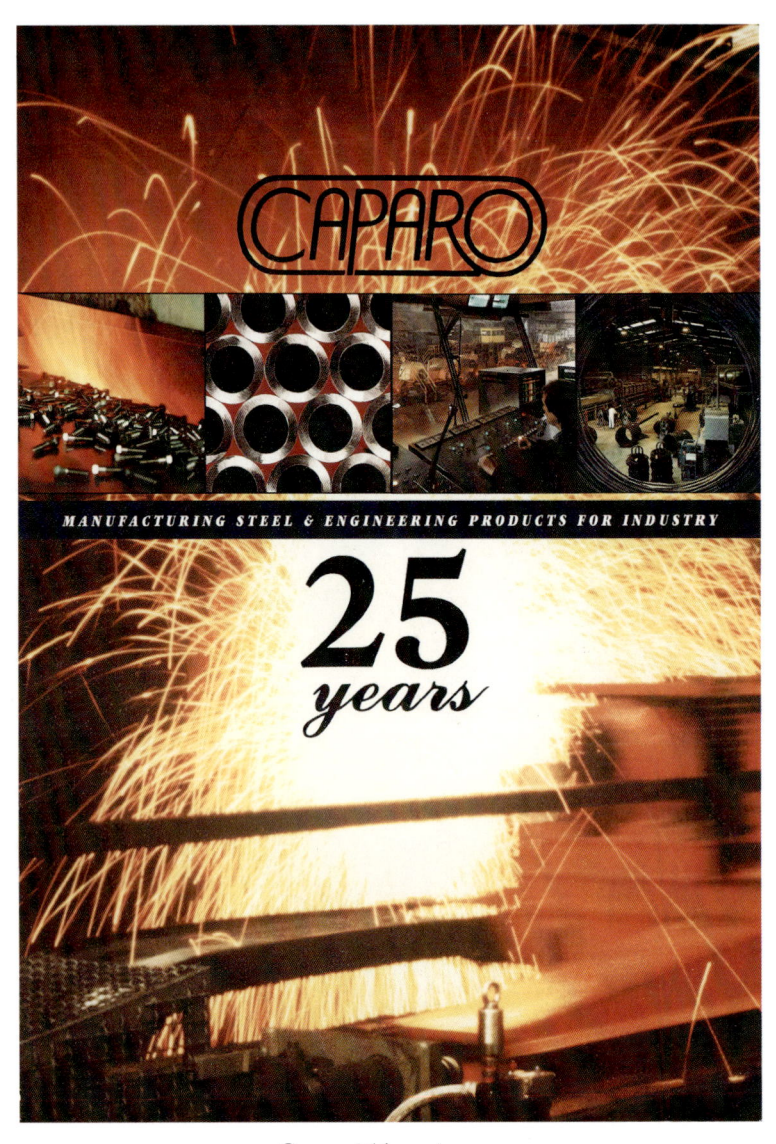

MANUFACTURING STEEL & ENGINEERING PRODUCTS FOR INDUSTRY

25 years

Caparo 25th anniversary

(Left to right) Ambar Paul and his wife Gauri, Anjli Paul, Angad Paul, Nisha with her husband Akash Paul

A happy couple: Aruna and me

8

Peerage and Parliament

I have spent the greater part of my life in London. This makes me a creature of two cultures—one by birth, the other by choice. I have fortunately felt comfortable in both settings and never sensed being displaced in either. India gives me my values and heritage; Britain has extended to me opportunities to freely express myself. I am thankful to both. Britain is today multicultural. This wasn't the case when I arrived here. Yet, a traditional society like Britain allowed a relative stranger like me to make good.

The cultural dissimilarities used to be quite stark. Lord Louis Mountbatten, the last British viceroy and the first governor-general of India, was a man of planning and precision. So, typically, he wanted to ensure that when he died, his obituaries would cover all aspects of his life. Thus, in 1978—unknown to him that his end was nigh, for he died in an explosion triggered by the rebel Irish Republican Army (IRA) while cruising on a boat off the Irish coast the following year—he was working on this.

Upon hearing that Jagjivan Ram, then deputy prime minister of India, was visiting London, he asked me to arrange for him to be interviewed. Ram was already a minister in the Indian government when Mountbatten was viceroy and governor-general in India. However, the latter was unaware that it was taboo in the Indian tradition to talk about the death of a living figure. So, when I approached Ram with Mountbatten's request, he was outraged. 'Mountbatten has gone mad. So have you. Do you think I am also mad to discuss a living person's death?' he reacted.

Mountbatten created an annual Nehru Memorial Lecture, which I used to attend. We maintained regular links with each other. But when I invited him to a dinner in Indira Gandhi's honour in 1978—when she was out of power—he chose not to come. He was afraid his presence would be interpreted as political support for her at a time when the Janata Party government in India were hounding her for alleged—ultimately unproven—misdeeds during the State of Emergency she imposed in the mid-1970s. He did, however attend the first Indo-British dinner as our chief guest.

Over the decades, I have had the pleasure of getting acquainted with many an eminent and prominent British personality, including Her Majesty Queen Elizabeth II, who sadly passed away in September 2022 at the age of ninety-six. On 8 July 2009, she kindly appointed me a member of her Privy Council—the first person of Indian origin to be so selected. She was always very gracious towards me.

On an occasion in 1998, she granted me the honour of having me sit immediately to her right at a lunch hosted by her at Buckingham Palace, her London residence—generally by protocol reserved for the chief guest. HRH the Duke of Edinburgh was also present at the meal.

I had the opportunity of meeting the Duke on various occasions. We had a common interest in reviving the London Zoo. He was very friendly towards me, as has been his son Prince Charles, now King Charles III.

I had the honour of interacting with King Charles more often when he was still Prince of Wales and heir to the throne, partly because I was vice chairman of one of his organizations, The Prince's Trust, an organization that helps people aged eleven to thirty get employment, launch a business or simply build confidence. We collaborated again when I joined Business in the Community (BITC), a network of business members leading a movement to create a fair and sustainable world in which to live and work. Formed in 1982, with King Charles as the Royal Founding Patron, BITC is the largest and longest-established membership organization dedicated to responsible business.

I have also occasionally enjoyed being in the company of HRH Princess Anne, the Princess Royal, since I was happy to join the board of one of her charities, UK Youth. She was also involved with the YMCA which I too supported. Later, we were members of the London Olympic Bid Committee and took part in London's successful bid to host the 2012 Olympic Games.

I got to know King Charles's first wife Princess Diana, too, reasonably well. In 1992, while they were still married, she visited Mother Teresa's Missionaries of Charity in Calcutta. In March 1997, after their separation, she invited me to lunch at her Kensington Palace apartment in London for the purpose of following up on her interest in the Missionaries of Charity. The other invitee was the celebrated pop singer Sir Cliff Richard, who was born in India. I remember vividly her charm and her insistence on opening my car door when seeing me off. She dropped me a line thereafter saying, 'I enjoyed meeting you and very much look forward to hearing about the progress which can be made with the Leprosy Mission in Calcutta.' Strangely, Princess Diana and Mother Teresa died within five days of each other in 1997.

I had contacts with Princess Margaret, sister of Queen Elizabeth, as well. She made me a committee member of one of the charities she chaired, the National Society for the Prevention of Cruelty to Children (NSPCC). It was delightful to host a dinner in her honour at The Viceroy of India restaurant near Baker Street, which I then co-owned.

If one settles in a country, I believe you should be committed to making it work like it is your own. People of South Asian origin in the United Kingdom have by and large made an outstanding contribution. We have proven to be highly productive and our reputation for industry has been justly earned. Nowadays, more and more of us are participating in public life. The British government under Boris Johnson boasted as many as four Cabinet ministers of South Asian origin, including those holding top portfolios like home secretary and chancellor of the exchequer. Following the failed premierships of Boris Johnson and Liz Truss, Rishi Sunak was the preferred choice of Conservative Party MPs as prime minister.

In my case, adhering to core Indian customs and being devoted to family life have been guiding principles. And in my view, those who have migrated should not forget India is their motherland, but that Britain is now their homeland.

After launching Caparo, I circumstantially encountered political leaders of both Labour and Conservative parties, especially the former. The first British prime minister I was introduced to was Sir Harold Wilson. When I began constructing Caparo's first steel plant in Wales, he was head of government. The project, though, was completed when James Callaghan, himself a Welshman, had succeeded him. I came to know him, too. I of course know his daughter, Baroness Margaret Jay, better. She was Leader of the House of Lords between 1998 and 2001, when Labour was in government. At that time, I too belonged to the Labour Party.

Tony Benn was a committed socialist and an uncompromising believer in state control of industry. However, it was during his tenure as secretary of state for industry that the ball was set rolling for my private investment in the steel mill in Wales, although it was Michael Foot who played a key role in the process. It was in his parliamentary constituency that the manufacturing unit came up. Michael was associated with V.K. Krishna Menon's Indian League, which agitated in London for Indian independence before 1947.

From the mid-1970s onwards, my interaction with Foot and his wife Jill increased. He encouraged my interest in Labour and was the godfather of my subsequent involvement with the party. Indeed, I learnt immensely from him. He himself became leader of the party in the early 1980s, succeeding James Callaghan.

It was an era of highs and lows for the left-wing movement and quite a traumatic period in its existence. But those of us who remained consistent in our support for the cause never doubted that a stronger, more competitive organization would emerge.

I was invited to speak at Michael's seventy-fifth birthday celebrations, where I was moved to say, 'History has a special place for good people in public life. This has nothing to do with success or failure, victory or defeat. It is a place for those who have rare virtues and values—loyalty, commitment, sincerity, wisdom and justice. Michael will rank high among these saints of civic endeavour.'

Labour has been a congenial ideology for me because its bedrock philosophy addresses social justice. Having lived my youth in Gandhi's India, this ethic held a special appeal. The ideals of fairness to all communities and special concern for the underprivileged was part of the political air I had breathed. Gandhi taught us colonialism was bad, but that colonialism within societies was worse. These notions, together with my gratitude for Labour's anti-imperial record as far as India was concerned, made me feel I belonged to it.

Roy Jenkins, who became home secretary in the Callaghan government, but later formed the breakaway Social Democratic Party and was sixth President of the European Commission, and Peter Shore, who held Cabinet responsibilities for trade and environment, were good friends as well. There was a Hungarian restaurant called the Gay Hussar in the Soho district of London, where we used to go regularly for lunch.

I first met Margaret Thatcher in 1978, when she was Leader of the Opposition and I accompanied Indira Gandhi to their meeting in London. I of course sat in the background as the two conversed. In 1979, Labour was defeated and the Conservatives, with Thatcher as prime minister, captured power. She warmed towards me because she knew I was close to Mrs Gandhi. Aruna and I were invited by her to the British prime minister's official country house at Chequers in Buckinghamshire. I remember she requested me to sit next to her in the presence of quite a few of her ministers. Besides that, before she paid her first trip to India after entering office, she called me to Downing Street to discuss her upcoming talks. She also spoke to me on the phone on the eve of her departure for Delhi.

Mrs Thatcher was joint chief guest at a dinner hosted by the Indo-British Association, of which I was chairman, when Mrs Gandhi came to London in 1982. At this event, the British premier was characteristically drinking wine, while Mrs Gandhi and I sipped Perrier mineral water from France. Turning to me, Mrs Thatcher, pointing to the Perrier bottle, asked, 'Mr Paul, why not Malvern?' I was a bit anxious as I didn't understand what she meant. Mrs Gandhi then quickly explained, 'She is inquiring why you aren't serving Malvern, which is British bottled water from the Malvern Hills of England.' It was of course half in jest, half in seriousness. Mrs Gandhi also pointed out that Mrs Thatcher was drinking wine from France.

Mrs Thatcher was extremely distraught by the assassination of Mrs Gandhi. She travelled to Delhi for the funeral. Sitting next to me, she went up to the pyre to place sandalwood on it. Before leaving Delhi, she made it a point to personally express her condolences to Mrs Gandhi's son Rajiv, who had stepped into his mother's shoes as prime minister, and his wife Sonia at their residence. I mentioned to Mrs Thatcher during that journey that her government should look at ways to control the Sikh extremist movement in Britain, otherwise India would be disquieted. Efforts were made to do so.

Sir Eldon Griffiths and Sir Peter Walker, both Conservatives, served on my company Caparo's board of directors. Baroness Liz Symons, a former minister of state for trade and investment, also joined the Caparo board for five years. I have had good relations with Michael Heseltine, who became deputy prime minister under Prime Minister John Major. He is now a colleague in the House of Lords. And

James Prior, who was secretary of state for employment under Thatcher. His son David is a fellow member in the Lords. Nigel Lawson, who was for a time Thatcher's chancellor of the exchequer, inaugurated Caparo's plant at Scunthorpe in Lincolnshire—a joint venture with British Steel—with highly encouraging words.

John Major became prime minister after Conservative MPs ousted Mrs Thatcher in 1990. He was coincidentally Member of Parliament for Huntingdon, where I started my first steel production unit. So, in 1994 when Caparo celebrated the twenty-fifth anniversary of its formation, I organized a lunch in the town to mark the milestone. John and his wife Norma were our chief guests.

Michael and Jill Foot introduced me to Neil Kinnock, who succeeded Foot in 1983. Neil is a man of courage and great warmth who drew me further into the Labour fold, partly to rebrand it as a party friendly to business. With determination and moderation, he guided Labour in a manner that made it much more acceptable to the average voter. Neil later became an adviser to Caparo. He was a wise and helpful counsellor before moving on to a ministerial role at the European Commission.

Kinnock gave way to John Smith as Labour leader after the former was narrowly beaten in the 1992 elections. John was Britain's lost leader, for he died prematurely of a heart attack in May 1994. He would have been a fair and forthright leader of the United Kingdom. Few individuals in politics have had his honesty. As one newspaper headlined at the time of his death: 'John Smith was the best prime minister Britain never had.'

Politics has changed drastically in the twenty-first century. The requirements from leaders have altered accordingly. Media skills, and now social media savviness, have become integral for communication. New methods of operating party organizations, processes and systems have become essential to efficiency and prospects. John figured on the cusp of this transformation.

John was a Scotsman, as was Robin Cook, who became foreign secretary in 1997 in the first Tony Blair government. Both were very cordial towards me, as was Tony. I also knew Peter Mandelson. But after he switched his allegiance from Gordon Brown to Blair in the leadership issue between the two, our relationship cooled.

Tony was elected as Labour leader after John's death and fully grasped the new politics, while retaining an inspirational flair for motivating others. It was therefore hardly surprising that he won three elections in a row, was prime minister for over a decade and retired undefeated, making way for Gordon.

I once asked Indira Gandhi what was the single most important quality a prime minister required. She replied, 'The capacity to say "no" and stick with the decision.' Tony had that ability. He was also constantly searching for creative answers to intractable questions.

I was kept busy during the 1997 election campaign. There were two groups I was assigned to canvass among: the business community and South Asians. My message to business was that Labour would be entrepreneur-friendly and supportive of the private sector. I knew this to be true, and the Conservative propaganda to the contrary was nothing but scare tactics. In any case, most corporate executives were no longer with the Tories. As for people from the Indian subcontinent, I asked them: Which party do you think will protect your interests better and provide more opportunities for your children? There was little else that needed to be said.

As election day neared, Labour presented a dynamic alternative to the tired Tories bereft of ideas. After eighteen years of the Tories in government, voters wanted a change. The Conservatives were undermined by sharp internal divisions and low morale—a situation that was replicated in the 2024 elections! In contrast, then as now, the Labour team functioned methodically and looked fit for office. Tony proved to be a star at the hustings.

On election night, 1 May, when results were pouring in, Aruna and I drove to Hampstead in north London to join Michael and Jill Foot's party. The guests were Labour supporters. The mood was upbeat. Exit polls forecast a big lead for Labour. Cheers went around the room.

From Hampstead we moved to the BBC television studios, where people from all political parties were gathered. By that time, the outcomes were being declared seat by seat. In the first sixty constituencies where winners were announced, there wasn't a single Conservative. It was obvious that a landslide victory was in the offing. The Tories in the room looked downcast. They weren't expecting such a one-sided trend.

From the BBC, we proceeded to the Royal Festival Hall on the south bank of the Thames. Here, an official Labour Party function was being staged to thank its workers. It was a notably lively atmosphere. At 2.45 a.m. came the confirmation that Labour was certain to win at least 330 seats in a house of 650, which was obviously more than the absolute majority mark. Thus, it was certain that it would form the next administration. A resounding roar greeted the news!

As information filtered through about the defeat of several Conservative leaders, the spirits rose even higher. The enthusiasm was amazing to watch. Many in the crowd were too young to remember the last Labour victory in 1974. For them, it was a wholly new experience which they relished. It was a night to cherish. The joy and jubilation washed away the pain and struggle of the path to success. It was one of the finest hours in Labour's history.

The architects of the triumph began to arrive. Everyone was delighted to see Neil. Around 4 a.m., Gordon and Robin entered to a warm welcome. Then, at 4.15 a.m., Tony arrived to a tumultuous reception. He had flown in from his constituency in Durham and looked every bit the prime minister designate. The applause was so thunderous that the beginning of his speech was drowned by it.

With Gordon Brown, it was admittedly a special relationship. It is no secret that I believed he would make a very capable prime minister. He was solid as chancellor of the exchequer under Tony, who handed the baton to him in the summer of 2007. The British press were full of speculation about how much I had donated to the Labour Party over the years. Now they claimed I had bankrolled Gordon's elevation to the premiership. The fact is that his premiership was inevitable and did not require any bankrolling.

The same year, I bought a country house in Buckinghamshire, a beautiful county to the west of London. The property was previously used as a location for the popular British television crime drama *Midsomer Murders*. On 9 September 2007, the pro-Conservative, anti-Labour newspaper *Mail on Sunday* wrote, 'The acquisition of the Georgian mansion and 250-acre farm on the edge of the Chilterns establishes Lord Paul, seventy-six, as one of the first British Asians to join the ranks of the landed gentry.'

It went on, 'The industrialist's new Buckinghamshire base will also give him easy access to Gordon Brown, who uses

Chequers, the prime minister's official country residence, for weekends with his family.' I cannot deny Aruna and I were Gordon and his wife Sarah's first guests for lunch at Chequers on 21 July 2007. But we were not exactly partaking of their hospitality every weekend.

I must confess I never warmed to David Cameron, who was elected Conservative prime minister in 2010 in place of Gordon and was at the helm for six years. He will go down in history as the British prime minister whose misguided referendum gave rise to Britain's exit from the European Union (Brexit). I also never got along with Ed Miliband, who replaced Gordon as party leader

I first met Boris Johnson when he was a journalist. This was in Delhi at the home of Indian writer Khushwant Singh. The mother of his second wife Marina—to whom he was married for twenty-five years and with whom he had four children—Dip was previously married to Khushwant's younger brother.

When Johnson was mayor of London, he would quite often invite me for lunch in the City. After addressing an audience at London's Bharatiya Vidya Bhavan, he asked, 'What did you think of my speech?' I told him, 'You said everything you wanted to say, but you made everyone laugh.'

But to rewind, in the summer of 1996, I heard through the grapevine that Tony, then Leader of the Opposition, had recommended my name to Prime Minister John Major for a peerage. On 5 August, I in fact received a letter from Major, which stated, 'I am writing to let you know, in strict confidence, that I shall shortly be recommending to Her Majesty The Queen the creation of a number of Life Peers in a special list to increase the working strength of the House of Lords.' It continued, 'I have it in mind to submit your name to The Queen with a recommendation that Her Majesty may be graciously pleased to approve that the dignity of a Barony of the United Kingdom for Life be conferred upon you.' It concluded, 'I hope that you will be able to let me know as soon as possible that this would be agreeable to you.'

I naturally indicated my acceptance immediately. Around 21 August, Aruna and I were on a cruise when the captain of the ship communicated the news that I had been made a Peer. On our return to London, we were overwhelmed by people personally conveying their good wishes, sending cards, cables and flowers. My office was deluged by over 10,000 messages of congratulations. The telephone didn't stop ringing. Many letters came from people in Britain and India whom I didn't know. I was joyous, yet humbled by the honour. I was touched that so many had affectionately identified with my Peerage as a symbol of their own aspiration.

I chose the designation of Lord Paul of Marylebone, which is in the City of Westminster—one half of modern-day central London, the other being the City of London—where I have lived and worked throughout my stay in Britain. Marylebone is also where I sometimes attend the famous All Souls Church built by the architect John Nash in 1825.

On 12 November 1996, I was introduced to the House of Lords. I was only the second person of Indian origin in the modern era to be so ushered in. It was a solemn ceremony. The new Peer, attired in his regalia and robes, is presented by two sponsors. Mine were Lord Simon Haskel, an old friend, and Baroness Elizabeth Smith, widow of John Smith. As I walked into the chamber accompanied by them and witnessed from the galleries by my family and close friends, I could scarcely control my emotions. Tears welled up and it was with forced restraint that I managed to navigate the oath-taking.

Memories came flooding back. How happy and intrigued I thought my parents would have been to see their son, who belonged to an Indian nationalist family, being accepted in an assembly that once decided India's destiny. My brothers Jit and Stya shared my sentiments. But I missed Surrendra's sense of humour. He had tragically been killed by extremists in a tea garden in the north-eastern Indian state of Assam. He would surely have had a joke up his sleeve about Lord Paul! I also grieved at Ambika's absence.

Before the introduction, there was a luncheon in the House of Lords Cholmondeley Room. Many kind words were expressed here. Yet, the camaraderie and cordiality was tinged with a degree of sadness. Several near and dear ones with whom I would have loved to share these moments were no more.

The House of Lords is an institution where you participate according to your own volition. It is the second legislative house—the other being the directly elected House of Commons—where the 'working' lawmakers undertake a substantial amount of parliamentary work. Until pruned down, the Lords had over a thousand hereditary and life Peers. It now has about 800 members, but the regular attendance is about 300 Peers.

I resolved to actively engage in proceedings. I had been proposed as a member by the Labour Party and was therefore affiliated to the Labour Parliamentary Group and sat on its benches. I felt I was obliged to play an active part to fulfil the purpose of being admitted to the house. I saw no point in being a Peer for ornamental reasons.

I sat on various select committees including the Science and Technology Committee and the Committee for Economic Affairs.

A new Peer can deliver his or her maiden speech at any time. Some take months, even years, to do so. Others have a greater recognition of urgency. The debut statement customarily outlines one's outlook rather than focusing on any specific agenda or topic. The panelled walls have heard notable speeches and observed high points of history. The House has been a venue of majestic debates wherein celebrated orators have waxed eloquent. During the Second World War, when the Commons was damaged, Winston Churchill's stirring speeches were rendered in the Lords. Bearing in mind such events, I rose to speak a mere sixteen days after entering the chamber.

'My Lords,' I submitted, 'I come to this House conscious that the roots of my heritage and philosophy are not conventional to the membership of this august assembly. Yet, I believe Your Lordships recognize that they symbolize a contribution to the new Britain which we are all engaged in constructing.'

I added, 'At this moment, I am also mindful that my presence among Your Lordships signifies another convergence—the reconciliation and friendship between the land of my birth and the country which is my home.'

The House of Lords is a serious assembly, without the crosstalk, interjection or sharp retort that enlivens business in the Commons. Regardless of their affiliations, the relationship between members is not fractious. Discussion is conducted in a calm atmosphere. Whenever the House has been in session, I have attended regularly and taken part in debates on education, corporate and economic matters, not to mention subjects connected with India. Parliamentary work has, in fact, motivated me much more than I expected it to. It has been a thoroughly enjoyable and parallel second career.

Over the years, I have spoken on multiple occasions in the House. On 14 November 2008, I took part in a debate on immigration. I recorded,

> The status Britain has enjoyed through history compared with its size and population is largely due to the fact that we welcome immigrants from all over the world and have recognized their value and contribution. In my experience, immigrants bring in fresh ideas, more vigour and a greater desire for success. That is natural because to be a success in a new country, one has to work at least 25 per cent harder to be counted at par. I know this from my personal experience and forty years of hard work here. If Britain did not have an immigrant community—as I know myself, from running an industrial business—we would not have a labour force, the same productivity or an economy of the size we have today. We would have lower standards of living, higher inflation and very little influence in the world, which would reduce Britain to a second-rate country . . . Finally, I say that globalization, which has benefited all of us, cannot be complete without the free movement of people.

Debating the Queen's Speech on 8 December 2008, I summed up,

> The UK has a manufacturing base of which we can be proud. The government has taken steps to address some of the short-term challenges that we face, but some issues remain. Manufacturing must continue to play a key role in the economic future of the United Kingdom. It is high time

that the government listened more to the people who run manufacturing industry.

The Commonwealth was in the business of the House on 17 October 2013. I highlighted,

> India's Prime Minister Jawaharlal Nehru took the decision for India to stay in the Commonwealth. This encouraged the notion of a multidimensional organization, diverse in its activities and membership . . . To date, the position of head of the Commonwealth has been vested in the monarch of the United Kingdom. It has been admirably filled by Her Majesty The Queen, to whom we are all indebted for her wholehearted commitment and genuine interest in the Commonwealth. She has set an extraordinary precedent. Looking to the future, I think that what needs to be considered is a clear succession protocol or procedure.

In May 2014, India voted in a government led by the Bharatiya Janata Party. The House took up this development on 23 October that year. I analysed,

> At these polls, Indians transcended old divisions of caste and religion, largely leaving behind sectarianism, to vote for national concerns such as employment and anti-corruption. A new leader—we must congratulate Mr Narendra Modi—was able to secure a one-party majority and a stable government after many years of minority or coalition rule.

Pranab Mukherjee, then President of India, sent me a letter of appreciation on 12 November 2014 in which he said, 'Your thoughts are a reflection of your deep understanding and insight into Indian politics as well as the unique nature of India-British relations.'

On 23 July 2018, Lord Qurban Hussain, a Peer of Pakistani descent, asked what steps the British government would take 'to assist the implementation of the recommendations of a United Nations report concerning human rights abuses in (Indian-controlled) Jammu and Kashmir to hold an independent international inquiry to investigate abuses'. I intervened to say, 'Both India and Pakistan are very active members of the United Nations. Will the government say what purpose it will serve to discuss this point here?'

My friend the Conservative government Minister of State Lord Tariq Ahmad responded,

> Her Majesty's Government, as the noble Lord has rightly said, is a friend to both governments, India and Pakistan. Our position remains that it is primarily for India and Pakistan to come together. They are countries tied together by history, culture and families. Indeed, my parents hailed from India and my wife's parents from Pakistan. Communities and families can come together. Perhaps I am living proof of that.

In December 2008, I became the first person of Asian origin to become deputy speaker of the House. This meant overseeing proceedings, sitting on the Woolsack—a large red seat stuffed with wool—in the absence of the Speaker. In this capacity, I coincidentally presided over a debate on India on 18 December 2008.

However, the House also inflicted on me a four-month suspension after long-running media investigations into

Parliamentary expenses. In October 2009, *Sunday Times* reported I had unjustifiably claimed Parliamentary expenses of £38,000. This related to Peers' 'second home' allowance if their main residence was outside London. Every week *Sunday Times* named different Peers who had also wrongly claimed expenses on this basis, so I was not alone. Even the Lord Speaker Baroness Helen Hayman had erroneously claimed some £200,000. Baroness Thornton, a government minister, claimed £22,000 a year saying that her mother's home in Yorkshire was her main residence. Lord Ryder, a former acting chairman of the BBC, claimed more than £100,000 by saying that a converted stable on his parents' country estate was his main home. None of these claims were formally investigated. In my case, the moment a disputed amount of less than £40,000 was brought to my attention, I returned that amount in full and asked the Clerk of the Parliament to investigate the matter as I did not believe I had done anything outside the rules governing expenses at that time. This was not formally acknowledged until the report on the whole proceedings was published on 18 October 2010—a full year later.

What happened instead was that I was first asked to appear before the Sub-Committee on Lords' Conduct. This newly convened sub-committee had been hastily formed as the investigating arm of the full seventeen-member House of Lords Committee for Privileges and Conduct. It was chaired by Eliza Manningham-Buller, previously head of MI5 and only recently ennobled. Also on the committee was Lord Derry Irvine, who himself had been criticized for lavish expenses relating to the refurbishment of his official apartment in the House of Lords[*]—spending for which he refused to apologize.

---

[*] BBC News, 4 March 1998.

So the fact that he was sitting in judgement of fellow Peers in similar circumstances seemed to me ironic.

The sub-committee's findings said that while I had repaid the full amount of the disputed expenses, I had not made the original claims 'in good faith' and therefore recommended I make a full statement of apology to the House and be suspended for six months.

I immediately appealed to the Committee for Privileges and Conduct and appeared before it. Following its own deliberations, the committee concluded I had *not* acted dishonestly or in bad faith. If my office had claimed expenses I was not entitled to, this committee agreed it had been done out of ignorance. But I was nevertheless suspended for four months. I disagreed with the finding and felt it was unreasonable. On 22 June 2011, I called for reform and revision of the structure of the House's constitution.

'If there are any investigations or allegations regarding members of this House,' I asserted, 'all those concerned must be treated equally; selective application of rules against some and exculpation of others is discriminatory. When it is known that many have done what only a few are castigated for, that can only be a gross transgression of British justice.'

I further argued, 'As far as I know, retrospective violations have no status and are not recognized in the courts of law. Why, then, should they be the basis of punishment for members of this House?'

Finally, I stated, 'When this House or its committees conduct investigations or examine evidence, it is essential that all relevant documents be made available. Scrupulous care should be taken that nothing is omitted or withheld.'

The entire episode was inspired by inter-party politics, and I had become a victim of media and rival hostility. On

21 October 2010, with Gordon no longer prime minister and to avoid continued targeting by the Tory press, I abandoned the Labour whip to become a non-affiliated member of the House.

In November 2010, I resigned as deputy speaker to uphold parliamentary conventions and proprieties. Writing to the Speaker, I placed on record: 'I have decided to resign despite the fact that the Committee for Privileges and Conduct and indeed the House itself has cleared me of any dishonesty and bad faith. Although I have several reservations, I have accepted the suspension imposed upon me in keeping with the traditions of parliamentary practice.' I also impressed on him, 'To my mind, this situation is fraught with gross injustice and violation of what I had come to believe are the norms of British fairness.'

It was a different concern that prompted Lord Waheed Alli of Norbury to intervene in the expenses affair.

A successful television executive who helped create some of Britain's most popular programmes—*The Word*, *Big Breakfast* and *Survivor* among them—he joined the Labour Party and became a valuable part of Tony Blair's strategy for extending the party's appeal to a younger, more modern generation.

What bothered Alli was this: of the thirty-one members of the House of Lords who were investigated over their expense claims in 2009 and 2010, only four were hauled before the Conduct Sub-Committee for questioning (not counting Hanningfield and Taylor, who were investigated by police). Of those four, three were suspended. All three were of Asian origin.

I was suspended for four months; Lord Bhatia of Hampton for eight months; Baroness Uddin of Bethnal Green until the end of that parliamentary session (then eighteen months away). The fourth MP to be questioned was Lord Clarke of

Hampstead, a former English trade unionist who was found to have wrongly claimed overnight allowances but was required only to apologize after repaying the amount involved. Clarke admitted to a 'terrible error' and said, 'I was told you claim the full amount . . . the impression I got was that if I didn't do what (other) people did, it could bring a bad light on somebody else.'

I had also apologized to the House and repaid the full amount involved without being asked to. In fact, I repaid more than the amount I would have been asked to, but this has never been acknowledged.

On 21 October 2010, a few days after my appeal was turned down, Alli stood up in the Lords chamber. 'I have thought long and hard about whether or not to intervene in today's debate,' he said. 'There are those who advised me to keep quiet and not rock the boat, but I have some serious worries.'

He mentioned his concerns about procedural failures, the sub-committee's standards of proof and the lack of legal representation afforded 'any noble Lords facing such a serious set of allegations'. Then he arrived at what he described as 'the element of race'.

Alli hastened to add that he was not accusing anyone of racism. 'But it cannot have escaped your Lordships' attention that the only three members of your Lordships' House who were referred to the Committee for Privileges and Conduct . . . were all Asian'. He had reviewed numerous cases involving expense complaints but had failed to detect 'any constant pattern' for the referrals to the committee. 'When one combines inconsistency in approach and the disproportionality of the sanctions, my concerns deepen,' Alli said. 'Something has clearly gone wrong.'

The Leader of the House, Lord Strathclyde, took several months to come up with a response. He wrote to Alli in June

2011 and said he was satisfied that the House had dealt 'fairly and appropriately' with the complaints against Lord Bhatia, Baroness Uddin and me. He pointed out that Lord Dholakia, an Asian member of the Conduct Sub-Committee, had 'detected no discrimination'.

Alli was not satisfied as the whole investigation appeared flawed. For example, among the Peers whose cases never reached the sub-committee was Baroness Mary Goudie of Roundwood, who declared her 'main residence' to be a small flat in Glasgow. Yet, she also owned a home in central London where she lived most of the year with her barrister husband. Goudie was accused of claiming around £250,000 worth of allowances related to the Glasgow flat—more than six times the amount that was an issue with me.

A preliminary investigation by the Clerk of Parliaments concluded: 'It is not clear that the designation of Glasgow as her "main or only residence" is really based on actual residency'—the same charge levelled against me. Yet, the case was not referred to Manningham-Buller's sub-committee and no sanction was imposed after she apologized and repaid an agreed amount. Again, why wasn't I treated the same way?

Alli decided an independent investigation was needed and commissioned a study from Imran Khan, a high-profile London human rights lawyer who had represented the family of Stephen Lawrence, the black British teenager stabbed to death by a group of white youths in 1993. The key question was not how badly or otherwise Lord Bhatia and Baroness Uddin had behaved in submitting questionable claims, but whether the House of Lords had treated them fairly and impartially.

Khan soon established that the House's internal disciplinary procedures did not reflect any recognized principles of English law. He concluded that the rules governing reimbursement of expenses were 'not sufficiently clear, certain and precise'. In fact, by the time his report appeared, the Lords had already tightened its definitions of what constitutes a 'main residence'.

Khan then raised the matter of the defendants' right to an 'independent and impartial tribunal'. He said that committee members presiding over the expenses cases may have been influenced in different ways. The *Sunday Times* allegations had triggered 'widespread and intense media, public and political criticism . . . accompanied by calls for radical reform', Khan wrote. 'There was clearly a risk that members of the Sub-Committee and the Committee felt pressure to find against those members they were investigating', to demonstrate that the House was taking the issue seriously. 'They had a direct interest in restoring the reputation of the House.' And someone had to shoulder the blame.

Also, the interrogators and their subjects would likely have known each other. 'There was a danger that, for example, any personal antagonism might have influenced a panel member's view.' The report went on: 'We are concerned that the complaints against the three members were not investigated by an independent and impartial body as the legal term is understood and applied in comparable tribunals.'

Then there was the House's ban on legal representation, which meant some of Britain's most senior lawyers were examining witnesses who were not allowed lawyers of their own. This showed what Khan described as 'at least an apparent inequality', with the inquisitors' ranks including Lord Irvine, the QC and former lord chancellor, and, on the full committee, Lord Scott of Foscote, a former Appeals Court judge. The only person I was allowed to have accompany me in the proceedings was my long-term PA, Elizabeth Allan, who is not a lawyer and, in any case, wasn't allowed to speak.

Khan's conclusions were critical of what he described as 'the wholly different treatment' accorded to the three Asian Peers, compared to those whose cases were investigated but dropped. In his report, he cited the 'apparently inconsistent' treatment of Lord Clarke, who was found to have claimed bogus allowances for staying in London when he had in fact returned to his home in Hertfordshire.* Why weren't the Peers treated the same?

Khan was unable to reach a decisive conclusion about the bearing of racial factors based on his review of all the documents in the case. However, the final paragraph of the report concludes: 'In our view, judged by the standards they have set themselves (the Committee for Privileges and Conduct and its sub-committee) have failed to conduct fair hearings in the cases of Lord Bhatia, Lord Paul and Baroness Uddin.'

---

* *Guardian*, 5 February 2010.

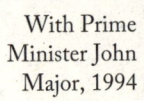

With Tony Blair
at the House of
Commons, 1996

With Prime
Minister John
Major, 1994

With Neil Kinnock at the House of Commons, 1993

With British Foreign Secretary Robin Cook at Lancaster House, 2005

At the Court at Buckingham Palace

THE 8th DAY OF JULY 2009

PRESENT,

THE QUEEN'S MOST EXCELLENT MAJESTY
IN COUNCIL

This day Lord Paul was, by Her Majesty's command, appointed a Member of Majesty's Most Honourable Privy Council.

Privy Councillor appointment, 2009

राष्ट्रपति
भारत गणतंत्र
PRESIDENT
REPUBLIC OF INDIA

November 12, 2014

Dear Lord Swraj Paul,

I would like to express my appreciation for the stimulating speech delivered by you on the outcome of the 2014 General Elections in India in the House of Lords on October 23rd, 2014.

Your thoughts are a reflection of your deep understanding and insight into Indian politics as well as the unique nature of India-British relations. I am happy that you were able to point out the need to provide new energy to India-Britain relations and avoid some of the mistakes of the past. I am sure your views have been listened to carefully and will result in concrete action leading to renewed momentum in India-Britain relations.

Please accept my best wishes for the good health of your family and you.

With regards,

Yours sincerely,

(Pranab Mukherjee)

Lord Swraj Paul,
Chairman, Caparo Group,
Caparo House, 103 Baker Street

Letter from Pranab Mukherjee, 2014

10 DOWNING STREET
LONDON SW1A 2AA

THE PRIME MINISTER
IN CONFIDENCE

5 August 1996

Dear Swraj,

    I am writing to let you know, in strict confidence, that I shall shortly be recommending to The Queen the creation of a number of Life Peers in a special list to increase the working strength of the House of Lords.

    I have it in mind to submit your name to The Queen with a recommendation that Her Majesty may be graciously pleased to approve that the dignity of a Barony of the United Kingdom for Life be conferred upon you.

    I hope that you will be able to let me know as soon as possible that this would be agreeable to you.

Yours sincerely,
John Major

Swraj Paul Esq

Letter from John Major about my peerage, 1996

Anjli Paul, Michelle Paul, Sarah Brown, me and Angad Paul at Chequers, 2007

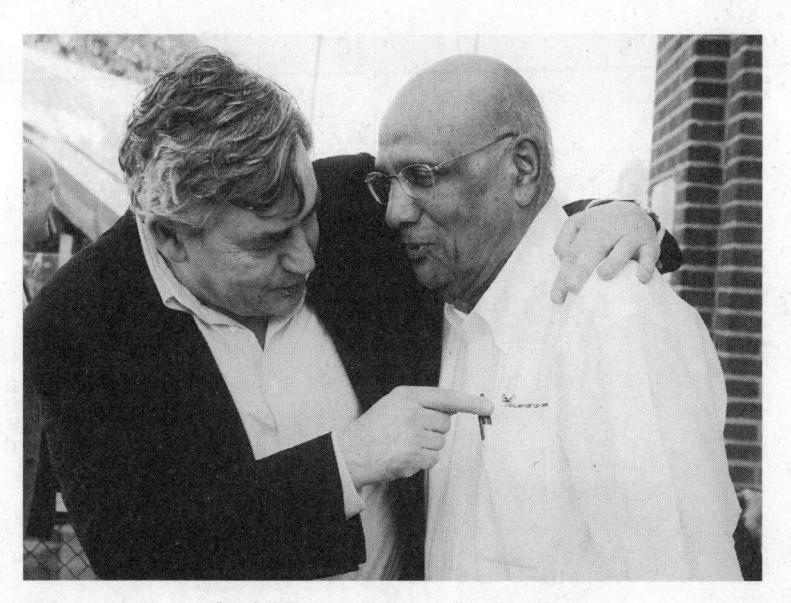

Gordon Brown and me at London Zoo

BUCKINGHAM PALACE

In the 1844 Room
At 1.00 p.m.
Dress: Lounge Suit

Seating Plan   Wednesday, 4th March 1998.

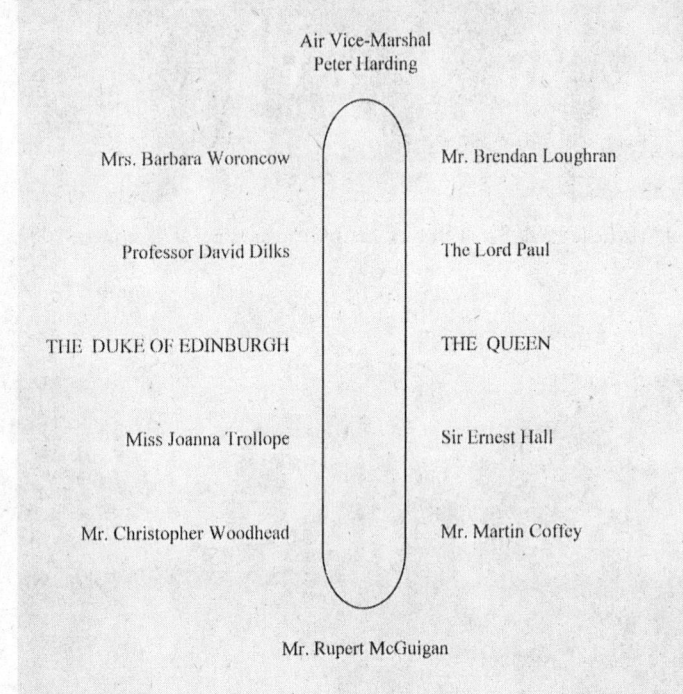

Air Vice-Marshal
Peter Harding

Mrs. Barbara Woroncow   Mr. Brendan Loughran

Professor David Dilks   The Lord Paul

THE DUKE OF EDINBURGH   THE QUEEN

Miss Joanna Trollope   Sir Ernest Hall

Mr. Christopher Woodhead   Mr. Martin Coffey

Mr. Rupert McGuigan

↑ ↑
ENTRANCE

Buckingham Palace lunch with HM the Queen, 1998

9

Universities and Education

I have been privileged to receive fifteen honorary degrees from universities all over the world:

Honorary Doctor of Philosophy in Management Sciences, Maharshi Dayanand University, Haryana, India, 2007; Honorary Doctor of Philosophy, Dr B.R. Ambedkar National Institute of Technology, India, 2006; Honorary Doctor of Punjab Technical University, Jalandhar, India, 2005; Honorary Doctor of the State University of Management, Moscow, Russia, 2001; Honorary Doctor of Commercial Science, University of Hartford, Connecticut, USA, 2002; Honorary Doctor of Philosophy, Thames Valley University, UK, 2000; Honorary Doctor of the University, University of Central England, Birmingham, UK, 1999; Doctor of Science, The University of Buckingham, UK, 1999; Honorary Doctor of Philosophy, Guru Nanak Dev University, Amritsar, India, 1998; Honorary Doctor of the University of Bradford, UK, 1997; Honorary Doctor of Letters, University of Westminster,

UK, 1997; Honorary Doctor of Humane Letters, Chapman University, USA, 1996; Honorary Doctor of Economics, University of Hull, UK, 1992; Honorary Doctor of Philosophy, American College of Switzerland, 1986; Corporate Leadership Award, Massachusetts Institute of Technology, in recognition of distinguished corporate leadership and contribution to economic strength (MIT equivalent to Honorary Degree), USA, 1987.

My first university post was pro chancellor at the University of West London (then called Thames Valley University) under its Vice Chancellor Mike Fitzgerald in 1994, and I held that position until I was made chancellor in 2000–01. During that time, it was a great pleasure for me to award an honorary doctorate to my elder brother, Stya Paul, to commemorate his achievements and contribution to education throughout his life.

Starting with a small school in Jalandhar in 1967, Stya established sixteen schools and eight institutions of higher learning over the next five decades under the aegis of Apeejay Education, which are recognized as symbols of excellence in their various disciplines. The year 2010 also saw the realization of his lifetime dream of setting up the Apeejay Stya University, a seat of global learning designed to bring about the transformation of society through value-based education, personal development and nation-building.

After graduating from MIT in 1952, I kept in close contact with my alma mater and inaugurated the Swraj Paul (1952) Scholarship which is awarded to graduate and undergraduate students from India or of Indian origin to enable them to study at MIT. I am delighted to be able to give something back to the institution that has helped shape much of my thinking and career path. I sat on MIT's Mechanical Engineering Visiting

Committee between 1998 and 2001, when we established the Ambika Paul Mezzanine and Study Space. We have also established the Swraj Paul and Angad Paul Theatre there, as mentioned earlier in the chapter on MIT. In August 2020, Aruna and I were invited to become members of the MIT Charter Society in recognition of our philanthropic commitment to MIT.

In 2005, I was approached by the vice chancellor of the University of Westminster, Dr Geoffrey Copland, to ask whether I would become that university's first chancellor. The position of founding chancellor was one I was delighted to accept, and my installation took place at The Banqueting House, Whitehall in London on 9 October 2006, where the guest of honour was The Rt Hon. Gordon Brown, then chancellor of the exchequer.

I had first met Geoffrey a decade earlier when we were both board members of the Central London Training and Enterprise Council (CENTEC), a body that had been set up by John Major's government to form strategic partnerships between local businesses, local authorities and education. My remit as the university's first chancellor was to assist Geoffrey in raising the profile and the status of this most central London university. Geoffrey said, 'I am delighted you accepted the position of chancellor. You are the right person for that role, bringing your influence and experience to help the University.' I headed the Court of Governors and on a personal note, was delighted that our charitable foundation was able to provide necessary funding to repurpose a huge underground space, once used for concrete construction, into the Ambika P3 Gallery. Opened by Sarah Brown in 2008, Ambika P3 is an award-winning distinctive space for contemporary art and architecture that presents a public programme of solo and group exhibitions, education projects, talks and events. Its size is unique for an exhibition space in crowded central London's West End. Dedicated to innovation, experimentation and learning, Ambika P3 operates as a laboratory and meeting place for practitioners, industry and academia. It has hosted many fashion and design shows in addition to the Sunday Art Fair in London every October. The P3 has proved to be a major asset to the university and is much used.

I decided to resign as chancellor after leading the university's 175th anniversary celebrations at Westminster Abbey in 2014 and I am gratified that I was able to contribute much to its expansion and progress throughout my nine-year involvement.

In 1982, I was selected to attend the Harvard Business School Leadership programme, a prestigious three-month course designed specifically for owner/managers of SME companies.

In the 1980s and 1990s, I collaborated with the University of Cambridge to fund the Nehru Chair, a professorship established to help forge closer links between the Indian and other international economies and to promote understanding of India's interests and its place in the world economy.

I attended an academic dinner in 1996 and found myself sitting next to James Doti, the president of Chapman University, Orange County, California, who mentioned that he had a problem. A few years after the fall of the Berlin Wall, one of the university's alumni had found pieces of graffiti-clad concrete on sale in Berlin and had bought 'a three-ton chunk' which he offered to the university, provided they paid the transportation costs. Chapman's president approached another alumnus who ran an international shipping business and who agreed to transport this Cold War relic, now a worldwide symbol of freedom, to California. The problem, Jim said, was that no funds were available to Chapman to construct a suitable memorial space to display the giant slab. Coincidentally, in November 1989, I had attended a World Steel Association conference for steel company presidents in Berlin. Aruna came with me and, while we were in our meetings, our wives went on a city tour where they witnessed the Wall being torn down. Thus, we were present for a unique moment in history, and so I did not hesitate when, seven years later, Jim Doti told me about his plan for a 'Liberty Plaza' in Orange County, California.

I said I would support the project. That piece of wall now stands in an oval pool in a leafy corner of the Chapman campus. The inscription on the plaque includes the words: 'Dedicated on May 4, 1999 in memory of Ambika Paul with gratitude to Lord Swraj Paul and family.' More recently, the tributes to Ambika have also included tributes to Angad.

I was a member of the President's Cabinet for Chapman University until 2016.

Wolverhampton

In 1998, the newly appointed vice chancellor of the University of Wolverhampton, Professor John Brooks, asked me to become its chancellor, a position I was delighted to accept given Caparo's ties with the West Midlands region. I was installed as chancellor at a ceremony in St Peter's Church, Wolverhampton on 9 May 2000. In my oration, I said that the purpose of education went beyond the acquisition of information and credentials; that the values of integrity and industry, of faith in people and faith in oneself, of endurance and enterprise, were no different from one culture to another. I quoted T.S. Eliot, whose words still resonate today, ninety years after he wrote them: 'Where is the life we have lost in living; where is the wisdom we have lost in knowledge; where is the knowledge we have lost in information.' I went on to say that 'I believe we must educate, not only for a city or a region or a country, but for the world in which we live.' I am still chancellor of the university today and the longest serving chancellor in the UK.

Wolverhampton is known as 'The University of Opportunity'. We are increasing opportunities for the thousands of students who may come from immigrant or from poorer backgrounds and help them get fulfilling careers.

It is a public university located on four campuses across the West Midlands, Shropshire and Staffordshire in England. The roots of the university lie in the Wolverhampton Tradesmen's and Mechanics' Institute, founded in 1827, and the nineteenth-century growth of the Wolverhampton Free Library (1870), which developed technical, scientific, commercial and general classes. The Technical College was built in 1931, the year of my birth, in the grounds of St Peter's Collegiate Church. The College merged in 1969 with the Municipal School of Art, originally founded in 1851, to form the Wolverhampton Polytechnic. It was granted university status in 1992.

The university has four faculties comprising eighteen schools and institutes. It has 25,000 students and currently offers over 380 undergraduate and postgraduate courses. The city campus is located in Wolverhampton city centre, with a second campus at Walsall and a third in Telford. There is an additional fourth campus in Wolverhampton at the University of Wolverhampton Science Park.

The year 2000 saw the launch of a multimillion-pound refurbishment programme and the opening of two major facilities. Plans for a further £45 million investment in the city campus were announced in December 2012, with redevelopments including a new Business School building that now bears my name. In 2013, the university celebrated its twenty-first anniversary since being granted university status on 17 June 1992.

In 2015, we saw completion of the Lord Swraj Paul Building (home to the University of Wolverhampton Business School), and a £10 million investment in engineering at Telford Innovation Campus, where the Angad Paul building is located, together with a new courtyard and catering facilities at City Campus, and the development of the new Springfield Campus, a national centre for excellence for construction and the built environment. The Lady Aruna Swraj Paul building was formally inaugurated on 25 June 2024 and contains the School of Architecture and Built Environment.

In 2015, I donated £1m to the university, which is its largest single donation ever received, setting up the Chancellor's Fund to cover three key areas of university activity: to pump prime new initiatives in research, innovation in teaching and learning, and business engagement.

I have worked with six vice chancellors at the University: John Brooks, Caroline Gipps, Geoff Layer, Ian Campbell, John Raftery and Ebrahim Adia. All of them have been excellent vice chancellors with whom I have been happy to collaborate and help drive this expansion. And I look forward to an ongoing relationship so long as I can add value to an institution of which I am extremely proud.

During my time working with John Brooks, we embarked on an ambitious plan to rationalize campuses in Wolverhampton,

Walsall and Telford. In February 2003, The Rt Hon. Gordon Brown, then chancellor of the exchequer, accepted our invitation to formally open the Millennium City Building and receive an Honorary Doctorate in Social Science from the university.

In March the same year, The Rt Hon. Charles Clarke, Secretary of State for Education and Skills, opened the Learning Centre and the Charles Clarke Classroom of the Future. He was awarded the University's first honorary foundation degree in public service.

During this busy period, John particularly remembers a visit in September 2001 to the State University of Moscow (SUM), which had awarded me with an honorary degree in management to celebrate and cement the relationship between Wolverhampton and SUM. A huge banquet was held in our honour.

Of our time together, John said recently, 'Wolverhampton made an excellent choice when we asked you to become chancellor. I remain thankful that you accepted.'

In 2005, John left Wolverhampton and a new vice chancellor was installed, Professor Caroline Gipps, whom, coincidentally, I had known for some time as her husband, Jo, was the director of ZSL and London Zoo, with whom I had been working for a decade on our projects there.

Under the vice chancellorship of Caroline Gipps, we awarded an honorary degree to Sarah Brown in 2007 to mark her contribution to charity and to educational causes. The following year, we launched the Wolverhampton-India initiative. And in 2010, I was delighted to open the Ambika Paul Student Union Centre at the university with Sarah as our guest. That year also saw a major visit to India where, at a specially convened ceremony in Delhi, the university conferred honorary degrees on President and former finance and defence minister, Pranab Mukherjee; India's finance minister and BJP stalwart Arun Jaitley; and N. Ram, prominent journalist and director of the Hindu group of publications. The following year, we conferred an honorary degree on Indian President Dr A.P.J. Abdul Kalam, India's eleventh President, whose enthusiasm for, and work in, the space industry contributed so much to India's recent dark side moon landing.

Wolverhampton University has diversified and expanded immensely in the twenty-five years that I have been associated with it and my own family's contribution has been significant.

Under the vice chancellor Geoff Layer, who succeeded Caroline Gipps, the university built and inaugurated The Ambika Paul Building (2015), the Lord Swraj Paul building (2016) and the Angad Paul building (2019) at its various campuses. Geoff says of our time together:

> Swraj, as he became to me, and I worked hard to promote the university in the UK and abroad and he was always willing to use his immense range of connections to help the university. He loved to come to the university and to meet colleagues, business leaders but most importantly, our students. He always seemed happiest talking to students. Our students from India and those local students of Indian heritage all knew who Swraj was and were really keen to talk to him and especially to have a photo opportunity. This demonstrated to me how much he is respected within all the communities that he engages with.
>
> As chancellor of the university, I worked with him on a number of university projects over the period of ten years. He was very keen to drive engagement with business and to provide opportunities for young people.

The Ambika Paul building houses the Learning Information Services, the Students' Union and the Careers and Employment Services. The Lord Paul building houses the Business School, the centre for a wide spectrum of business disciplines, including MBA programmes, HR, corporate governance and CSR, and entrepreneurship. It was officially opened on 22 March 2016.

The Lady Aruna Swraj Paul building was inaugurated on 25 June 2024 and houses the school for Architecture and the Built Environment.

The Angad Paul building, opened in March 2019, is used for student–staff initiatives like support for early careers researchers, nursing programmes, engineering programmes, individual and group teaching excellence reward initiatives and to fund student entrepreneurial initiatives.

At the inauguration of this building, Geoff Layer said, 'Angad was an industrialist so it is fitting that his memory and legacy will go on to support the next generation of entrepreneurs.'

In addition to working with the vice chancellor's office, I attend the university graduation ceremonies and hold a dinner every year for honorary graduates. I also host annual gatherings at the House of Lords so that the university can showcase its talents to a wider audience in the fields of education and government.

I have made several ambassadorial visits to India and Nepal and opened doors for links to Sri Lanka and Bangladesh. The visits to India were always major occurrences where I hosted events on the university's behalf to ensure that we were continually able to develop partnerships and engagement in India. In Nepal, I attended the closing ceremony of the university's ten-year project on deforestation. Since then, the university's links with Nepal have increased.

Organizations either evolve or they cease to exist. The University of Wolverhampton has proven its resilience. It has been in existence, in various forms, since 1827. It has evolved in response to the national and educational environment over almost two centuries, forty-five prime ministers, two world wars and, as of 2024, has some 22,000 students and 2200 staff.

The university's world has changed, though, with, among other things, a new regulator, inescapably forensic public information about learning outcomes and repeated, unfunded increases in pension costs. The latter has given rise to unplanned, multi-million-pound additions to payroll costs entirely outside the control of the vice chancellor and the board.

By the end of 2021, I was becoming increasingly concerned. At the same time, the university, under interim vice chancellor Ian Campbell, should be credited with taking tough, but wise, decisions in 2022 to refresh its portfolio and ensure it looked forward to the future of work, not back to the past. The painful closure of the previously illustrious glass and ceramics and the opening of a new film school is an illustrative example. The university had also been investing in new facilities at Telford, Hereford, Walsall and the Springfield campus, in which I had been taking a particular interest, but it had undeniably reached a low point with diminished financial reserves, student outcomes and a consequent loss of confidence in itself and its mission. As we approached the end of 2022, it was clear the university needed new and vigorous leadership.

Following a global search, February 2023 saw the arrival of John Raftery, the Irishman credited with saving London Metropolitan University from bankruptcy, leaving them with a large surplus of financial reserves, rising graduate employment and a repaired reputation. Raftery's home is in Cambridge,

Massachusetts, where, from his eighth-floor apartment, he has a view of my alma mater, MIT, from one window, and Harvard, where he had studied at the Kennedy School, from the other. This proved to be a good omen for me, as an MIT alumnus who had undertaken executive education at Harvard. Raftery had a reputation for intensity, insight and energy, all of which would be needed in abundance. I later discovered that he had a good knowledge of India, was widely read and familiar with Tagore and Anglo-Indian writers such as Jhumpa Lahiri and Amitav Ghosh, and had met and closely studied the work of Bengali economist Amartya Sen, the Nobel laureate. Although he had not visited Jalandhar, he had made many business trips to the Punjabi state capital Chandigarh and to New Delhi, Kolkata and Mumbai.

Upon learning each other's stories and sharing reflections on our life experiences, it became clear that we would soon become friends as well as close colleagues, a chancellor and vice chancellor working together to serve the university. As far from a stereotypical British VC as it is possible to be, Raftery, the son of an orphaned Irish immigrant, had gone on to a PhD in economics and, by the time he was successfully tempted to leave Massachusetts for Wolverhampton, had accumulated four decades of top leadership experience. In his earlier career, he had worked on assignments on risk in major public infrastructure projects valued at more than $20 billion, and on cartels and restrictive practices in Hong Kong, Finland and the UK. He had served as an adviser to the UK prime minister's Initiative Research schemes for UK-India and UK-India-US and had held many board appointments in the UK, including the Office of the Independent Adjudicator, the Open University National Role Advisory Board and Access HE, and had served on the Council of Ruskin College Oxford. Bringing with him a reputation as a troubleshooter and turnaround specialist, Raftery came to visit me in London on 18 February 2023, my ninety-second birthday.

Over the following months, I would hear him say, in private and in public, that 'universities change lives, over generations, that this is important, honourable work, and that it is important to do it well, to be bold, not reckless, to be intentional and resolute, ensuring no one is left behind.'* It was unusual for me, as chancellor, to be working with a vice chancellor who had both academic and business credentials. Raftery was fond of saying 'we should begin with the end in mind'. The 'end', which he identified and which we worked on together, was to help the university towards sustained improvement in benchmarked indicators of educational quality and financial resilience. In short, these were the themes that marked our time working together.

Throughout his time as interim VC, he would visit me regularly in London and to this day, we speak weekly on the phone. Our Friday phone conversations take place as he is having his mid-morning coffee break in Cambridge, and I, my afternoon tea in London. In our London meetings, he would tell me about the progress he was making with the university and, as he would often say, seek a 'sanity check' as he tested ideas for the future and enable me, as university chancellor, to use my contacts and advocacy to help where possible. In that intense year of 2023, my twenty-fifth as chancellor, we were able to draw a line under the events of the previous few years, stabilize the organization, ensure continuity of services to students and community, create ambitious yet achievable

---

* *Wolverhampton Express and Star*, 24 February 2023.

plans for the future, and see early results from a major change in organizational culture and communications.

Of course, 2023 was important in another aspect, as personal as it was professional. On 22 September, the university hosted a dual celebration for the then first lady of Sri Lanka, Maithree Wickremasinghe, on the award of her honorary professorship and to mark the twenty-fifth of my chancellorship, making me the longest serving chancellor at a British university. Professor Wickremasinghe was accompanied that day by her husband, then President of Sri Lanka.

Here are the welcome remarks on 22 September 2023 by vice chancellor, Professor John Raftery, on the occasion of the twenty-fifth anniversary of Lord Paul's chancellorship at the University of Wolverhampton, in the presence of the President of Sri Lanka, Ranil Wickremesinghe:

> Your Excellency and First Lady, Professor Wickremesinghe, Lord Paul, High Commissioner Sirisena, Lord Mayor, honoured guests, you are all warmly welcomed to our university today as we mark both the award of an honorary professorship to Dr Maithree Wickremesinghe, First Lady of Sri Lanka, and the twenty-fifth year of the chancellorship of Lord Swraj Paul of Marylebone.
>
> We will proceed to the convocation, following this lunch, where we will hear an extended, formal encomium recognizing the achievements, dedication and academic work of Professor Maithree Wickremesinghe, who will be recognized today with the award of honorary professor. The students, staff and I are also looking forward to hearing Professor Wickremesinghe's remarks to the university community.

So let me turn now to my friend and chancellor of the university, Lord Swraj Paul of Marylebone. We are assembled here today to mark the twenty-fifth year of Lord Paul's chancellorship, making him the longest serving chancellor of a British university. But Lord Paul has been much more than that. Uniquely in British higher education, he has been advocate, friend, benefactor as well as chancellor to this university for more than a quarter of a century. As he himself put it earlier this year, 'Chancellor for twenty-five years and still going', the exact words which are inscribed on the celebration pen you will each find in front of you.

For the mathematically inclined, Lord Paul's chancellorship covers one-eighth of the total life of this 200-year-old institution. Lord Paul's generous donation of £1M this year brings his philanthropic support to our community to a symmetrical £2.5M over the last twenty-five years. Lord Paul is by far the university's most generous benefactor, with no other individual coming close to the levels of his support.

You do not court publicity and I am aware that this will embarrass you, Lord Paul, but I hope you will forgive me for sharing, in a spirit of gratitude, with our guests today, just a small selection of the work which has been supported by your philanthropy.

Since 2016, when we opened Lord Swraj Paul building, home of the Wolverhampton Business School, more than 8000 students have graduated with degrees in business studies. A further 2500 MBA graduates have benefited from the Caparo Executive Development Suite. The restored Chancellor's Hall has enabled the university to host hundreds of events, including the launch of the Centre for Sikh and Panjabi Studies, the Annual Alumni Awards and the Annual Women in Business Conference. Your donations to the employability fund have, over the past three years alone, enabled sixty students to undertake international and domestic work placements to support their career paths.

The Lord Paul Enterprise Fund has awarded £52,000 to student business start-ups in the last two years, including Motorsport 3D, which manufactures components for motorsport using ALM techniques, and SymbioTex, which uses biodegradable seaweed to manufacture consumables for the health industry. The Lord Paul Research Fund has funded fourteen PhDs across diverse projects recently, including antimicrobial biomaterials for pandemic preparedness and cyber security.

In conclusion, let me turn to our plans for your generous gift pledge totalling £1Million from the Aruna and Ambika Paul Foundation. This gift is being acknowledged through the naming of the award-winning Lady Aruna Swraj Paul building at the Springfield Campus. Our intention is to use the funds to support both undergraduate and research students. Most importantly, as we continue to experience unprecedented global change, this generous gift will enable the university, where appropriate, to respond in an agile way to meet crisis relief and emergent (currently unknown) needs in support of our students.

When Raftery arrived, he had said his overarching objective was to leave the institution in better shape than he found it. As 2023 came to a close, it was clear to me from my networks that this was indeed the case. The university had a perceptibly increased sense of confidence, clear-eyed plans for the future and a new permanent appointment as vice chancellor, Professor Ebrahim Adia. Professor Ebrahim Adia joined the University of Wolverhampton as vice chancellor on 1 October 2023.

Formerly pro vice chancellor (academic leadership) at the University of Central Lancashire, Ebrahim has a national and international profile and brings to the role a wealth of experience, serving as chair and member of several high-profile boards.

Born and raised in Bolton, UK, he was the first in his family, and one of the few from his school, to attend university, which has helped to shape his views on the role of higher education. As a result, Ebrahim has striven in both his professional and personal life to create opportunity. Under his leadership, I am confident the university will prosper. I look forward to working with Ebrahim and continuing my close association with the university for the foreseeable future.

The Installation of
the First Pro Chancellor of
Thames Valley University

29 June 1998

Thames Valley University installation, 1998

Presenting Wolverhampton University honorary degree to N. Ram, editor-in-chief, *The Hindu*, with Vice Chancellor Caroline Gipps, May 2011

Outside the Lord Swraj Paul Building, Wolverhampton University

University of Wolverhampton

Programme

Friday 7th February 2003

To commemorate the
Official Opening of the Millennium City Building

by the

Rt Hon Gordon Brown MP
Chancellor of the Exchequer

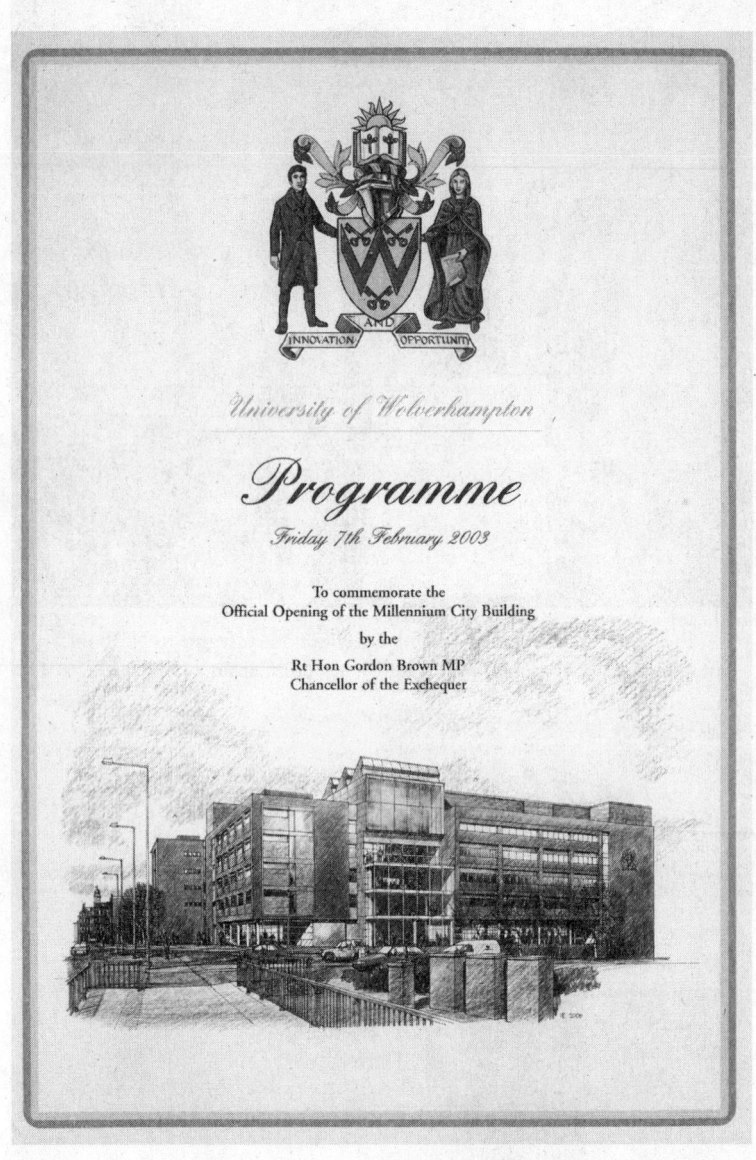

Opening of Wolverhampton University Millennium Building

My portrait as the first chancellor of the University of Westminster, with Vice Chancellor Geoffrey Petts, July 2010

My brother Stya receiving an honorary degree from Thames Valley University

Me with Sarah Brown receiving her honorary degree at Wolverhampton University, and Vice Chancellor Caroline Gipps, September 2007

Me with Gordon Brown, chancellor of the exchequer, at my Westminster University installation ceremony, 9 October 2006

Me with Dr Geoffrey Copland, Vice Chancellor and Terry Wright, Chairman, Court of Governors at my installation as the first chancellor of Westminster University, 2006

Me with children of Doaba Primary School, Jalandhar, 2000

The Installation of Lord Paul of Marylebone

as

Chancellor

of the

University of Wolverhampton

on

Tuesday, 9th May 2000

in

The Collegiate Church of St Peter, Wolverhampton

Installation as chancellor of Wolverhampton University, 2000

Arun Jaitley receiving an honorary degree from Wolverhampton University, May 2011

Angad Paul Building inauguration, Wolverhampton University

10

Other Activities Including Government Appointments

After receiving my peerage in 1986 and following the start of Tony Blair's new Labour government in 1997, I was appointed Ambassador for British Business (ABB) by Robin Cook, who was the foreign secretary in the Blair government. This appointment carried Cabinet rank. My brief was that whenever I travelled on business, I should allocate an extra day during my trip to promote British trade, industry, exports and investment.

It enabled me to meet a great many of our own ambassadors and high commissioners along with their counterparts. I addressed nearly 100 meetings and symposiums and the list of countries, ambassadors and high commissioners I met are given in the appendix, together with a selection of speeches I made.

Some of the highlights were visiting Dubai and Abu Dhabi, where I stayed at the Royal Palace and visited the President. Then Nepal, where I was invited to stay with the Indian ambassador, but the British ambassador insisted that he was duty-bound to be my host, so I had to stay one night with each. While there, I also met the King of Nepal, Birendra, who, with his brother Prince Gyanendra, was keen for me to do something to help the Central Zoo at Kathmandu. I liaised with the Zoological Society of London in its work to upgrade the Central Zoo, to educate visitors about the uniqueness and appeal of Nepal's native species and the opportunity to conserve them. The King was grateful for my interest and input.

The following year, I met Their Majesties the King and Queen of Norway at a dinner held in honour of my visit by the British ambassador.

Another initiative of Foreign Secretary Robin Cook was to establish the India-UK Round Table (IUKRT) in April 2000. With his counterpart, Indian Foreign Minister Jaswant Singh, the remit was to examine all avenues for ways to regenerate and strengthen the bilateral relationship. It consisted of thirty individuals drawn from different backgrounds and I was called upon to be the UK co-chair while K.C. Pant, one-time Indian defence minister and chairman of the Tenth Finance Commission, headed the India side. He was succeeded by Hamid Ansari, India's vice president. The round table has debated the importance of IT and biotechnology and put forward proposals for collaboration in research in these areas. Culture, tourism, air services, biodiversity, cultural and educational exchanges, and legal services are among the many other issues that have been discussed.

The efforts of the round table were acknowledged in the New Delhi Declaration of 6 January 2002, signed by the two prime ministers. The bilateral relationship was upgraded to a strategic partnership during a meeting of Prime Minister Manmohan Singh and Prime Minister Tony Blair in London in September 2004. In a joint declaration, it was agreed that the two countries would intensify cooperation in civil nuclear energy, space, defence, combating terrorism, economic ties, science and technology, education and culture. A number of summit meetings were held after the strategic partnership in 2004. UK Prime Minister Tony Blair visited India in September 2005, Indian Premier Manmohan Singh visited UK in October 2006 and UK Prime Minister Gordon Brown visited India in January 2008. It was during Gordon Brown's visit in 2008 that he and Sarah visited the Caparo India plants.

In 1999, I was approached by the UK Department of Trade and Industry to join the Industrial Development Advisory Board for a period of six years. The board advises the secretary of state and ministers on applications from companies proposing to start capital investment projects as it is important that public funds for supporting industry are allocated appropriately and deliver value for money. Board members include those who, in the opinion of the secretary of state, have wide experience of, and have shown capacity in, industry, banking, accounting and finance.

When Ken Livingstone became mayor of London in 2000, he approached me to join the Board of the London Development Agency (LDA), the executive body of the Greater London Authority, responsible for London's economic development and regeneration.

Three years on, I became a board member of London 2012, the group formed to bid for the London Olympics which, as everyone knows, successfully won the bid for the Olympic and Paralympic Games to be held in London in 2012.

At the time, there was great opposition to the 2012 Games being held in London, but the LDA under Mayor

Ken Livingstone worked hard to overcome this and had the determination to see it through.

And two years later, I was asked to chair the London Olympics Delivery Committee, which was responsible for delivering the land and infrastructure for the London 2012 Olympic Games. This huge project was completed on time and on budget. As the then Minister for Sport, Tessa Jowell, said, 'Lord Paul, your leadership, dedication, energy and imagination as a member of the London 2012 board was absolutely crucial to its success.'

In 2002, Sarah Brown founded the charity PiggybankKids with the initial aim of supporting scientific and community research to help the most vulnerable children get the best start in life. She asked me to chair this, which I was pleased to do. We established the Jennifer Brown Research Laboratory at the University of Edinburgh in 2004. It launched with a small team of scientists and clinical experts from the New Royal Infirmary Edinburgh and four research fellows—all women—to lead the way in bringing obstetric and neonatal work together in one lab. I remained as chairman until 2015 after the charity changed its name to *Theirworld*. In addition to continuing its core work, it now also acts as a global initiative to recognize the importance of supporting quality education and learning for children and young adults worldwide.

In 2004, I was asked to join the Council of the Royal Albert Hall for a period of five years. This is the charitable body that is ultimately responsible for the Hall, its assets and activities. The council meets five times a year and I thoroughly enjoyed my involvement with this world-famous bastion of the arts.

In the course of my lifetime, I have received a number of awards and honours, including fifteen honorary degrees from universities in the UK, the US, India, Russia and Switzerland. In 1983, the Government of India conferred upon me the Padma Bhushan, making me the first British citizen to be given the honour. In 1989, I received the Corporate Leadership Award from the Massachusetts Institute of Technology. The same year, I received the Bharat Gaurav Award from the Indian Merchants Chamber, Mumbai. The Freedom of the City of London was granted to me in 1998, as was the Lifetime Achievement Award from Asian Business Awards. In 1995, I received the Donald C. Burnham Manufacturing Management Award, Society of Manufacturing Engineers in the US. The first Asian of the Year Award, Asian Who's Who, was given to me in 1987 and the Asian Woman Magazine Lifetime Achievement Award was conferred in 2008. PowerBrands Hall of Fame nominated me Global Indian of the Year 2011.

I was chosen as the 'International Indian of Decade' for outstanding achievements in the fields of industry, education and philanthropy on the occasion of the twentieth anniversary of the publication of *India Link International*, a monthly magazine, on 15 November 2013. In 2014, I was presented with a Lifetime Achievement Award by the Black Country Asian Business Association for 'outstanding achievements in the fields of industry, education and philanthropy'. In the same year, I received another Lifetime Achievement Award in recognition of my promotion of India-UK educational ties from the Global Skill Tree Consortium, an India-based think tank, which is engaged in promoting India as a global hub of international education through its 'Great Place to Study— India' programme.

In July 2014, I was given the 'International Icon of the Decade Award' by the World Consulting Research

Corporation at its Global Indian Excellence Summit in London, in recognition of my 'outstanding achievements in the fields of manufacturing, education and philanthropy'. In April 2018, I received two awards during a trip to India: IOD Golden Peacock Award for Lifetime Achievement in Business Leadership and Global Punjabi Society Lifetime Achievement Award. In May that year, I was given the WCRC International Iconic Leader Award for Lifetime Achievement in the UK and Asia Business Awards ceremony in London. In October 2018, I was awarded the Mahatma Gandhi Honour by the NRI Institute at its thirtieth anniversary celebrations. In June 2018, I was awarded the prestigious Honorary Fellowship by the Zoological Society. In June 2016, I was presented with the keys to the City of St Louis and in August 2020, Lady Paul and I were made members of the MIT Charter Society in recognition of our philanthropic commitment to MIT.

I was also proud to receive the Mother Teresa International Award in 2019 for outstanding achievement in the field of social work.

Politics and Leaders

I was privileged to meet all the prime ministers of India, but one of my greatest memories was meeting Mahatma Gandhi, who came to lunch at our house in Jalandhar in 1942 when my eldest brother, Stya, was arrested and jailed by the British because of his activities with the freedom fighters. I was only eleven years old, but the sheer force of the Mahatma's personality affected me deeply.

I later met Pandit Jawaharlal Nehru, India's first prime minister following Independence in 1947, when I was at MIT in the US and its then president, James Killian, held a reception in Nehru's honour. Nehru's sister Vijaya Lakshmi Pandit accompanied him on his trip to Boston, since she was then the Indian ambassador to the United States.

When Nehru died in 1964, he was succeeded by Lal Bahadur Shastri, an able politician, who signed the Tashkent Agreement with the President of Pakistan, Ayub Khan, to end the second Indo-Pakistan War over Kashmir. He died only two years into his term of office and was succeeded by Gulzarilal Nanda, who performed a caretaker role until the landslide election victory of Mrs Indira Gandhi in 1966.

I have written earlier in this book about Mrs Gandhi and her remarkable leadership. Also, her premature death at the hands of her Sikh bodyguards in 1984. She was a great statesman and India's greatest prime minister, who moved the country towards a new era and the twenty-first century. She helped to establish Bangladesh and was well-received on the world stage. She forged an enduring friendship with Britain, particularly with Prime Minister Margaret Thatcher. I met Mrs Gandhi on numerous occasions and when I was chairman of the Indo-British Association, we held a dinner in London in her honour, attended by both prime ministers.

Her son, Rajiv Gandhi, who succeeded her in 1984, was also assassinated by terrorists in 1989, but alas, was unable to replicate his mother's political prowess or carry on her legacy.

P.V. Narasimha Rao I met and corresponded with several times and he was a very good prime minister during his five-year term. However, I had rather more to do with Atal Bihari Vajpayee, who was in power during the same time I was co-chair of the India-UK Round Table. He tried to bring India on to the world stage and I met him on various occasions with

Robin Cook, UK Foreign Secretary, to discuss Indo-British relations, which were burgeoning under the two governments at that time.

There is no doubt in my mind that India's brightest stars were Pandit Nehru and Mrs Gandhi. Their legacy is now being enhanced by another star, Narendra Modi, who has brought glory back to India, and may God bless him with a long and fruitful life. He is a champion of the working man and is committed to making life better for the ordinary people of India by revitalizing the economy and reforming labour laws. His greatest challenge has been in eradicating the corruption that has held India back for so long. It is something that Mrs Gandhi worked hard to do but her efforts were sabotaged, and she lost her first premiership through the machinations of various industrialists and ministers, whose bribery of government officials was endemic.

Presidents of India

I enjoyed good relations with most Presidents of India. Rajendra Prasad, the first President, I met while I was still working and living in India. He served with distinction for twelve years and was succeeded by S. Radhakrishnan for the next five years and Zakir Husain for a short two-year term. V.V. Giri, Fakhruddin Ali Ahmed, B.D. Jatti and Neelam Sanjiva Reddy all made good contributions.

In 1984, I received the Padma Bhushan from President Giani Zail Singh. He was a wonderful person, very respectful, and treated me like a younger brother. Like my brother Stya, he had also been a member of the Freedom Party during the days of the Raj and was injured when British troops rolled him under a cart.

When HM the Queen and the Duke of Edinburgh visited Delhi in 1983, President Singh mentioned to Prince Philip that 'Swraj is our gift to Britain,' which was a heart-warming moment.

Zail Singh was succeeded by Ramaswamy Venkataraman, a former finance minister and very good President. Venkataraman served as President of India starting in 1987, where he worked with four prime ministers, and appointed three of them—V.P. Singh, Chandra Shekhar and P.V. Narasimha Rao—during his five-year term, which saw the advent of coalition politics in India. His successor S.D. Sharma was the only other Indian President in twentieth century to work with four prime ministers and appoint three of them. K.R. Narayanan, the first Dalit to be elected President, hosted Queen Elizabeth II during her 1997 state visit to mark India's golden jubilee of independence.

Abdul Kalam, whom I met often while co-chairing the India-UK Round Table, was a great President and an extremely nice person. A distinguished scientist, he mainly developed India's nuclear programme and contributed greatly to its space exploration programme too. While his space endeavours were remarkable, Dr Kalam's most enduring legacy is his contributions to India's defence capabilities. Spearheading the Integrated Guided Missile Development Programme (IGMDP), he propelled India's ballistic missile technology to new heights. Widely referred to as the 'People's President', he returned to his civilian life of education, writing and public service after a single term. He was a recipient of several prestigious awards, including the Bharat Ratna, India's highest civilian honour. I was proud and pleased to award him with an honorary degree from the University of Wolverhampton, where I am chancellor.

Pranab Mukherjee, who took over from Pratibha Patil (India's first woman President) in 2012, was a remarkable President who had already done an excellent job for India in his roles as foreign minister and finance minister. A great supporter of Indira Gandhi throughout her life, he was also a great friend to me and someone who made an outstanding contribution to the nation.

Other good friends whom I met in the Government of India were Arun Nehru, the home minister and Arun Jaitley, home minister and finance minister who, in addition to being great friends, were also extremely hard-working and impressive modernizers for India. Arun Jaitley's early demise was a great shock to me, and I still miss his friendship and wise counsel.

Soon after establishing the Caparo Group, I decided to form the family's own charitable organization, the Ambika Paul Foundation, which now operates as the Ambika and Aruna Paul Foundation. Through the foundation, we have supported many educational projects around the world, most of which I have mentioned in this book, but substantial donations have also been made to the Prime Minister of India's Relief Fund, the President of Pakistan Relief Fund and the Sri Lanka Relief Fund.

With the Duchess of Edinburgh at London Zoo, 2022

With Prime Minister Narendra Modi

With Pranab Mukherjee and Arun Jaitley, May 2011

With Pranab Mukherjee, 2018

With N. Ram, editor-in-chief, *The Hindu*, at their offices, examining the special tribute to Mahatma Gandhi, on *The Hindu's* 125th anniversary

With Labour Party leaders Neil Kinnock, James Callaghan and John Smith

With K.C. Pant as co-chairmen of the India-UK Round Table (IUKRT) and Buddhadeb Bhattacharjee, CM of West Bengal, at the IUKRT 7th meeting, Kolkata, January 2004

With Foreign Secretary Robin Cook at the India-UK Round Table

With Gordon Brown, London Zoo, 3 July 2017

Addressing CII lunch,
Chennai, January 2004

Lady Paul and me with HRH Princess Anne at the Indian YMCA in London

Inaugural meeting of the India-UK Round Table

Hasim Abdul Halim, speaker, West Bengal, me, Lord Bhatia and
Ashok Kumar, MP, of the UK Commonwealth Parliamentary Association at
Bengal Legislative Assembly, April 2008

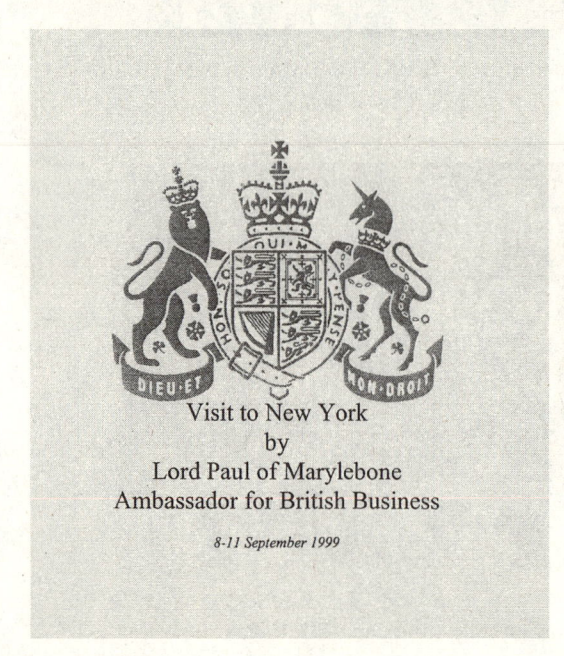

Ambassador for British Business programme

Visit to New York
by
Lord Paul of Marylebone
Ambassador for British Business

8-11 September 1999

The Sunday Telegraph

NOVEMBER 23 1997

Business elite to promote Britain on trips abroad

by DAVID WASTELL

ROBIN Cook, the Foreign Secretary, is recruiting a group of successful business leaders to act as unpaid "ambassadors" for Britain while travelling abroad.

But Richard Branson, the Virgin chief who 10 days ago criticised the Government for its decision to exempt Formula One racing from its ban on tobacco sponsorship of sport, is absent from the list of 30 high-flyers who have been approached by the Foreign Office to take part.

Among those who have agreed to assist Mr Cook's drive to promote business links with Britain is Sir Colin Marshall, the chairman of British Airways, which is in bitter competition with Virgin. One senior figure within Virgin said: "If Marshall is involved that may explain why we are not."

Others who have accepted the invitation include John Brown, the chief executive of BP; Sir Iain Vallance, the chairman of BT; Anita Roddick, of The Body Shop; Paul Smith, the men's fashion designer; and Lord Paul, the industrialist who was ennobled at Tony Blair's suggestion last year.

Under Mr Cook's plan, the "ambassadors" will be asked to help to promote the benefits of doing business with Britain by allowing extra time during overseas trips for speeches, dinners and lobbying government ministers.

Although they will be unpaid, the Foreign Office will pick up the bill for extra travel, meals and accommodation involved in assisting the drive for exports and for inward investment.

A spokesman for the Foreign Secretary said: "We will be asking them to give up half a day or even a day of their time to promote trade with Britain and British companies generally."

The move reflects a pledge by Labour to inject more practical business experience into the Foreign Office's activities. It follows the announcement in July of a system of short-term attachments by senior businessmen from 15 companies to assist British embassies.

A spokesman for Mr Branson said he already worked hard to promote Britain. "He is one of the few British businessmen of the moment to have really made a mark in the Japanese and American markets. He has always thought that British businesses should get out and sing more widely overseas."

Ambassador for British Business announcement

Addressing a press conference at British High Commission, Delhi,
October 2002

11

Angad

In early 1996, I handed over much of the day-to-day running of Caparo to my sons. Twins Ambar and Akash became chief executives of Caparo Industries, and my younger son Angad was appointed group director, with me continuing as chairman with a broad policy-making portfolio. This gave me freedom to pursue other interests while permitting me to participate in planning Caparo's future.

Angad, unlike my other children, was born in London. I remember how in 1978, when he was eight years old, he came running to me, visibly upset, to ask, 'Will we have to leave London?' He told me he had just heard Margaret Thatcher, then Conservative Party leader but before she was elected prime minister, say something to the effect that there was the prospect of an end to immigration. I was sufficiently upset by the reaction of my British-born, British-educated son to her statement that I arranged a meeting with Mrs Thatcher because I felt very strongly that an eight-year-old boy should have been hurt by her words. Mrs Thatcher was very gracious. I said to her, 'Madam, I'm not looking for anything' but I told her about Angad and said, 'I feel as a person from India living here, I don't think Britain can be the kind of country that is talking about an end to immigration.' She assured me that she had heard my concerns, and the following year, as prime minister, invited me to the prime minister's country residence at Chequers as a gesture of further assurance.

I sent my sons to Harrow School partly because Winston Churchill and Jawaharlal Nehru had studied there. My sons, however, evolved their own styles of management and also had varying plans for their and the group's future. This is reality and a father cannot expect the next generation to duplicate his path. To me, it was enough if they shared the values that inspired me to create Caparo.

I was disillusioned with India after the DCM-Escorts affair and it was Angad who comforted me by saying, 'I know you love India, but that experience frustrated you. Let me go there.' He was fascinated by India and its prospects.

He took charge of Caparo's joint venture with Maruti to manufacture automobile components in Gurgaon near Delhi, which had started in 1994. Soon, he was opening more plants as the demand for vendors grew rapidly in a fast-expanding car-making environment in India. I was naturally thrilled. As Caparo developed its component production in India—adding General Motors, Honda, Mazda and Leyland to its list of Indian joint ventures—Angad began to talk of expanding the company's interests into brakes, chassis, drivetrains, transmissions and, not least, automotive research and development. Caparo's future, for Angad, lay not in metal bashing, but in providing the know-how for high-tech.

When Angad took over the Caparo reins, it was essentially a manufacturer of steel products and engineered products. By 2007, it was more sub-assembly and systems and design engineering with a greater brand recognition. Steel plants were very twentieth century. Angad saw Caparo's future in innovation and expertise.

I have always maintained that Angad was the most brilliant child in the family. He excelled academically at Harrow, played rugby and acquired a deep appreciation of music; he even played the drums. He then graduated in economics and media arts and sciences from the Massachusetts Institute of Technology, my alma mater. He predictably powered Caparo to further growth. There is no better feeling than having your children outperform you; Angad did well. The company expanded exponentially in England, Europe, the United States and India in steel products manufacturing and engineering.

Angad was enterprising and unorthodox. He loved business and was enthusiastic about it. At MIT, he befriended Sir Richard Attenborough, the director of the Oscar-winning film *Gandhi*, who then introduced him to the filmmaker Guy Ritchie. In 1998, Angad part-funded and was executive producer of Ritchie's feature film *Lock, Stock and Two Smoking Barrels*, which became a significant commercial and critical success. It cost £860,000 and recovered £18.5 million at the box office. The sequel *Snatch* in 2000, another crime comedy, grossed £55 million. His other film credits include *The Liability* (executive producer, 2013); *Truth or Dare* (executive producer, 2012); *Best Laid Plans* (executive producer, 2012); *The Tournament* (associate producer, 2010); *Lesbian Vampire Killers* (co-producer, 2009); *Pledge This!* (executive producer, 2006); *School for Seduction* (associate producer, 2004); *Pasty*

Faces (executive producer, 2001); and *Bombay Boys* (associate producer, 1998).

At the time of the premiere of *Lock, Stock*, I hadn't visited a cinema for perhaps twenty-five years. I told Angad I would go to watch it only to see his name on the screen. I must admit it had some very bad language. But then I am a conservative in certain respects. I recognized very few of the celebrities who attended the show. But several came up to me to say, 'I owe my career to Angad.' That was uplifting. We continue to get royalties from this investment.

Angad also set up the television channel *Film24* before selling it to Sony Pictures in 2010. And he co-founded the exclusive London nightclubs Chinawhite and Aura.

Most innovatively, under the banner of Caparo Vehicle Technologies, he backed the development and manufacture of Caparo T1, a remarkable mid-engine, rear-wheel drive sports car. He worked with design director Ben Scott-Geddes and engineering director Graham Halstead, who were previously involved in the construction of McLaren F1. The Caparo T1 was motivated by the Formula One concept but was planned to be a road-legal racer. It was initially priced at £211,000 and comprised 80 per cent Caparo components. It is an illustration and showcase of Caparo's strong design engineering capabilities.

The exterior of the T1 closely resembles a Formula One car. It has an aerodynamic carbon fibre low-drag body. The interior is a two-seat configuration, where the passenger seat is set slightly back from the driver's seat, allowing the seats to be placed closer together, thereby reducing the overall width of the vehicle. It has a head protection system and six-point harnesses for the driver and passenger. The dashboard is multifunctional, with race data logging and speed sensors for traction control and launch control.

The T1 has an estimated maximum speed of 205 miles per hour on a low downforce set-up. From a standing start, it is calculated to achieve 0-62 mph under 2.5 seconds and 99 mph in 4.9 seconds, depending on the tyre set-up. This easily broke the *Top Gear* circuit record. During this test, Jeremy Clarkson, the programme's presenter, reportedly screamed, 'God Almighty, you can forget Ferrari Enzos, you can forget Koenigseggs; this is a different league!'

The car is still being sold to select customers by the Norfolk-based Stratton Motor Company (SMC). Unfortunately, Angad didn't get a chance to push the project further. Roger Bennington, managing director of SMC, remarks, 'Angad was the instigator of building the Caparo T1. It was his ambition and his baby.'

Angad then had the idea that the lightweight composite amalgamation that constituted the car could have profitable spin-offs in India in completely different spheres. He realized that the metal would be applicable in constructing composite housing, which was quicker to produce, cheaper to erect and stronger than conventional building materials. It would also be appropriate in the making of city buses.

Following the financial crisis in 2008 and the downturn in 2013 in India, Angad initiated, through Caparo India, a number of projects to address growing needs, particularly in India's rural areas.

The company's in-house R&D team designed the manufacture of high-quality battery-operated electronic autos (e-rickshaws) in India under the aegis of a subsidiary company, Caparo AT Autotech Limited, to provide an energy-efficient, reliable and affordable means of transport to be used in big urban centres and as an alternate means of transport in smaller towns and the countryside.

Battery-operated cycles can revolutionize urban transportation by having lower operating costs and nil emissions, which are environmentally desirable. An essential feature of these cycles is a smaller battery size that can be charged via solar panels. Multiple usage includes short journeys, educational institutions and health centres.

Human waste disposal in high altitudes, railways, ships, big cities, mines and remote areas is increasingly an endemic problem in India. Caparo set up a facility to manufacture bio digesters for environment-friendly toilets, a product conceptualized and endorsed by the Government of India to revolutionize waste management techniques by providing completely sludge-free removal of human waste in a portable and highly durable manner. Bio digesters can also be used for power generation, with the methane gas produced used as an input in alternative energy generation.

To cater to India's increasing demand, Angad's plan was to offer affordable housing solutions. Caparo planned to ensure optimization of technology to provide high-quality, affordable housing to the masses. Houses use composite and bamboo base for earthquake resistance with structural and dimensional stability, which greatly contribute to uplifting the lifestyles of the underprivileged sections of society while providing an opportunity for aesthetic growth of the surrounding areas.

Angad and I made many visits to the Indian plants from 2005 to 2015 and we welcomed many distinguished guests there, including Prince Andrew, Sir Mervyn King (now Lord King), Governor of the Bank of England, Sarah and Gordon Brown (when he was UK prime minister) and Robin Cook.

In 2009, Angad began a large-scale agriculture entity across the developing world devoted to helping restore the food balance by focusing on renewable agricultural land banks to plant staple food crops—sustainable projects in Sierra Leone, collectively supported local economies, feeding upwards of 20,00,000 people in West and sub-Saharan Africa while employing over 5000 skilled and unskilled labourers.

Few people know that Angad also co-founded and was chairman of Established and Sons, which provided architecture in the form of reconstructing thatched cottages, carbon-neutral concrete and giant sloping roofs, among other services, plus interior and furniture design. The firm quickly reached a turnover of £1 billion.

In 2012, Accles and Pollock, a division of Caparo, provided tube-work and engineering expertise to CERN (the European Organization for Nuclear Research) for the Large Hadron Collider, the particle accelerator that identified the Higgs Boson particle (the first word comes from British physicist Professor Peter Higgs and the second is an adaptation of the surname of Indian physicist Professor Satyendra Nath Bose) that year.

He entered the wind energy sector in India, where he co-founded and was a significant shareholder of Caparo Energy (now named Mytrah Energy). Mytrah Energy (India) Pvt. Ltd has the largest wind data bank in India, being the only independent power producer that has over 200 wind masts across the country. It is now owned by Ravi Shankar Kailas.

He also created and became chairman of Caparo Financial Solutions Ltd, an Indian non-deposit-taking financial services entity lending to small companies and providing advisory services to both small and large companies.

He further consolidated Caparo's steel operations in the US, where he spotted and pursued an opportunity to redevelop St Louis's city centre. To start with, in partnership with Steve Smith of the Lawrence Group, he identified an empty multistoreyed building, formerly the Missouri Theatre, built in 1927, in the city's Grand Center Arts District, a cultural complex with the second largest movie theatre in America. He converted this into a boutique property now known as the Angad Arts Hotel. There is a separate chapter on the redevelopment of St Louis in this book.

There was always a caring side to Angad. The delivery of his wife Michelle Bonn's first baby was a difficult one at St Mary's Hospital in Paddington. Following this, he donated new incubators for the entire ward of the hospital. The old ones, still in good working order, were sent to Ghana at the request of the nurses. Angad had married Michelle, a media lawyer, in 2004. It did not matter that he was Hindu and her parents were Jewish. They have a daughter, Amalia, and a son, Arki.

We had a marvellous celebration of their wedding. It began with a civil ceremony at the Landmark Hotel on Marylebone Road; then came a larger party at the London Zoo, followed by a series of parties in India, including tea with the President of India, A.P.J. Abdul Kalam, then at the Udaipur Maharaja's palace and finally the British high commissioner's residence in Delhi. A few months later, I held another reception to celebrate the union at the historic Lancaster House, a nineteenth-century British government mansion in London's St James district bordering Green Park. Among the speakers were my good friends Gordon Brown and Robin Cook.

Angad was also patron of an education charity, SHINE, alongside David Beckham, Lord O'Neill and Sarah Brown.

SHINE was founded in 1999 and its mission is to support additional educational initiatives that encourage children and young people to raise their achievement levels.

He was open-hearted, helping to support charities as far away as Sierra Leone and Kenya, and was always willing to help family and friends who needed any kind of assistance.

His public appointments included being a non-executive director (from April 2008 to September 2012) of the Imperial College Healthcare NHS Trust; a member of the advisory panel of the Imperial College Department of Materials; a member of the Saudi British Joint Business Council; and adviser to the UK-India Business Council.

In 2015, the Paul family's net worth was around £2.2 billion. The Caparo Group had an annual turnover of £1.5 billion. We had also entered financial services in India with a view to ultimately establishing a bank. But after the collapse in steel prices, the business climate for British manufacturers like us was extremely stressed.

Caparo Holdings went into administration in October 2015. The catastrophe of Angad's death occurred the following month. He was only forty-five. I had no inkling he could commit suicide, neither did his wife Michelle.

His public presentations at seminars as late as 2015 were lucid and relaxed. He confidently and knowledgeably spoke about the challenges facing business around the world after the 2008 global meltdown.

In 2004, Caparo profited from China's demand for steel products. But after only two years, the country had become a net exporter of steel. Subsequently, by 2014, the massive investment in its infrastructure was slowing down, thereby creating a surplus of steel stocks. To offload these, China began dumping its excess of metal pipes, tubes and sheets on the overseas market at a cut-throat price. The European Union's Trade Commissioner Cecilia Malmstrom described this as 'unfair competition from artificially cheap exports' and pledged not to allow it. But action did not immediately match words.

As Angad pointed out to the press at the time, the situation in Britain was compounded by a strong pound. Forty per cent of Britain's steel exports were to the EU. I also believe it was more the value of the pound than Chinese dumping that hit Caparo UK. The strength of the pound meant we couldn't sell our products abroad competitively.

Indeed, the combined impact of the two negatives inflicted widespread misery on the British steel industry across the board. The biggest producer, Tata Steel UK, laid off hundreds of workers in England and Wales and mothballed plants in Scotland.

The banks were not interested in the issues that caused the unprecedented stress. They panicked. They wanted their money back forthwith. One of our executives presented restructuring options to Caparo's board but we didn't find any of these to be workable. We had already staked £10 million in Caparo UK, pegged to shares in Caparo's enterprise in India. Now the lenders, Barclays Bank and Royal Bank of Scotland, wanted Ambika House, the family's private residence in Portland Place, and Caparo's office building on Baker Street to be provided as collateral.

Needless to say, we have a deep and abiding attachment to Ambika House, named after my daughter who tragically left us as a child, shattering our lives. I asked the banks, 'When have I ever defaulted on a loan with you?' But they were in no mood to listen. Thus, while our businesses in the United States and India were unaffected, Caparo UK went into administration on 19 October 2015.

It was a devastating time for me for I had painstakingly built the company brick by brick and nurtured it over forty-seven years. It was no less crushing than losing an offspring. And it was made more painful when the business, rather strangely and speedily, ended up in the hands of an ill-equipped entity after it was snatched from our control.

Angad was distraught when Caparo UK went into administration. He felt it was the wrong outcome and agonized over his helplessness to avert the situation. He took the blow very personally, thinking people would say he was responsible.

At the inquest following his death, Michelle told the coroner that he had a history of depression, for which he had been prescribed medication, but had never expressed suicidal thoughts to her.

I was aware he took medication but never imagined his condition was a matter of exceptional concern. Angad would in fact make light of it. At first, there were no noticeable after-effects of withdrawing from his treatment.

He became fascinated by the Amazon forest and its tribes. He visited the area in 2010 and told everyone he met about his moving experience, which, as well as helping the indigenous people, was intended to be beneficial in a more holistic approach to help his mental processes. He came back full of praise for the region and its way of life. In September 2015, he returned to the region to reignite the spiritual connection. But he came home disillusioned. He was a sensitive soul. He was disappointed that the indigenous people had become commercialized and were losing their identity.

About his earlier self, Michelle said, 'He was the happiest person I ever knew.' But after the second Amazon trip, Angad told her it had 'all gone wrong' and asked what they could do.

In October 2015, Angad admitted himself into Capio Nightingale Hospital, where he was prescribed new medicines. I went to see him there and was deeply distressed. He was, however, discharged after about twelve days when he was assessed as not being a suicide risk. But he was soon perturbed by the loss of jobs at Caparo when he returned to the office. In hindsight, I wonder if he should have stayed longer at the hospital.

By early November, Angad was once more not feeling too well. So Dr Elza Eapen, the specialist at Capio, examined him on 5 November. She found no evidence he was actively considering suicide. In fact, he told her he could not consider this because of the effect it would have on his wife and children. Dr Eapen later told the coroner Dr Shirley Radcliffe, 'I wouldn't have let him leave my office if that was the case.'

On the morning of 8 November, Angad told Michelle he wanted to be left alone. Michelle told him that was not going to happen. However, she stepped out of the building for a coffee, leaving him and the children in their penthouse flat on the top storey of Ambika House.

Angad would generally come down to the flat Aruna and I occupied on one of the lower floors to see us in the morning. On this day, he didn't make an appearance. So I went upstairs to inquire about him. Michelle was back, but neither she nor I could find him. We assumed he was in the bedroom, but he wasn't there. Michelle then observed the kitchen door to the balcony was open. When she looked over the edge, she was horrified by the sight of Angad lying on the first-floor roof. I was shaking, completely stunned!

The coroner ruled Angad 'had died as a result of severe head injuries'. In retrospect, my judgement is that his coming off the original medication was destabilizing his mental health. It probably made the difference between life and death.

It took five months for the Westminster coroner to reach a decision. But the police were clear from the start: there was no foul play. The autopsy recorded there were no drugs in his system.

At the inquest, Michelle described Angad as 'a devoted father and a beyond amazing husband'.

A month earlier, my older sister Prakasho had passed away in India aged ninety-three. All through my life, I had been very close to her. She had taken care of me when I was a little boy after we lost our mother prematurely, so her passing was an immense loss. With the thunderbolt of Angad's death, my cup of sorrow was full. God was indeed punishing me.

One of Angad's partners and designers in Established and Sons, Sebastian Wrong, said after his death, 'Without him, Established and Sons would not have existed. He was responsible for enabling an important period in contemporary design.' He described Angad as a 'special man with a big heart, great passion and humour' and that he 'believed in championing design innovation.' Finally, that 'his inspired vision created a unique collection that will be a lasting legacy to his enthusiasm that united so much talent.'

In fact, tributes poured in from all over the world and even through our sadness, Aruna and I were astonished to see how much Angad had been loved and how many people's lives he had affected for the good. His memorial at London Zoo and his funeral at Golders Green Crematorium were packed with mourners.

The filmmaker Matthew Vaughn and director Dexter Fletcher dedicated their film *Eddie the Eagle* to 'our friend Angad'; Lady Paul and I were guests of honour at the premiere in Leicester Square in 2016.

Angad was by my side when I decided to buy The Grange, the family house in Beaconsfield, where I hoped members of the family would congregate at weekends under one roof and where the grandchildren could enjoy playing in the extensive gardens. There are trees planted there now in memory of Ambika and Angad, which I like to look at whenever I visit.

I love all my children as any normal father would. But unlike the fast track laid out for children within business families in India, I wanted them to work their way up the Caparo ladder from junior positions, notwithstanding their engineering or MBA degrees. I had, after all, begun life by sweeping the floor of my father's office in Jalandhar.

Akash, who did a great job at our joint venture plant with British Steel in Scunthorpe and at our steel conversion factories in Spain, is married to Nisha and their children are Arush and Ashma. Ambar was a great manager of our engineering establishment in the West Midlands out of Birmingham, and now heads the steel tubes business in St Louis in the United States and our hotels in England. His wife is Gauri and their children are Akhil and Anika. My daughter Anjli looks after Caparo's interests in the United Arab Emirates and London. Her children are Shalin and Shaila. All I want for them is that they be happy in their own ways.

Angad Paul

Angad Paul Building, University of Wolverhampton

World of Established & Sons

With Lady Paul, grandson Arush and the Caparo T1, London Motor Show, 2006

PRESS RELEASE

Caparo's T1 smashes BBC Top Gear's lap record

Angad Paul throws down gauntlet

Ultra high-performance car beats previous lap record by seven seconds

The world's fastest ever track-biased, ultra-performance road car, the Caparo T1, has smashed the lap record on BBC TV's popular motoring programme Top Gear. The two-seater sports car, which utilises lightweight materials and technology more commonly found in Formula One cars, set a new lap record time of 1:10.6; an astonishing seven seconds quicker than a modified Koenigsegg CCX which held the previous record.

Caparo's engineers have utilised some of the most advanced materials and technologies available. The cars are constructed using a carbon composite tub, giving it a dry power to weight ratio of more than 1,000bhp per tonne. The car's high performance brakes, built and designed by Caparo AP Braking, also provide awesome stopping power. High-strength aerospace grade aluminium billet is used for the six pot race calipers on the front and the four pot calipers on the rear, capable of bringing the car to standstill from 100mph in under three seconds.

Indeed, commenting on braking power of the T1, it was stated on the show that, "you couldn't stop more quickly if you went into a tree."

Despite its record breaking time, Top Gear viewers will not see the T1 at the top of the Power Lap board yet. The programme makers specified that in order to appear on the board, cars must be capable of driving over a speed bump. In their opinion, the T1 would not have been able to do this and was subsequently removed from the top of the leader board.

"We certainly hope that the Caparo T1 is given another chance by Top Gear to take its rightful place at the top of the leader board even if they put a speed bump on the track, we are confident of our success. To have beaten the previous leader by seven seconds is a truly astonishing achievement," says Angad Paul, Chief Executive of Caparo Group.

The model supplied to Top Gear was one of the final engineering vehicles without adjustable ride height and electronic active driver control systems which are standard on our production models. When driver's select the 'road' setting, the car is more tractable in slower speed conditions and the ride height is fully adjustable to bring the car up to 90mm clearance, making it more than capable of driving over speed bumps

Angad Paul is the chief executive officer of Caparo Group, a worldwide manufacturing company specialising principally in steel, aluminium and composite products for all industries. The group was founded in 1968 by Lord Paul and remains wholly owned by the Paul family.

The Caparo T1 has been developed by Caparo Vehicle Technologies, part of the Caparo Vehicle Products Division of Caparo Group.

Top Gear Press Release

Me with Paul Osborn of Cars International and Caparo T1, 20 July 2006

Me and Steve Smith with Angad portrait, Angad Arts Hotel, St Louis, USA

Angad Paul, cover picture, *Director* magazine, January 2008

History of the Angad Paul Building, St Louis, USA

THE ANGAD PAUL BUILDING

Angad Paul was passionate about design and creativity. He challenged conventional thinking and sought innovative solutions to ordinary problems. Angad would say:

*"What is art, but seeing the world in a different way.
What is life but a series of experiences connected together."*

It was his vision and leadership that led to the restoration of this historic building. We dedicate this building in memory of Angad.

NAMED BY THE RT HON THE LORD PAUL, PC 31 AUGUST 2017

Angad Paul Building, St Louis

Angad Paul Building inauguration, Wolverhampton University

Angad Paul Building inauguration, St Louis, 31 August 2017

Angad Paul and Caparo T1

Angad Paul and Caparo T1 team

12

Aruna

In the chapter about my life in Calcutta, I mentioned that I met and married Aruna Vij in 1956.

Aruna, also a Punjabi residing in the city, was charming and exquisite. It was love at first sight! She was a student at Loreto College, a leading Catholic missionary institution, as well as a teacher at Loreto House, which was the school under the same order, the two located in the same compound at Calcutta's Middleton Row.

Aruna was a very good student. She was much liked at Loreto and was one of the most beautiful girls at her college. She was also a well-respected teacher.

In 2013, Aruna and I were delighted to contribute to the expansion of Loreto College with the building of the Lady Aruna Paul Wing and together, we laid the foundation stone. This was formally inaugurated in 2017 and won significant praise for its construction.

But to go back to the beginning of it all, I had hosted a party for the then chief minister of Punjab, who was visiting Calcutta. Aruna attended this party with somebody else, and I admired her immediately. A family friend, P.C. Gaur, noticed my interest in her and invited her with her parents to his house the next day. I was also invited, and I had an opportunity to talk to her properly. I quite simply asked, 'Will you marry me?' She was understandably a little shocked and replied, 'Ask my mother.' I said, 'I am not asking to marry your mother. I am asking to marry you. This proposal is for you.' So she went to her mother; her mother then came to me and said they would be happy with our marriage. The next day, we tied the knot.

Aruna's parents had another man in mind and had by previous arrangement informally agreed to the match. This understanding was obviously broken for our betrothal to go ahead. Her former fiancé was heartbroken.

I wanted a quiet wedding, so it was a very small gathering. Part of the ceremony in Hindu matrimony is known as *kanyadaan* or giving away the bride. By tradition, the priest presiding over the nuptials is paid a fee for conducting this part of the service. I negotiated him down to the minimum to carry it out!

Straight after the marriage, Aruna accompanied me to our factory and the following morning, she was at work in the office, where she handled the administration. She was simply wonderful as a wife and as a partner. From that day forward, I discussed all manner of business proposals with her, and her advice was always wise and welcome.

Aruna was just twenty years old and strikingly attractive. I was twenty-six. Satyajit Ray, the legendary Indian filmmaker, was shooting a movie in our house in Alipore in Calcutta, and when he saw her, said that he would like to cast her in his production. She, however, turned down the offer. Aruna said her first job was as a housekeeper, her second an office administrator and her third looking after her husband. Many years later, I was asked on a BBC interview why we chose each other. I responded, 'I married her for her money, and she married me for my looks!' which caused some laughter.

As well as helping me in the office after our marriage, she ran our household in an exemplary fashion and really looked after other members of the joint family who resided with us. Jit and Surrendra lived in the same house. Stya was of course in Jalandhar or Delhi.

While in Calcutta, Aruna was also entrusted with the running of Flury's, the Swiss confectionery and cafe that Apeejay bought.

A wonderful person with a caring nature, she was devoted to the family and took care of all family members. It was a quality that remained with her all her life. When Surrendra married in 1963, she warmly welcomed his spouse, Shirin. To me, Aruna was a special friend and an amazing wife.

Life was great in Calcutta, where a varied social life was almost compulsory. Aruna and I would go to the Calcutta Club, the Hindustan Club and the Royal Calcutta Turf Club. While I had of course to continue travelling abroad for business purposes, Aruna came with me on quite a few of these trips.

Our twin sons Ambar and Akash arrived in December 1957. Daughter Anjli was born in November 1959. Then came Ambika in November 1963. Aruna chose the names of our children, all beginning with the letter 'A'.

Aruna and I had made it a ritual to host a summer tea party at the London Zoo in the first weekend of July. It was an annual remembrance of Ambika, when many of our friends and relatives would join us to enjoy the lovely surroundings in Regent's Park. In 1997, the event was especially significant. It was the first such gathering after I had been made a Peer and the previous winter, Aruna and I had completed forty years of marriage.

Together, we had shared both joy and sorrow. Aruna's encouragement, good humour and patience had steadfastly sustained me during times of tribulation. She showered me with extraordinary happiness. Whatever I have achieved has been founded on the stability I invariably enjoyed at home.

I wanted to publicly acknowledge my debt to Aruna. So, unknown to her, I requested the London Zoo authorities to curate an attraction in her honour. In discussion with them, I looked at the range of options that would add value to the zoo, particularly to visiting children. After various consultations, it was decided that they would create a unique pygmy hippopotamus enclosure. This rare African species was threatened with extinction and it was a wonderful opportunity. *'The Baroness Paul Pygmy Hippo Enclosure Dedicated to Aruna Paul'*, the plaque said, to Aruna's utter surprise and delight at the dedication ceremony to mark our fortieth wedding anniversary in 1996. She often joked that other men gave their wives jewellery for their wedding anniversaries while she received a couple of hippopotami, even if they were the pygmy ones. Our friend, Frank Dobson MP, who was secretary of state for health in the first Blair government, performed the opening ceremony.

Subsequently, a couple of unfortunate falls and resultant injuries partly impaired her vision and mobility. But these did not undermine her spirit. Her children and grandchildren adored her, as did members of our extended family and friends. Always very generous with her time and gifts, Aruna was also charming and erudite company.

Throughout her life, Aruna was always interested in helping those less fortunate and took a great interest in the arts. She was an early member of the Women's India Association (UK), which works to empower women and children from disadvantaged backgrounds through education, entrepreneurial and vocational skills, rehabilitation and life skills. It also provides financial aid in areas of natural disasters and emergencies. She was a committee member and then a patron of this organization up to the time of her death.

She was also a patron and great supporter of the Bharatiya Vidya Bhawan in London. Known as 'The Home of Indian Arts', it is the largest centre for Indian classical arts in the UK. The Indian Gymkhana Club in Osterley, England, which we have both supported for many years, has recently dedicated a new hall on its premises in both our names.

In the spring of 2022, I had been admitted into a nursing home off High Street Kensington in London to receive medical attention. Aruna would visit me regularly at this nursing home and did so on the afternoon of 3 May, when we took afternoon tea together. There was no indication of her being physically uneasy. Yet, after returning home that evening, she suddenly passed away. She was eighty-six.

I wasn't informed until the next morning. Soon, I was flooded with messages of condolence. Among these were a couple from our close friends, the ever-supportive erstwhile British Prime Minister Gordon Brown and his wife Sarah.

'Aruna was a wonderful, kind, welcoming and brilliant friend to all of us and together, you were the best team in the world!' Gordon said in a hand-written note, adding, 'We will miss Aruna greatly and know that your lifelong partnership was second to none.'

Sarah penned, 'Oh Swraj—I am so very sorry to hear of Aruna's passing . . . We are thinking of you.'

Aruna was cremated at London's Golders Green Crematorium on 11 May, the same place where Ambika and Angad were cremated. Speaking at her funeral, another good friend, Cherie Blair, eminent barrister and wife of another former prime minister of the UK, Tony Blair, remarked, 'It isn't easy to build a life in a new country as Aruna and Swraj did here in the UK . . . their achievements were marked by Swraj's elevation to the House of Lords for his services to industry and to the Labour Party and many Labour leaders including Tony welcomed and listened to his advice; and therefore, I know they were listening to Aruna's advice.'

I have made innumerable references to Aruna throughout this book, including our first meeting and subsequent marriage in 1956, our travels together, her steadfast loyalty to our family and friends, her unique support during the course of my tumultuous business and political career, her generosity, and most of all, her love and compassion during the times of our deepest sorrow and family tragedies.

In an effort to give people a wider understanding of her strength and goodness, it has been a pleasure for me to create memorials to her around the world. Some of these are in our joint names, but they are really my gifts to her. They include the Lady Aruna Paul wing at the Loreto College in Kolkata, the various London Zoo memorials, the memorials at Ambika House, the Lord and Lady Paul Hall at the Indian Gymkhana Club near London, the Aruna Paul theatre in St Louis and, now, the outstanding new building at the Springfield site, University of Wolverhampton.

The Lady Aruna Swraj Paul Building, which was officially inaugurated on 25 June 2024, is within Europe's largest Architecture and Built Environment campus. The school contains laboratories, a lecture theatre, a super studio and a research centre focused on developing modern methods of building in partnership with the construction industry. I know Aruna was passionate about education and would be delighted to see that we are supporting the University of Wolverhampton to produce workforce-ready graduates and helping to create a more sustainable and productive society.

In December 2016, we were thrilled to receive a message from Her Majesty Queen Elizabeth II congratulating us on our diamond wedding anniversary, sixty years of marriage. Aruna and I bonded for over sixty-five years and were emotionally dependent on each other. Losing her is an irreparable loss. As I said from my heart at her funeral, 'Aruna, I will miss you. Goodbye my dear. I love you. I will always love you.'

With Wolverhampton University Vice Chancellor Ebrahim Adia at the unveiling of the Lady Aruna Swraj Paul Building, 25 June 2024

Statue of me at Ambika Paul Children's Zoo from Aruna on my seventieth birthday

Our fortieth wedding anniversary. Aruna at the opening of the Pygmy Hippo Enclosure, London Zoo with The Rt Hon. Frank Dobson, Secretary of State for Health, 1997

Lady Aruna Paul Student Recreation Centre
Dedicated to the sweet memory of
Late Lady Aruna Paul
An industrious student and an illustrious teacher in Loreto College, Kolkata
by her husband
Rt.Hon. Lord Swraj Paul, P.C.
An alumnus of Doaba College, Jalandhar &
Massachusetts Institute of Technology, USA.
May God look after her forever

Lady Paul Building, Doaba plaque

Lady Paul and me with Cherie Blair and son Leo, July 2002

Lady Aruna Paul, dedication at Indian Gymkhana Club, London

Lady Aruna Paul portrait

Lady Aruna Paul memorial at London Zoo

Lady Aruna Paul and Margaret Thatcher, March 1982

Lady Aruna and Swraj Paul Hall, Indian
Gymkhana Club, the UK

Aruna, bottom row right with friends from the Women's India Association

Aruna and me unveiling the Lady Aruna Paul Foundation plaque at Loreto, Kolkata, April 2013

13

Where We Are Now and Going Forward

I have never shirked hard work. But to return to hands-on duties at Caparo after Angad's passing wasn't easy. Yet, it had to be done; I didn't have a choice. Regardless of the fact that I was in my mid-eighties, I was determined to ensure our business outside Britain remained stable and profitable. Indeed, where there was scope of expansion and growth, I believed we should capitalize on such opportunities.

Caparo UK had operated thirty-six steel-related establishments in Britain and continental Europe. All were now out of our control after the crisis in 2015, except for the Osborne Hotel in Torquay on the south-west coast of England, and our real estate interests. I much regret this. But our investments in North America, India and the United Arab Emirates remained unaffected and continue to be so. They promise much for the future.

I maintain a strong and watchful presence over all the companies but particularly those in the US, where we have diversified into the property development arena.

Caparo's engineering and steel tube manufacturing business in North America operate under the banner of Caparo Bull Moose Inc., after our first acquisition of the Bull Moose company near St Louis in Missouri in 1988. Today, there are eight Bull Moose Tube plants in North America: Casa Grande, Arizona; Chicago Heights, Illinois; Elkhart, Indiana; Gerald, Missouri; Masury, Ohio; Trenton, Georgia; Sinton, Texas and Burlington in Ontario, Canada.

Additionally, Bull Moose Industries acquired two units producing XL specialized trailers in Manchester, Iowa. XL is a leading designer and manufacturer of highly engineered and customized trailers used in heavy haul trucking, construction, agriculture, wind energy and oil and gas industries.

In fact, we didn't stop there and diversified into further development projects.

Urban development in downtown St Louis is powering ahead in a joint venture with Steve Smith, a practising architect. His Lawrence Group, which was started in 1983, has developed into a national design and development firm. He was first introduced by our lawyer in America, James Dankenbring, to my son Angad, who was at the point also considering relocating Bull Moose's corporate office in the US—which was in suburban St Louis—to the city centre. Angad needed a planner and builder for the purpose.

Steve and his team were invited to Dankenbring's office in St Louis to be interviewed by Angad in August 2014. The Lawrence Group was on a shortlist of potential developers for the contemplated project. Angad had determined that the

Bull Moose headquarters needed to move to the heart of town because all the innovation was happening there, as opposed to being in the suburbs.

Steve says, 'I was one of five that were interviewed on that August day. The two things I remember are that there was great chemistry and Angad was a visionary. Happily, we were selected and Angad and I decided we would become partners.'

In May 2015, Steve came to London to meet me at Caparo's head office on Baker Street. Angad brought him into my room, we had a pleasant conversation and then went out for lunch. We confirmed our legally binding partnership in real estate development in St Louis.

The project involved not only creating offices, but also a hotel. After Angad's unexpected death in November 2015, Steve called sometime later that month to ask if it would be 'okay' to name the hotel after Angad. It was a thoughtful suggestion. I readily agreed. Also, in practical terms, the partnership subsequently evolved into one between Steve and me.

Construction began in what is St Louis's theatre district in early 2017. Next door to the site is the base of the St Louis Symphony, the second oldest symphony orchestra in the US. Across the street is the Fox Theatre, a former movie palace, now a splendid performing arts centre that reopened in 1982.

When our complex, formerly the Missouri Theatre, built in 1927, opened on Diwali 2018, the hospitality component of the property was named the Angad Arts Hotel. The main building is called Angad Paul House. The Governor of the State of Missouri, Michael Parson, and the Mayor of St Louis, Lyda Krewson, joined the unveiling.

Angad Arts Hotel is markedly different as a hospitality location. It was immediately accorded acclaim in the US and internationally. Its interior is uniquely designed to reflect life's experiences intertwined with seeing the world in a different way.

It became, we believe, the first hotel in the world where you could book a room by your colour and emotional preference—red for passion, blue for tranquillity, green for rejuvenation or yellow for happiness. This means, for instance, in a red room, the walls and ceiling are painted red, the wardrobe is red, the curtains are red and even the bathtub is red.

USA Today newspaper named it as one of the five most creative new hotels in North America. It won the Best in Show prize at the St Louis Interior Design Award Ceremony. In 2022, *River Front Times* voted it the best hotel in St Louis. We were off to a great start. The total investment between Steve and myself was $63 million.

A second opportunity to partner with Steve came along in 2016 when he identified a nine-acre brownfield plot which had previously been the location of a large steel foundry that had closed decades ago. It was in downtown St Louis as well and near the Angad Arts Hotel. It was environmentally contaminated. The idea was to buy the site and convert it into a mixed-use commercial centre.

The proposal sounded viable and I decided to join Steve in the project. He kindly remarked that 'Lord Paul's early involvement was critical for us to move forward.' And he said of me, 'It's a testament to his vision and his comfort at taking risks.' Building work started in the middle of 2018 and a large mixed-use compound has evolved, offering space for entertainment, live music, offices, restaurants and shops. City Foundry, as the development is called, is a $230 million joint investment.

Completion of the venture was unfortunately delayed by fifteen months because of the COVID-19 pandemic. It was eventually launched with great fanfare in August 2021. City Foundry was ranked number one in 'commercial historic redevelopment' in the US in 2018. *Forbes* magazine named it one of the ten best commercial opportunities in developments utilized in the US in 2019. The multipurpose facility has generated 1000 new jobs in St Louis and is one of the city's largest sales tax payers. The centrepiece of the development is the food hall, which was recently recognized by *USA TODAY* as the third most popular food hall in the United States. Currently, over 2.4 million people a year come to visit City Foundry, making it one of the top tourist attractions in St Louis. Besides which, the zone around City Foundry—it having acted as a catalyst—is presently exploding with a building boom.

Steve's plan didn't provide for residences in the construction. Instead, he earmarked land available adjacent to City Foundry, which would lend itself to a strategic place to live. He inquired if I would be interested in partnering on this, too. The cost was coming to $102 million. I approved, and Vande East, with homes and a small office segment, was soon underway. The Vande East apartments will be among the most luxurious properties in St Louis, comprising a fourteen-storey luxury residential tower located adjacent to the City Foundry development. With 270 apartments, the property features an innovative design with two elevated parks that sit seven storeys above the street, making it among the most desirable properties in St Louis.

Nearby, the Lord Swraj Paul Theatre is a 250-seat auditorium that features the most state-of-the-art audio and visual technologies in the St Louis market. With over seventy audio devices, a 60-foot-wide screen and fully adjustable seats allowing the guest to customize their experience, it is the most sophisticated and advanced viewing experience in St Louis.

Currently in preparation, with construction completion expected by the end of 2024, the Aruna Paul theatre will feature a 1200-person capacity live music performance centre. Located in the Grand Center Arts District, the Aruna Paul Theatre will complement many of the other neighbouring live music venues, including the St Louis Symphony, the Sheldon Concert Hall and the Fox Theatre. Aruna was steadfast in her enthusiasm and support for the arts all her life. I am sure she would have been delighted to see this memorial in her name, which will make a great impact on the thriving artistic scene in St Louis.

Caparo has, over the years, significantly widened its footprint in India. After our foray into this market in the shape of Caparo Maruti Limited in Gurgaon, in Haryana state, we extended this joint venture by creating two more such plants—in Bawal, also in Haryana, and Halol in Gujarat. Maruti Suzuki is the largest carmaker in India. We provide sheet metal stamping, weld assemblies and, in certain cases, complete modules to them.

Following the success of Caparo Maruti Limited, we formed Caparo Engineering India Limited in 2000 to cater to the needs of various other original equipment manufacturers (OEMs). In fact, Caparo India now has twenty offices and state-of-the-art manufacturing units across the country, many of these being greenfield projects. Caparo's core capabilities are stamping, producing sheet metal, forging, aluminium die casting, fasteners and steel tube manufacturing. Apart from catering to the needs of major OEMs in the passenger and commercial vehicles and off-highway segments, we forge heavy and critical fabrication parts for the Indian Railways.

Caparo Engineering India Limited's sheet metal plants are based in Greater Noida, Bawal, Chennai, Halol (two units), Jamshedpur (two units), Pithampur (two units), Pune, Rudrapur and Sanad.

In 2005, Caparo India Limited set up AYATTI, another of Angad's ideas, to create a modern socio-cultural facility spread across twenty-one acres of landscaped lawns in Greater Noida, near Delhi. It is used for meetings, conferences, concerts, exhibitions and weddings.

The following year, Caparo MI Steel Processing Limited was incorporated through a joint venture with Marubeni-Itochu Steel Inc. of Japan to extend customized laser welding services for large sheet metal panels for automotive body applications. This is based in Bawal.

Indeed, it would perhaps be true to say that Caparo in India is looked upon as a supplier of choice by global automotive majors.

We entered the energy sector in 2012 with a 26-megawatt gas-based group captive power plant, also in Bawal, with Finnish major Wartsila as our partners. Caparo Power Limited is also based in Bawal, Haryana, and supplies uninterrupted electricity in the region.

The Caparo Group today employs more than 10,000 people spread across the UK, North America, India and the United Arab Emirates, where Caparo Middle East produces polyvinyl chloride (PVC) tubes and is located at the Jebel Ali Free Zone in Dubai. It also sells steel tubes imported from Caparo India.

We have stakes in financial services, medical products and private equity as well. Our workforce would have been bigger but for our unfortunate setback in Britain in 2015.

My son, Akash, heads the Indian operations with his son, Arush, acting as chief executive. My daughter, Anjli, oversees the UAE businesses.

So, as an industrialist back at the wheel in his nineties, I look back with a degree of satisfaction at Caparo's overall accomplishments over more than half a century. But also with a tinge of disappointment relating to the blow that befell us in terms of losing our original UK division.

I am optimistic about the future, despite the downturns occasionally affecting the global economy in the form of a once-in-a-century pandemic, disruption in the supply chains or recession. These obviously dampen demand, and it means we must be constantly vigilant, detect tempestuous trends early and ward off such destabilizing waves to remain buoyant.

Caparo's quest for expansion is undiminished. In September 2024, following my tour of the various US facilities, I announced the expansion of our operations with a new steel pipes and structures plant in Gerald, Missouri, near the company's headquarters in St Louis. The $25-million Bull Moose Tube plant is slated to begin production in early 2026 and will strengthen our position as the largest producer of steel pipes and structures in the US.

My whole life has been devoted to the Paul family and to our business ventures. I look back over the years with mixed feelings of joy and sorrow. I am proud of what has been achieved and I am grateful to all those people, too numerous to mention, whose input was vital to this success. I acknowledge their efforts and thank them for their hard work and loyalty.

With employees of XL Specialized Trailers, Manchester, Iowa, USA

Vande East Apartments, another Caparo-backed development in St Louis, Missouri, USA

Steve Smith of Lawrence Group outside Lord Paul Theatre, St Louis sign

Steve Smith accepting honorary doctorate, 7 July 2024

Lord Paul Theatre, St Louis, interior

Lady Aruna Paul Theatre, St Louis, ready for restoration in 2025

Hon. Akash Paul accepting Wolverhampton University honorary doctorate, 7 July 2024

City Foundry, part of the redevelopment of St Louis, USA

Bull Moose, Sinton, Texas, USA, First Bundle Group, 24 May 2023

Bull Moose, Sinton, Texas, USA plant

Bull Moose Trenton, Georgia, USA employees, 2024

Bull Moose Gerald, Missouri, USA employees, 2024

Bull Moose employees, Sinton, Texas, USA, and memorial trees for Lady Paul, Angad Paul and Ambika Paul, 2024

Bull Moose employees, Elkart, Indiana, USA, 2024

Bull Moose Burlington, Ontario, Canada plant

Epilogue

The writing of this book has taken many months and significant research into company and family archives. While I have tried to cover as much detail as possible, there are many reminiscences that have occurred to me at random.

The first, and most disturbing of these, is my unease at the inquest into the death of my beloved son, Angad.

He was the brightest and most ambitious of my children and even though he was experiencing mental anguish in the weeks leading up to his demise, I still find it hard to believe he took his own life. We know he was besieged by difficulties that may have impacted his mental processes, yet he was still a wonderful father to his two children and loved them unconditionally. I cannot accept that he wilfully left them in such cruel circumstances. To my mind, the verdict at the inquest was inconclusive because there were many important questions raised, yet several relevant ones were not investigated when they could have been and certainly were not answered on the day. It will haunt me forever.

My remaining children, Ambar, Akash and Anjli, have taken on most of the day-to-day running of Caparo in the US, India and UAE, respectively, where they work with their local executive management teams. I still take an interest and oversee much of the activity, though I'm aware that different generations see and do things differently. But as I mentioned in the Caparo Ethic, there is no substitute for hard work with integrity.

My niece, Sushma, who is Stya's only child, I remain close to, and she has taken on the responsibility of chairing the Apeejay Education, the Apeejay Stya and Svran Group, and the Apeejay Stya Education Research Foundation, as well as being chancellor of the Apeejay Stya University in India. Sushma is very much a humanitarian and, like her father, is devoted to the cause of education.

I am fortunate to have met so many influential people on the world stage, who have all been engaging characters. For example, the times I spent with Rupert Murdoch and his son James during and after the Gordon Brown government years. In general, our exchanges were very lively, and we discussed many things pertaining to global politics and industry. He is a great businessman, a wise and interesting conversationalist.

Another treasured memory is my visit to see Pope John Paul II with Mrs Gandhi in November 1981. We felt blessed to be received by such a great spiritual leader.

Likewise, Mother Teresa, whom Aruna and I met in Kolkata not long before she died. Mother Teresa's headquarters in Kolkata were very close to the Apeejay offices on Park Street. My brother Jit and I were great supporters of her work, and she often used to come to our office, or we to hers, for tea and a chat.

Epilogue

I have been privileged to meet His Majesty King Charles III on many occasions, the first being when he was a young Prince of Wales and inaugurated the first Caparo factory, Natural Gas Tubes, in 1977. Whenever we meet, he always asks me how that plant is progressing.

After Princess Diana died and before he married the present Queen, Camilla, he hosted a dinner at Windsor Castle to which Aruna and I were invited. Aruna sat on the prince's right while I was seated next to Camilla. When he and Camilla were married, he again invited us both to Buckingham Palace.

HM the Queen Mother asked me to tea at Clarence House and later, I met her again when the Duke of Edinburgh and Prince Charles hosted a dinner at St James's Palace in support of the World Wildlife Fund. The WWF later took me on a tour of their site in Ranthambore to see the tigers.

When I met Pandit Nehru at MIT, he told all us Indian students that we must make it a priority to do something for India. After I returned and was married in 1956, I went to Delhi with Aruna the following year. I rang his secretary to ask for an appointment and was given one for the following day. Aruna and I went to tea and met Mrs Gandhi, who was also there, and I recall she was petting a tiger, which rather scared us.

In 1983, when Her Majesty Queen Elizabeth II and the Duke of Edinburgh were visiting India, we attended a reception held by the then President Giani Zail Singh, who said to the Duke of Edinburgh in my presence that 'Swraj Paul is India's gift to Britain.' The Duke replied, 'We accept him with pleasure.'

Another great friend was the novelist Barbara Cartland, and I visited her at her home, Camfield Place, many times. It was always a pleasure to talk to her as she had a wonderful sense of humour and was also a good friend of Mrs Gandhi.

President A.P.J. Abdul Kalam was another great friend who always invited us to lunch or dinner whenever we were in Delhi. He also held a reception at Rashtrapati Bhavan in honour of Angad's marriage, which was almost unprecedented.

More recently I have had the pleasure of enjoying a large birthday party to celebrate my ninety-third year organized by friends and colleagues at the Indian Gymkhana Club, where we opened the hall remembering Aruna.

At our annual London Zoo party this year, 2024, I presented honorary doctorates awarded by the University of Wolverhampton to my son Akash; to Steve Smith, my great friend and colleague in St Louis; and posthumously to Tom 'Mo' Modrowski, the CEO of Caparo US, who died suddenly, leaving behind a grief-stricken family and colleagues. He was a talented CEO, a very loyal Caparo employee and a beloved family man. Tom will be greatly missed by all who knew him. There is a road named after him at the Sinton, Texas plant.

Many years ago, I was being interviewed by the BBC and the presenter asked me whether I considered myself to be Indian or British. I replied, 'I am one hundred per cent Indian and one hundred per cent British.'

Although born in India, a country that I love and admire more with each passing year as I see it taking its rightful place on the world stage, I am also very much a product of Britain, my adopted country. In Britain, I have always been largely accepted and have thus been able to grow and diversify. As I have recounted in an earlier chapter, taking my seat in the House of Lords was a highly charged moment for me, not just as one of the first Asian Peers but because of all the family history and corporate responsibility that led to that moment.

I look back on a life well-lived. Though it was tempered by tragedy, I have been fortunate to meet some wonderful people and to see most parts of this extraordinary world, and I am still making plans to see even more. I thank God for the opportunities I have had, and I pray to Him every day, remembering those who are no longer here yet whose presence touched my heart and motivated so much of my success.

It is my dearest wish that the philanthropic projects to which I have been delighted to contribute over the years will flourish and benefit all the people for whom they are intended, whoever and wherever they are.

I very much hope that Caparo continues to prosper under the leadership of my sons, daughter, grandchildren and perhaps one day, my great-grandchildren.

We bring nothing into this world and can take nothing away. I do not want for anything in this life except to be remembered as having always striven to do my best and for leaving a legacy for the benefit of generations to come.

ZSL | LET'S WORK FOR WILDLIFE

Patron: H M The Queen
Vice Patron: HRH The Prince of Wales

The Zoological Society of London (ZSL), founded in 1826, is devoted to promoting and achieving the worldwide conservation of animals and their habitats

Regent's Park, London NW1 4RY
0344 225 1826
zsl.org

From the **President**

The Rt Hon. the Lord Paul
Caparo House
103 Baker Street
London
W1U 6LN

21 January 2019

Dear Lord Paul,

I am delighted to inform you that the Council of the Zoological Society of London would like to award you its highest honour, ZSL Honorary Fellowship, in acknowledgment of your exceptional commitment to ZSL London Zoo over the past 30 years. As it looks toward its third century, ZSL would like to formally recognise your extraordinary commitment and the ongoing support of you and your family, which enables ZSL to inspire, empower and inform people through our Zoos.

I would be very pleased if you would accept this appointment. We would be delighted to confer your ZSL Honorary Fellowship to you at our annual Awards Ceremony, which is being held next year on the 11th of June in the ZSL Meeting Rooms. Alternatively, we could award your Fellowship to you at your Summer Party on the 7th of July, with your family, friends and guests in attendance. Please do let us know which you would prefer in due course.

I send my warmest congratulations and look forward to welcoming you to the Society in a new capacity as an Honorary Fellow. I hope that you are willing to accept this title and continue to play a valuable part in our work to secure a world where wildlife thrives.

Yours sincerely,

Sir John Beddington, President
Zoological Society of London (ZSL)

Animals and their habitats face increasing threats across the world. Donate to ZSL to help build a future where animals are valued and their conservation assured. ZSL is a registered charity in England and Wales no: 208728

ZSL Honorary Fellowship

With The Rt Hon. Michael Foot, MP, on his seventieth birthday

With niece Sushma Paul, Jalandhar, 18 April 2018

Walking with President A.P.J. Abdul Kalam, in his Delhi garden, 2005

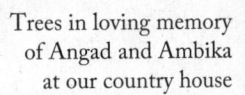

Trees in loving memory of Angad and Ambika at our country house

Statue of brother Jit Paul in Kolkata

My picture for 'World in London' Exhibition to coincide with the London 2012 Olympic Games

Remembering Lady Aruna, Ambika and Angad Paul

Sunday 2nd July 2023
ZSL London Zoo

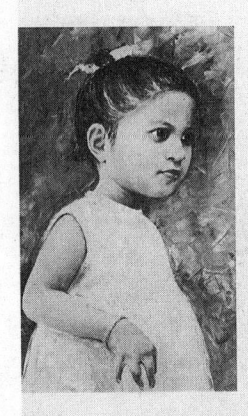

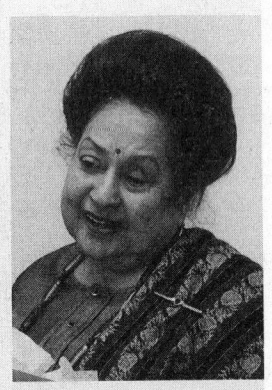

In memory of those I have lost

CAPARO
Caparo Group Limited and Caparo Industries Plc

Surrendra Paul
1935-1990

A Commemoration

Recital by Ustad Amjad Ali Khan

at the

Members' Dining Room
House of Commons
London SW1
on
Saturday 27th October 1990

In memory of Surrendra

Inaugural

Apeejay Svrán Dr. Stya Paul Memorial Lecture 2014

on

Industry, Education & Values

25th April 2014, New Delhi

by

Rt. Hon. Lord Swraj Paul
of Marylebone, PC

Stya Paul
(4th October 1919 – 7th June 2010)

Introduction by: **Sushma Paul Berlia**
President, Apeejay Stya & Svrán Group

In memory of Stya

AMBIKA PAUL CHILDREN'S ZOO

AMBIKA PAUL
MEMORIAL GARDENS

In memory of Ambika

12 NOVEMBER 1994

1500	Guests arrive and visit Ambika Paul Children's Zoo
1600	Unveiling Ambika Paul statue
1630	Tea, Regency Suite
1730	Depart

Family of Tom Modrowski accepting posthumous honorary doctorate from Wolverhampton University, July 2024

Aruna and me receiving my ZSL Honorary Fellowship from HRH Prince Philip, the Duke of Edinburgh, London 2019

93rd birthday party in London with Barry Gardiner, MP, 18 February 2024

Acknowledgements

My purpose in writing this book is to record the many instances that have informed my life and career path. Some of them have been the ordinary rewards for hard work and integrity; others quite extraordinary and unlooked for. I am grateful for a long life well lived albeit having to face more than a fair share of tragic circumstances.

I would like to acknowledge all those past and present who have assisted me in my life story and the following people for their help with this memoir.

The Massachusetts Institute of Technology (MIT) archives team

Wolverhampton University former vice chancellors John Brooks, Caroline Gipps, Geoff Layer, John Raftery and the present vice chancellor Ebrahim Adia. Also Kulvinder Chohan and Louise Tonks

M.K. Razdan, PTI

N. Ram, The Hindu Group

Professor Ralph Buultjens

Steve Smith

James Dankenbring

Elizabeth Allan

Jo Clarke

Zoological Society of London (ZSL) staff including former director Jo Gipps and Amelia Scudamore

David Knox, UK Archiving

My personal staff: Salma, Raju, Tara, Josephine and Jharna

Appendix 1

Ambassador for British Business	The Rt Hon. Lord Swraj Paul	1997–2005
30 December 1997	Kolkata, India	Deputy high commissioner lunch and press conference for British Business Group
7 January 1998	Nepal, Kathmandu	British Embassy, dinner and speech to British-Nepal Chamber of Commerce
12 May 1998	Delhi, India	Speech at high commissioner's reception for British Business Group
17 September 1998	Bonn, Germany	Speech at lunch for leading Anglo-German businessmen hosted by British ambassador
	Frankfurt, Germany	Speech at Automechanica Exhibition for leading manufacturers

23 September 1998	Helsinki, Finland	Speech at dinner hosted by British ambassador for Finnish-British Trade Association
5 October 1998	Pittsburgh, USA	Speech at reception for British American Board of Commerce
8 November 1998	Tel Aviv, Israel	Speech at lunch reception hosted by British ambassador
22 December 1998	Dhaka, Bangladesh	Meeting with prime minister and speech to Federation of Bangladesh Chamber of Commerce and Industry
24 December 1998	Kolkata, India	Speech at dinner hosted by British deputy high commissioner for Kolkata Chamber of Commerce
5 January 1999	Bangalore, India	Speech at lunch hosted by British deputy high commissioner for Confederation of Indian Industry
7 January 1999	Mumbai, India	Speech at lunch hosted by All India Association of Industries
1 March 1999	Istanbul, Turkey	Led British Trade Mission to Turkey. Speech at lunch hosted by Turkish-British Business Council
2 March 1999	Ankara, Turkey	Call on under-secretary of foreign trade. Speech at lunch, Ankara Chamber of Industry

9 March 1999	Hong Kong	Speech at lunch hosted by British ambassador for Hong Kong British Chamber
11 March 1999	Hong Kong	Speech at breakfast meeting for Royal Commonwealth Society
24 March 1999	Brussels, Belgium	Speech at lunch hosted by British ambassador for Belgian-British Chamber of Commerce
27 May 1999	Milan, Italy	Speech at lunch hosted by British consul-general for British-Italian Chamber of Commerce
30 August 1999	Chicago, USA	Speech at dinner hosted by British consul-general for business leaders
1 September 1999	St Louis, USA	Guest of English Speaking Union. Dinner and speech at the University Club
7 September 1999	Los Angeles, USA	Speech at dinner with British consul-general for British-American Chamber of Commerce
3 October 1999	Dubai, UAE	Speech at dinner hosted by British consul-general for British Business Group
5 October 1999	Abu Dhabi, UAE	Speech to a meeting of the British Business Group
11 October 1999	Karachi, Pakistan	Speech at dinner hosted by British ambassador for Overseas Investors Chamber of Commerce and Industry

Appendix 1

23 November 1999	Oslo, Norway	Speech to British Business Forum. Dinner hosted by British ambassador for Their Majesties the King and Queen of Norway
18 December 1999	Delhi, India	Speech at lunch hosted by the minister of external affairs
11 January 2000	London, UK	Lunch with Foreign Secretary The Rt Hon. Robin Cook at official London residence
3 April 2000	Marseilles, France	Inter-Parliamentary Union Conference on Security and Cooperation in the Mediterranean. Speech at lunch hosted by British consul-general for Chamber of Commerce
12 April 2000	Toronto, Canada	Speech at the Ontario Club, hosted by the British consul-general for British-Canadian Chamber of Trade and Commerce
13 April 2000	Washington D.C., USA	Speech to British-American Business Association. Lunch with British ambassador
22 April 2000	Muscat, Oman	Meeting with minister of commerce and industry. Speech at Oman Chamber of Commerce and Industry Meeting for British business interests hosted by British ambassador

Appendix 1

23 April 2000	Muscat	Speech to Economic Forum meeting at Indian Embassy. Dinner hosted by Indian ambassador
30 May 2000	Gothenburg, Sweden	Speech to Swedish Employers Federation at lunch hosted by British consul-general
16 October 2000	Budapest, Hungary	Reception hosted by British ambassador. Speech to British-Hungary Chamber of Commerce
18 October 2000	Warsaw, Poland	Meeting with deputy minister, Polish Treasury Ministry. Meeting with Polish Auto Chamber and speech at Warsaw Chamber of Commerce
		Lunch and speech, British Polish Chamber of Commerce. Dinner hosted by British ambassador
22 December 2000	Delhi, India	Speech at Association of Indian Diplomats
2 January 2001	Chennai, India	Speech at Madras Chamber of Commerce. Lunch hosted by British deputy high commissioner. Press conference, reception and dinner hosted by British deputy high commissioner

4 January 2001	Kerala, India	Meeting with Kerala chief minister. Speech to Kerala Industrial Infrastructure Development Corp. Meeting with HRH The Maharajah of Travancore
5 January 2001	Mumbai, India	Speech to Indian Merchants Chamber. Dinner hosted by British high commissioner
26 March 2001	Prague, Czech Republic	Call on Czech President and prime minister. Meeting with deputy prime minister and minister of finance. Meeting with minister of industry and trade
27 March 2001	Ostrava, Czech Republic	Lunch at Technical University of Ostrava. Visit to Ostrava steelworks.
28 March 2001	Bratislava, Slovakia	Lunch at British ambassador's residence. Speech to Slovak business community at Chamber of Commerce and dinner with Slovak business leaders
29 March 2001	Vienna, Austria	Speech at Economics Industry, Chamber of Commerce Industriellenvereinigung. Dinner at British ambassador's residence with leading bankers and industrialists

30 March 2001	Vienna	Visit to Castrol plant, Austrian Stock Exchange and meeting major Austrian banks. Interview with *WirtschaftsBlatt*
7 May 2001	New York, USA	Lunch hosted by British deputy consul-general and New York City Fellowship alumni. Speech and reception hosted by British consul-general for the European Union Studies Center
9 May 2001	Chicago, USA	Breakfast meeting hosted by British consul-general at British Consulate
14 May 2001	Washington D.C., USA	Lunch at British Embassy hosted by British ambassador
21 June 2001	Moscow, Russia	Speech at Russo-British Chamber of Commerce. Dinner hosted by British ambassador
3 August 2001	Delhi, India	Speech to Indian Institute of Directors
6 August 2001	Noida, India	Speech to Noida Development Agency and Indo-British Partnership
	Delhi, India	Speech at dinner hosted by Associated Chambers of Commerce and Industry

23 August 2001	Port Said, Egypt	Meeting with Governor of Port Said. Meeting with members of the Chamber of Commerce, hosted by the Governor
19 October 2001	The Hague, Holland	Speech at the Dutch Institute of Directors. Dinner hosted by British ambassador
2 January 2002	Hyderabad, India	Meeting with Governor and chief minister, Andhra Pradesh. Meeting with industrialists
28 January 2002	Rome, Italy	Speech to SMEs at British Embassy. Dinner hosted by British ambassador
29 January 2002	Rome	Meeting with the mayor of Rome and representatives of the Rome Industrial Association
30 January 2002	London, UK	Speech at Greater London Authority and Trade Partners UK Conference
7 March 2002	London, UK	Speech to Russo-British Chamber of Commerce, Economic Round Table, UK
6 June 2002	Naples, Italy	Speech to the Economics Faculty, University of Naples
20 June 2002	Moscow, Russia	Speech to Expert Council for Metallurgy and Steel Production. Reception hosted at British Embassy by the ambassador

Appendix 1

3 July 2002	London, UK	Speech to Belgian Luxembourg Chamber of Commerce, Belgian Embassy. Dinner hosted by Belgian ambassador
19 August 2002	Gibraltar	Meeting with governor-general and lunch for Gibraltar businesses
26 September 2002	Geneva, Switzerland	Lunch for Swiss-British business hosted by British ambassador
21 October 2002	Jalandhar, India	Keynote speech, Jalandhar Outreach Programme. Meeting with Governor of Punjab. Reception hosted by director of trade and investment promotion
23 December 2002	Delhi, India	Dinner hosted by President of India, Rashtrapati Bhavan
31 December 2002	Kolkata, India	Speech at lunch hosted by Rotary Club of Kolkata
8 January 2003	Mumbai, India	Meeting with Governor, Reserve Bank of India
11 January 2003	Mumbai	Speech at lunch and conference organized by Rotary Club of Mumbai
10 April 2003	Bern, Switzerland	Speech at dinner hosted by British ambassador for UK Trade and Invest Programme
26 April 2003	Indore, India	Lunch hosted by Indore State Government. Speech to Confederation of Indian Industry

Appendix 1

8 October 2003	Dhaka, Bangladesh	Speech to Metropolitan Chamber of Commerce. Meeting with prime minister
13 October 2003	Kolkata, India	Speech to Kolkata Chamber of Commerce
2 January 2004	Chennai, India	Speech at lunch hosted by Confederation of Indian Industry
6 January 2004	Colombo, Sri Lanka	Speech at lunch hosted by Council for Business with Britain Group. Meeting with prime minister
15 February 2004	New Delhi, India	Meeting with Institute for Integrated Learning Management at India International Centre
1 June 2004	New York, USA	Speech at European Union Center of New York
4 June 2004	Chicago, USA	Dinner with president of British-American Chamber and British consul-general
27 June 2004	Vienna, Austria	Speech to SMEs at British Fashion Exhibition
28 June 2004	Bratislava, Slovakia	Speech at lunch hosted by the ambassador at the British Embassy for Slovak-British business interests
4 May 2005	Lilongwe, Malawi	Dinner hosted by British ambassador at British Embassy for Malawi-British commercial interest

Appendix 2

British Business Forum, Oslo
23 November 1999
Changing Britain: A New Business Environment
Lord Paul

Ambassador, president and members of the British Forum.

It is a great pleasure to be once again in Norway. The congenial relations between Britain and Norway extend over most of the twentieth century. They are, in many ways, a model for the ways in which nations associate with each other.

But there is another very personal reason why Norway touches my heart. As you know, my early years were spent in India. This was the time when the ideas and the spirit of Mahatma Gandhi infused public life. Anybody who went through this experience was profoundly affected by it. And today I feel that Norway—the land of peace and peace endeavours—

reflects those sentiments that so affected my youth. But let me move from nostalgia to current reality.

At the outset, let me say how pleased I am by the presence of the ambassador and his colleagues. We in Britain are very appreciative of the work of our Foreign Office and their splendid efforts in representing our country abroad.

I have been requested to share with you some thoughts on the business environment in Britain. What changes there have been in the economic universe in which we function. In a larger perspective we have, of course, moved from a world of superpowers to a world of supermarkets. This is the story of macroeconomics in our time—where the imperatives of globalization, with all its benefits and drawbacks, are here to stay. There is no real retreat to where we came from. So, accommodation, adjustment, restructuring and other responses are now a way of life for all of us for whom business is a way of life.

In a more specific sense, I believe that the events of the past few months reinforce this message. The arrival of the Euro currency, the new pre-emptive programmes that the IMF is considering, the coming of world trade talks—all this suggests that we are on the cusp of a new economic era. It will take much of our ingenuity and dexterity to make our way through the times ahead. This will be a singular challenge for policymakers and those who organize national and international economies.

This is a world in which little can be taken for granted and the business-as-usual approach is no longer valid. Economies that have taken early steps to restructure themselves, to anticipate and prepare for the future, to cope with global conditions before being forced to do so—these economies are in better shape to respond to the new times. And, in this context, I would like to say a few words about Britain.

I believe most observers will agree that, for almost fifteen years, from the early 1980s onwards, the British economy has experienced quite radical modification. At the heart of this is a programme which has brought about extensive privatization, incentives for investment and enterprise, and technological upgrading. All this signifies some very major changes in both the British economic climate and condition in recent years.

Within this framework, let me make a personal reference. In many ways, my own business reflects the opportunities of this ethos. Thirty-three years ago, I migrated from India to Britain and began a small business activity with a modest loan. Today, the Caparo Group has a turnover of around US$ 800 million. From our British headquarters, we supervise operations in four countries, employ nearly 4000 people and believe that we are among the technological leaders in our field.

Much of this record has been, of course, due to the endeavours of our staff. But much has also been the result of the environment in which we operate. The atmosphere has been conducive to enterprise, and the willingness to adapt and innovate is extraordinary. The coordination and cooperation between labour and management has sustained consistently improving productivity.

All this has taken place in a society which increasingly recognizes that ethnic and cultural diversity is a singular social and economic asset—something which I know Norway appreciates.

In this context, let me discuss a few of the major policies that we have been trying to implement in Britain. When the Labour government was elected two and a half years ago, there were still some residual doubts about the direction of economic policy. There is now no doubt whatsoever. There is, at this moment, a remarkable consensus in British politics—a consensus that an enterprise society is good for Britain and good for Britain's relationships with the world. The words of our leaders make this abundantly clear.

Speaking in the House of Commons, the prime minister described business as the engine of growth for the British economy. Our secretary of state for trade and industry, in a major policy statement, said (I quote): 'There is a fundamental role for business at the heart of this government's thinking.' Earlier this month, our chancellor of the exchequer outlined to the Confederation of British Industry, policies that will encourage enterprise for all. In particular, he indicated support for skills and innovation, cuts in corporate and small business taxes, government support for modernization and encouragement of inward foreign investment.

These are not empty words or mere promises. Two national budgets have maintained both personal and corporate taxes at levels among the lowest in Europe. We strongly encourage open capital markets where international investment can come and go freely.

Another initiative is the creation of enterprise partnerships between public and business investment in a variety of different fields. Central to all these activities is a focus on trade. Those of you who have commercial relations with Britain will appreciate the efforts of our government to encourage trade. Historically, Britain has been a major exporting economy. But I think we realize that, in the modern world, trade must be built upon reciprocity and is not a one-way flow.

This is one reason why we have been so supportive of global trade liberalization. There is currently a tendency in some nations, a tendency induced by the economic situation, to restrictively regulate international trade. Britain vigorously opposes this. We also strongly encourage inward and outward investment. Those who invest in Britain today find a congenial climate for their capital. These are a few of the indications that tell you what our government is trying to do.

As a result, we hope to establish a macroeconomic framework that can provide stable, long-term growth, low inflation and sound public finances in the years ahead. Our message to the world is that Britain stands for hospitable and responsible internationalism, and that all segments of our society will cooperate in this endeavour.

Surrounding all this is perhaps the most important economic issue of the future for Britain—the question of participation in the Euro currency.

When you hear of political controversies in the UK, it might surprise you to know that we are now going through a period of intensive preparation in order that the British government, Parliament and people can make an informed decision on this fateful choice. Personally, I would have liked Britain to join in the initial phase. This is largely the view of most of the British business and commercial community. In the longer run, I think that this participation will take place.

However, the government of Britain has made a public promise not to join without going to the people on referendum. It will honour this commitment. We are, by nature, a prudent people. So, we are rather careful about overloading the system with major organic transformations. Yet, we are irrevocably committed to responsible change. That is a commitment which sustains our economy in today's world.

Some 200 years ago, Britain was a leader in the first Industrial Revolution—a revolution based on capital and machinery. The revolution all of us are now going through demands a different approach—huge investments in human capital, in knowledge and in the reorganization of structures. These are things that any one nation will find difficult to do alone in the modern age. However, through joint efforts with each other, we can profoundly benefit from complementary associations.

As we do this, you will find a Britain remarkably different from both stereotypes and from the past. We are a society eager to learn, conscious that now, more than ever, our economic destiny lies in our ability to interact with the world.

In our time, Britain has experienced a variety of economic conditions—gone from an imperial capitalist system to a largely state-owned system—to a free enterprise economy. What we are really trying to do is create some kind of balance between individual initiative and the collective needs of society—to affirm that we are a market economy but that we will not slide into a market society. This is not an easy task, but I think we are making progress.

As we do this, the historic affinities between your country and mine suggest that there are many things we can do together. The agreements that are to be signed today are symbolic of this collaboration and its possibilities. I congratulate the firms concerned and hope that this will be a harbinger of much more to come.

It is in this spirit that I bring you our government's assurances of cooperation and the enthusiasm that our business community has for deepening our engagements with Norway.

Appendix 3

British-American Business Association
Washington D.C.
13 April 2000
*The UK: The Place to Do Business
in the Twenty-First Century*
Address by Lord Paul

It gives me great pleasure to join you this afternoon. Although my mandate is to address you, occasions like this are learning experiences for me. In many ways, Washington has become the capital of global economic policymaking. I inevitably find that the informal conversations that I have with people like you provide me with enriching insights. Anyone engaged in international business today needs to have fresh perspectives continually.

At the outset, let me say how grateful I am to the British ambassador and his colleagues for arranging this luncheon. We, in Britain, are very appreciative of our embassies abroad and the splendid way they represent our country.

I have been requested to share with you my thoughts on the business environment in Britain. I would like to convey some of the changes that are taking place in both the British economic climate and condition—developments that have significantly changed our economy and made it more interesting for foreign business.

Those of you who do business in Europe will have seen how, in just a couple of years, the fundamentals have been swiftly transformed. Currencies are disappearing; the geography of markets has been totally reshaped; quite dramatic shifts are taking place in pricing differentials and in the financial structure. And these are just some of the challenges that confront international business. All these and other developments presented us in Britain with critical choices.

We had to change rapidly or our economy, and our standards of living, would deteriorate. This is why, for almost fifteen years, the British economy has been going through a quite radical modification. At the heart of this is a programme that has brought about extensive privatization, incentives for investment and enterprise, and technological upgrading.

Thirty-four years ago, I migrated from India to Britain and began a small business activity with a modest loan. Today, the Caparo Group has a turnover of around US$ 800 million. From our British headquarters, we supervise operations in four countries, employ some 3500 people and believe that we are among the technological leaders in our field. In fact, our American business, Bull Moose Tube Company, which we acquired in 1988, is now a major part of our operations.

Much of this record has been, of course, due to the endeavours of our staff. But much has also been the result of the environment in which we operate. The atmosphere has been conducive to enterprise, and the willingness to adapt and innovate is extraordinary. The coordination and cooperation between labour and management has sustained consistently improving productivity.

All this has taken place in a society which increasingly recognizes that ethnic and cultural diversity is a singular social and economic asset—and has sought to integrate our minorities into our economic mainstream. To achieve this, the government, management, labour, and even the public, had to change attitudes and expectations. Fortunately, we have administrations with the political will to sustain these policies—and I believe that political will is vital to the success of macro-economic change.

Here are a few of the major policies that we have been trying to implement in Britain. When the Labour government was elected almost three years ago, there were still some residual doubts about the direction of economic policy. There is now no doubt whatsoever. There is, at this moment, a remarkable consensus in British politics—a consensus that an enterprise society is good for Britain and good for Britain's relationships with the world. Indeed, I think that the present government is one of the most business-friendly administrations Britain has had.

During its tenure, the government has created a new framework for monetary and fiscal stability, including giving independence to the Bank of England so that monetary policy and the fixing of interest rates have been removed from political influence.

A major investment in modernizing education is underway. Taxes have been reduced to the lowest level in Europe and the tax climate for investors is very favourable. In fact, in last month's Budget, taxes on small and medium-size enterprises were so reduced that they are now the lowest in the developed world. Another new initiative is the creation of enterprise partnerships between the public sector and businesses in a variety of different fields.

There is, of course, a lot of unfinished business. But, as an entrepreneur, I believe we are on the way to creating a dynamic and competitive economy that can offer the best conditions for growth with stability. At the heart of these changes is the welcome we give to foreign investment. Britain is now more open to it than ever—a Britain reaching outwards. Historically, Britain has been a major exporting economy. But I think we realize that today, no national economy can be an island.

In the modern world, trade and investment must be built on reciprocity and is not a one-way flow. This is one reason why we have been so supportive of global trade liberalization. There is currently a tendency in some nations, a tendency induced by the economic situation, to restrictively regulate international trade. Britain vigorously opposes this. We also strongly encourage inward and outward investment. Those who invest in Britain today find a congenial climate for their capital, and labour conditions that are extraordinarily supportive.

Surrounding all this is the much-spoken-about question of Britain and Europe. Let me say this very clearly: Britain is categorically committed to being in Europe. Indeed, it is fair to say that this government is the most pro-European government Britain has ever had. As our chancellor of the exchequer recently put it: 'We can become the best competitive environment for business, not just because of the reforms we are making, but because we are part of one of the world's largest single markets—the European Single Market.' Right now, we are working hard to extend the single market to areas where it is still incomplete—in energy, utilities, telecoms and financial services. In doing this, we hope to also expand the Atlantic bridge which has traditionally linked Britain in an old relationship with America.

Now to the Euro. When you hear of political controversies in the UK, it might surprise you to know that we are now going through a period of intensive preparation in order that the British government, Parliament and people can make an informed decision on this fateful choice. Indeed, a national change-over plan is being tested throughout Britain today. Personally, I would have liked Britain to join in the initial phase. This is largely the view of most of the British business and commercial community. In the long run, I think that this participation will take place. However, the government of Britain has made a public promise not to join without going to the people on a referendum. It will honour this commitment.

Some 200 years ago, Britain was a leader in the first Industrial Revolution—a revolution based on capital and machinery. The revolution all of us are now going through demands a different approach—huge investments in human capital, in knowledge and in the reorganization of structures. This is why recent Budgets have dramatically increased public expenditure in education.

But there are, of course, limits to the things that any one nation can do by itself in our modern age. However, through increased engagement with each other, both America and Britain can profoundly benefit from a complementary association. If you explore these opportunities, you will find a Britain remarkably different from both stereotypes and from the past. We are a society eager to learn, conscious that now, more than ever, our economic destiny lies in our ability to interact with the world.

In our time, Britain has experienced a variety of economic conditions—gone from an imperial capitalist system, to a largely state-owned system, to a free enterprise economy. What we are really trying to do is create some kind of balance between individual initiative and the collective needs of society—to affirm that we are a market economy but that we will not slide into a market society.

As we do this, the historic affinities between America and Britain suggest that there are many ways in which the business community can expand their collaborations. We are, after all, the English-speaking gateway to an emerging single market of almost 400 million upscale consumers. In fact, it is my personal dream that, one day, we will see an Atlantic Common Market. But that is obviously some distance away and the subject of another discussion.

Right now, what I do want to leave behind in your minds is that Britain has one of the most welcoming and stable climates for international business. It is in this spirit that I bring you our government's assurance of a warm welcome and the enthusiasm that our business community has for deepening our economic relationships with America and the entrepreneurs of this country.

Appendix 4

Dutch Institute of Directors
The Hague, 18 October 2001
Lord Paul, Ambassador for British Business

First, I would like to thank the Institute for inviting me to speak to you today. It is a pleasure for me to be in The Hague again.

I have known your country for a long time. I began doing business here in 1953 with Hoogovens, now the Anglo-Dutch partnership known as Corus. The association between Caparo and Corus continues with our UK joint venture, Caparo Merchant Bar, and so it can be said we are partners with a Dutch company. My family's company in India has had a similarly long history with Organon.

Historically, the UK and the Netherlands have a very close relationship.

We have strong trading links that have stood the test of time over centuries of change.

Our economies are closely linked and both have a worldwide reach.

We also have strong commercial links, including some major UK-Dutch joint operations such as Shell, Unilever and Corus.

We are the fourth-largest export market for each other and we are the second-largest investors in each other's markets, after the US.

We also work together at the political level—I know that Tony Blair and Wim Kok have built up an excellent understanding and rapport.

For example: Two years ago, they agreed a framework for the future. As part of this, they proposed an annual bilateral conference aimed at further developing close relations and understanding between our two countries.

The aim was to bring together a broad range of British and Dutch thinkers and opinion formers for two to three days of discussions on popular themes. The first of these meetings took place in Apeldoorn in May last year, under the joint patronage of our prime ministers and foreign ministers. This year's conference will take place in Edinburgh next month.

In the defence field too, there is close cooperation. Our defence forces have worked with their Dutch counterparts in peacekeeping operations in Cyprus, Kosovo and Macedonia. Indeed, at the moment, British forces are under Dutch command in Bosnia.

As result of this close relationship, we also have many shared concerns and approaches. And this is particularly so regarding the European Union. This has been helped in no small part by Tony Blair's efforts since 1997 to ensure that Britain plays a much more positive and constructive role in Europe. The government has shown in the last four years what you can achieve by working with Europe, not against it. The successful outcome of the Lisbon Summit last year is a good example. And I will speak more about this later.

I believe, as does the UK government, that the UK—geographically, historically and economically—is part of Europe. But, very much like the Dutch, we are practical Europeans. We are pro Europe and pro reform in Europe.

I would like to focus tonight on the need for economic reform in Europe and—particularly from the business viewpoint—the importance of a well-functioning Single Market.

I would also like to say a few words about the role of business in ensuring that Europe makes these reforms a reality:

Single Market

- The Single Market has been one of the EU's major successes of the past twenty years.
- It is made up of over 370 million people and is the world's largest and richest market, accounting for 38 per cent of world trade. In an enlarged European Union, that market could be as many as 500 million people.
- There's no question that the Single Market has brought growth and prosperity to Europe for several years.
- But full realization of the Single Market is being thwarted, and so business is not reaping the benefits of a completed and effectively functioning Single Market. For example:
  - Monopolies in some local telecoms markets are frustrating e-enterprise.

- Much of Europe's gas and electricity markets have not been liberalized—leading to high energy costs;
  - A Single Market has not yet been established in services, including financial services;
  - Too much unfair state aid is still being handed out;
- And there is too much regulation, which hampers business and especially small business.

Since the early 1970s when the ECSC was formed, we in the steel industry have discovered the benefits of working closely together. We buy and sell a great deal in Europe, which adds to our mutual strength. Personally, as far as I am concerned, we should keep moving towards the Single Market, and the faster we do so, the better off we will be.

At the Lisbon Summit in March 2000, the EU accepted that its economic performance must catch up with the best in world, particularly with the United States. It set Europe the goal of becoming 'the most competitive, dynamic and socially inclusive knowledge-based economy in the world by 2010'.

The Summit was an important turning point in EU economic thinking. It moved away from a regulatory, legislative agenda towards creating the right framework for enterprise, innovation, competition and employment.

The Summit agreed a wide package of structural reform measures to modernize Europe, increase employment and promote growth in the next ten years. The package covered eight key themes

- Information Society
- Research and Innovation
- Enterprise and SME

- Internal Market
- Financial Markets
- Education and Training
- Employment Policy
- Social Agenda

But having a package of measures is not enough—it must be delivered. I am sure that the UK and Dutch governments will play a leading role in ensuring that economic reform in the EU is delivered. But the pressure must come from *all* governments and importantly from the business community as well.

Business influence

I strongly believe that business should *and must* ensure that it has a strong voice and play its part in influencing the European economic agenda. We need to ensure that governments (and community institutions) listen and take account of the views of business.

Because governments do not create jobs, business does.

And governments do not create wealth and prosperity, business does.

In short, it is the job of government to create the environment for business to operate; and it is for business to create jobs and so wealth and prosperity. I would urge you all, therefore, to make your voices heard and encourage your business partners throughout the EU to do the same. To spread the message, not just to the UK and Dutch governments, but to all fifteen EU national governments and, of course, the European Commission and the European Parliament.

It is in everyone's interest for the EU to get this right, and business must play its part.

Appendix 5

Ambassador for British Business
Lord Swraj Paul
India, January 2002

I am again in India as an ambassador for British business, because of the importance of the political and economic relationship between the two countries. Also, to me personally, while I visit many other countries in this role, coming to India is always very special.

Our bilateral trade grew by an impressive thirty per cent last year and is now worth £5 billion a year. British investment into India now means that the UK is the largest single investor—with investment exceeding £3 billion.

At the same time, we are now seeing an increasing amount of Indian investment going into the United Kingdom. I want to build on this impressive trading relationship, to improve trade and investment dramatically between India and the United Kingdom.

There are a number of ingredients to the success of our relationship in bilateral trade and investment, the most important being the hard work of individual Indian and British businessmen living the reality of day-to-day business—researching markets; knocking on doors; writing proposals; winning orders and building the long-term relationships on which business depends.

British trade and investment promotion staff under the banner of 'Trade Partners UK' have also played a great part, helped by an expanding commercial network in India. And at this point, I would like to commend the professionalism of the British Missions in India.

So, I welcome this opportunity to underline the importance of our trade and industry. I also want to say that we understand the significance of listening to your views if we are to succeed in building a business climate that rewards innovation and encourages growth, while ensuring social justice for all members of society.

These views are even more important, especially after the tragic events of September 11 in New York and Washington D.C. But those destructive acts must not be allowed to dent our confidence. They were attacks upon the values of democracy and fundamental freedoms. They were intended to destabilize world order and ruin prosperity. But they did not succeed and must not succeed.

Of course, there has been an impact on business confidence, and companies must do what they think is right to ensure the safety and security of their overseas staff and operations. But it is true that the most successful business relationships are long term.

And the businesses that continue to maintain close relationships with overseas markets—even in uncertain times—are the ones that will be best placed to secure future business opportunities.

Some sectors have obviously suffered more than others—the airlines and travel industry for example. But there are still good opportunities to pursue, and businesses should be ready and able to adapt to new opportunities, wherever they arise.

Even before September 11, there were fears that the US economy was slowing down and that difficult economic trading conditions would spread throughout the world. But it would be wrong to talk ourselves into an economic downturn. It is not all doom and gloom. In fact, in Britain, the fundamentals of our economy remain strong. Interest rates and inflation are low, unemployment is low, productivity is rising, and the economy is still growing.

Of course, Trade Partners is well placed to give advice in this area and has been working behind the scenes to assess global business prospects. Good indicators are emerging, not only for the US, but, for example, in the Middle East, where across the board there is little evidence of any adverse impact on business.

And in many places throughout the world, major events and exhibitions—with an expectation of good attendances—are continuing as planned.

Since we are talking about the importance of international trade, I should say something about the deal reached at the fourth WTO Ministerial Conference at Doha in November. This new trade round is important for encouraging global economic growth for promoting access to world markets and resisting protectionism. September 11 underlined the need for the communities of the world to band together to safeguard the institutions and boost the world economy.

This new deal sends a positive signal that international economic cooperation can succeed in the face of obstacles and uncertainties. It provides a well-timed lift to world economic confidence and will have a positive impact around the world.

And here I would like to congratulate your minister of commerce, Mr Murasoli Maran, on the courage and vision he displayed to protect India's interests.

Security and prosperity must go hand in hand through world trade. The reason why trade creates peace is that it is far more than simply a flow of money or products—it is also a flow of ideas, of knowledge and of people.

China, the most recent member of the WTO, was the most technologically advanced nation in the world five hundred years ago. Long before the West, China invented paper, printing, blast furnaces for smelting iron, and a water-driven machine for spinning hemp. Yet, by the eighteenth century, many of these inventions had fallen into disuse—and while Britain was leading the industrial revolution based on similar technology. Why did China not realize its potential? One of the reasons was the absence of a free market and a distaste for trade.

In contrast, Europeans were exploring and trading across the globe. Europe was open to new products and new ideas while China retreated into isolation.

We all know that, in the global economy, our most important asset is our people. In the UK, we acknowledge that it is the diversity of our people. Cosmopolitan cities, a multitude of ideas and beliefs, helps to make a dynamic and creative culture. The British Asian community provides the UK with direct ties to the Indian subcontinent. This new generation of British Indians are at home in the global economy.

Their ties with India are already the basis for the rapid growth we're seeing in trade between our two countries—now up to £5 billion a year—as many Indian companies are choosing to expand into the UK and many UK companies are expanding into India.

Now is not the time to retreat within our own borders. History has shown that companies that continue to invest and look for new opportunities and markets in difficult times are the ones best placed to take advantage once those difficult times are behind us.

As Prime Minister Tony Blair said in the House of Commons: 'The most important thing is that we carry on with confidence in the basic strength of the economy and our way of life, because the fundamentals of the economy have not altered.' This is the statement that everyone in Britain is agreed on. I hope we can continue in the same vein with our trade and investment opportunities to India and from India.

Appendix 6

The Rt Hon. Lord Swraj Paul
Maiden Speech, House of Lords, London
28 November 1996

My Lords, it was just sixteen days ago that I was introduced to your Lordships' House. However, the courtesy and kindness which your Lordships have shown me in this brief period encourage me to speak today. I come to this House conscious that the roots of my heritage and philosophy are not conventional to the membership of this august assembly. Yet, I believe your Lordships recognize that they symbolize a contribution to the new Britain which we are all engaged in constructing. There was a time when the strength of nations was measured by exclusion and exclusivity. Today we heed a larger truth—that there is more strength in diversity, more vigour in variety.

At this moment, I am also mindful that my presence among your Lordships signifies another convergence—the reconciliation and friendship between the land of my birth and the country which is my home. The underlying spirit in which Britain and India now relate to each other is a model for the world.

In its own modest way, my personal history reflects this. My family, who were ardent participants in India's independence movement, named me Swraj for their ideals of freedom and self-rule. Swraj means freedom—the eternal cry that resonated in my youth. However, had I known that one day I would have to address your Lordships and this House, I should have wished to be named 'fearless'.

After university in India, I continued higher studies at the Massachusetts Institute of Technology in the United States. At MIT, I learnt much about engineering, and much more about life. The two greatest things it taught me were always to aspire to excellence and never to abandon hope.

Thirty years ago I came to this country in search of medical treatment for my daughter whom we later, sadly, lost. For a while, I abandoned hope. But that tragic beginning unfolded into a new life and a successful career largely because of the opportunities which Britain provides. These opportunities, leavened with the support which hard work and determination still receive in this country, enabled me to revive industries which were largely abandoned or downgraded some decades ago.

Britain is a country where responsible citizenship earns many rewards. Whatever pressures arise, let us not close our doors to those who bring their skills to these shores.

My attention today focuses upon the Budget which Her Majesty's government have presented. Because of my long association with the manufacturing industry, I am especially concerned with those components of the Budget that address this sector of our economy.

I believe that in recent years the manufacturing industry has received less recognition than it deserves. For me, manufacturing is the bedrock of the British economy. It is what first provided stable and permanent employment to the masses in this country and in this part of the world—and it still does. This is why I am disappointed that the Budget has not given any specific encouragement to the need for capital investment in industry.

Britain's manufacturing base is at a critical stage in its history. There has been a prolonged erosion of this plinth on which our economy stands. The principal components of industrial competitiveness need to be re-examined and their requirements re-assessed. Capital investment has been limited, and this has inhibited the acquisition of modern technology. We have to find ways to increase capital inputs and so to upgrade plants and facilities. Today, we risk falling behind western Europe and Asia-Pacific, not only because our skills are inadequate but because our equipment needs modernization.

Ours is not human failure. During the past decade or so, some of our shopfloor managements and workforces have demonstrated competence and achieved levels of productivity comparable with that of any economy. But their reputation for innovation and quality cannot be maintained without high technology.

Another issue close to my heart is that of entrepreneurial businesses. The small and medium-sized companies which were once the pace-setters of industrial Britain are now losing ground. While publicly quoted companies find it relatively easy to raise capital, it is much harder for privately owned businesses to do so.

The financial community and those who make financial policy should look at private companies in a different light because it is those businesses that are often the source of industrial innovation.

In the investment climate which now prevails, it is easier to raise capital for football clubs than for industrial ventures. This is cutting the lifeline of some of the potentially best and brightest British firms. High-flying financial engineering may be the trapeze artistry of the commercial world, but the small entrepreneur forms the safety net of society.

The human and social costs of industrial neglect will soon come to haunt us unless we move rapidly to reinforce and renovate the most basic parts of our economy. We must enthuse a younger generation about the benefits and excitement of an industrial career. We must develop an approach that looks forward to the time when British manufacturers will evoke the respect they once enjoyed in global markets. Given our traditional talents, it is surely not difficult to elevate our industries to world-class excellence. But we can never achieve this with policies of indifference.

I have worked on the shopfloor; and I have managed large enterprises. I know the hope which the growing industrial economy brings to working men and women. We have an obligation to rekindle those hopes because I passionately believe that what is good for British industry is good for Britain.

Appendix 7

House of Lords
Debate on Minority Ethnic and Religious Communities: Cultural and Economic Contribution
Thursday, 24 May 2012
Speech by Lord Paul

My Lords, I congratulate my noble friend Lord Bilimoria on initiating this timely debate, and his excellent speech.

The Zoroastrian community has always been a minority community in whatever country it has existed. But by its conduct and its contribution, it has without exception been a model of good citizenship, holding its members to the highest standards of ethical behaviour. At a time when grievances are often provoked and expressed by violence, this approach has been a lesson for us all.

As Mahatma Gandhi said: 'An eye for an eye will make the whole world blind.'

I now move to the larger implications of the noble Lord's Motion: the contribution made by minority ethnic and religious communities to the United Kingdom. Too often, minorities are viewed by significant parts of the majority as takers and not givers. Of course, this is palpably wrong, as is evident from the minority involvement in every field of endeavour: from public life to commercial enterprise, from the arts to sport, from education to government services. Minority involvement is growing and is now irreversible.

I do not need to remind your Lordships that this has been somewhat slow in coming, not because minorities were reluctant or unqualified but because barriers were placed in their way. Recent times have seen these formal and informal obstructions being dismantled. We must continue these efforts and guard against any reversal and, in doing so, open up avenues of advancement to higher positions, a situation in which recent studies have shown there is considerable inadequacy.

People are not born with discrimination in their blood. They are socialized into it, as I know well. I visit London Zoo as often I can because it is partly a memorial to my infant daughter. I well recall how, forty-six years ago, her last tragic months were brightened by regular visits there and by being with other children of all communities. When London Zoo was in danger of closure in the 1990s, I was delighted to step in and help. My delight today is to see how children of various ethnic communities mingle freely and enjoy companionship without any regard to racial, religious or other backgrounds. In this camaraderie, small children have many lessons for their parents.

I have been, and am, chancellor of two British universities: the University of Wolverhampton and the University of Westminster. Both have overseas branches and consequently a sizeable student body representing a number of nationalities. It must be remembered that when these overseas students return to their countries, they continue to make a great contribution as ambassadors for Britain.

The noble Lord, Lord Bilimoria, succeeded me as chancellor of the University of West London. He will confirm that a majority of younger students is far less concerned with ethnic and religious differences than with joint activities. These are the very people who, as they grow into full adulthood, can harbour prejudices that are of much concern in this country. Responsibility for enlightenment cannot be left to the individuals alone. That is why I urge the government to make every effort to encourage the expansion of educational curricula to include more information and analysis of minority contributions.

These are difficult days in community relations, and economic distress often makes them more difficult as retrenchment takes place that often affects minority communities first. However, whatever areas are drawn down, that should not include cuts in the minority-related programmes. Small economic gains must never be at the expense of the social fabric of the nation.

Appendix 8

House of Lords
Debate on the Economy: Currency Fluctuations
Thursday, 17 November 2016
Speech by Lord Paul

My Lords, I thank the noble Baroness, Lady McIntosh, for introducing this debate. It is always an honour and a pleasure to listen to the noble Lord, Lord Skidelsky. I learnt a great deal. I declare an interest as chairman of a manufacturing company, Caparo, and chancellor of the University of Wolverhampton.

We face a period of more than usual uncertainty about Britain's position in the world. As our government start to tackle the daunting task of implementing Brexit, the world is also trying to guess how the new US administration will play their part on the world stage when they assume power early next year. Brexit and the US presidential election have been singled out by commentators as leading to significant fluctuations in the exchange rate over recent weeks. We have heard much doom and gloom from survey firms and others, keen for a good story, on the adverse consequences for the British economy that will surely follow. All are now very excited, and this has provided opportunities for the speculators to make money.

At the simplest level, it is easy to accept the received wisdom that wild fluctuations in the exchange rate create uncertainty and will deter investment in the UK. However, I believe that for Britain, a fluctuating pound is really just business as usual. Honda, Toyota and Nissan, some of our biggest overseas investors, have all reconfirmed their commitment to car manufacturing in the UK and further investment. Only this week, Google announced a further major expansion in the UK. The prime minister's most recent foreign policy initiative was a trade mission to India, about which I hear good things and must congratulate her; both countries can now look forward to doing more business together.

We need to distinguish between the step changes in exchange rates caused by major world events, of which Brexit may be one—although some would argue that it was merely an event that pricked an already overinflated pound—and the background noise of daily currency fluctuations fuelled by the financial chattering classes. These should be ignored. I come from a background that means I do not think any government in this day and age can really do anything to control exchange rates.

We should not be frightened of this change. We should reflect on the long history of this country as a trading nation and what that means. I have been involved with international trade throughout my working life, from the 1950s onwards, mainly in steel and manufacturing goods. Over that period, I have seen much change in the world economy and I know from experience that a trader thrives on change, which brings opportunity. Over the years and centuries, change has also brought many opportunities for Britain which were seized by the entrepreneurs of the day. These recent events will also bring opportunities for business and investment in the UK. If they are followed through, they will create jobs and generate tax revenues for the greater good. If I was a younger man, I would love to get involved.

We must therefore do everything we can in this House to enable British business to seize these opportunities as they arise. We need clear regulation and a certain tax regime; we need an educated and skilled workforce; we need modern infrastructure and good transport systems. These, I believe, are the things that matter to investors over the longer term, not the day-to-day noise of the currency markets. After all, if we can get all that right, we will have a strong Britain and a strong pound.

Let us look at the effect of a weaker pound on higher education. A weak pound means that studying in the UK is cheaper. Britain's international reputation means that it is the number one destination for international students. We cannot afford to lose that status; in fact, we must strengthen it. Universities are looking for an increase in the fee income from overseas students from the present £3.7 billion to £4.8 billion in 2018–19, and a growth in home and EU students of over 10 per cent. This is the time to really encourage overseas students to come here. Not only do they benefit from the experience but our own students benefit by interacting with people from different backgrounds. Bonds forged at university often last a lifetime and will open more doors to further trade and international collaboration in the future. However, encouraging more students is at odds with the current immigration policy, so we have to find ways to make sure that they return to their own countries when their studies end. The University of Wolverhampton, where I am chancellor, is doing all it can to promote these policies.

Let the government do everything they can to assist our businesses and universities to build a Britain that will be as great in the future as it has been in the past. The world still retains a respect for Britain as a beacon for democracy—a reputation that has been put to the test by Brexit. Personally, I have always supported being in Europe, including joining the euro to gain all its benefits, but the people have decided. Speaking as a democrat, for that beacon of democracy to continue to shine brightly, the government must be seen to act on the wishes of the people by engaging with the EU on implementing Brexit now. Decisive actions on these issues really matter for our businesses and universities in making their investment decisions, not the daily fluctuations in the value of the pound, but this is no simple task. The prime minister must now be allowed to move forward with Brexit in an orderly manner, without irrelevant distractions. That in itself will reduce currency fluctuations.

Appendix 9

NRI Investment in India
Lord Swraj Paul

The public debate about Non-Resident Investment (NRI) in Indian companies has tended to focus on this one issue. In fact, the implications of this matter go far beyond this topic. Among other things they concern:

First: The use and misuse of funds which government institutions hold in trust for the public and invest on its behalf.

Second: The investment of these public funds in public companies which are controlled by managements who have limited financial interest in these businesses.

Third: The impropriety of these managements and public accountability for the benefits they have extracted from public companies which they manage like private estates.

Fourth: The impact of the actions of these managements (like refusal to register legally acquired shares) on the structure of Indian business, on markets, on stockbrokers, on all owners of shares and other negotiable instruments, on the integrity of investments.

Fifth: The relationship between the overseas Indian community and the Indian business establishment at home.

All India Investors Association, Mumbai, 6 August 1983

Everyone involved in investment in India needs to be more vigilant. This means the institutional investors, the stockbrokers, the small investors, suppliers, customers, the financial press and employees. Too many easy deals are done 'under the table' and winked at by those who should be more alert. Until recently, there was a feeling that big business could be trusted—they had built companies, become well known, had wide influence and were widely quoted in the press. Well, my experience has shown that you can trust them like you can trust a python! Can you imagine so-called reputed business families selling their own shares on the stock market while not intending to transfer those shares to the new owners? If that is not fraud, what is?

Management Forum, Kolkata, 3 January 1986

My message has been a simple one: until, and unless, we in India end economic discrimination, provide opportunity for ability and learn to play by rules that are fair for all, India will be a divided nation. This is the truth about our business world, about the world of politics and about our society. Forty years ago, India was born out of the concept of equal opportunity.

This is what our great leaders—Mahatma Gandhi, Jawaharlal Nehru and Indira Gandhi—stood for and worked for. Yet today, in almost every area of society we have an unacceptable level of discrimination; equality of opportunity is a myth.

Lions Club, Kolkata, 29 December 1988

Scan QR code to access the
Penguin Random House India website